MERCER STREET

To the Class of 2020:

Welcome to New York University! An NYU education begins, in part, with writing. This practice reflects the University's longstanding commitment to the centrality of written inquiry to undergraduate education. In the twenty-first century, this centrality is more evident than ever before. A wide range of courses is open to you: from accounting to history to mechanical engineering to woodwind studies. No matter what field you choose, you will be using writing to think, analyze, investigate, and create. And no matter what path or career you choose after you graduate (as a scholar, educator, health practitioner, entrepreneur, artist, performer, lawyer, engineer, or activist), you'll be using writing to propose, to investigate, to analyze, and to represent yourself and your work.

The essays collected in this volume represent some of the best work written for courses in Expository Writing or the CAS Freshman Seminars over the course of 2015-16; most were written by first-year students. These essays are smart, moving, funny, analytic, creative, and—like us all, and like all written work—imperfect. They open up questions, problems, and puzzles that are not entirely solvable. The faculty of EWP hope that you will both enjoy and learn from them.

Take heart! College is a time to challenge yourself and to nurture your mind both in and out of the classroom. Your most surprising encounters—your most creative or insightful moments—may happen when you least expect them. Be interested. That is almost always the best way to begin.

With all best wishes,
Dara Rossman Regaignon
Director of the Expository Writing Program
Associate Professor of English

EDITOR'S NOTE

With this volume of *Mercer Street* we bring together an edifying collection of writing from last year's Expository Writing seminars. Hundreds of NYU freshmen competed this year for publication in *Mercer Street*, and many more achieved significant gains in their own writing practice. With this book we recognize everyone's commitment to something that is very highly prized among cultured persons everywhere: the ability to write and speak with clarity, distinction, and effectiveness—to mean what you say and to say what you mean.

This volume offers a foretaste of the topics, subjects, and disciplines you'll be studying across the College of Arts and Science and in your majors. Indeed, for the first time, we are dedicating a portion of *Mercer Street* to interdisciplinary writings from the Freshman Seminars. In our own Expository Writing courses, as you will see, students find ways to explore abiding passions such as music or politics, but just as often they are captivated by hardly known works in science, film, environmental studies, and the literary arts, taking up what is simply too perplexing to ignore.

A great reward for both students and teachers in our seminars is watching a project come to life over a period of weeks. Usually this process has humble beginnings. It then develops into a richer understanding of one's initial question or reason for writing. This movement takes place in language and by working with sources, but the more radical transformation is to the individual writer's mind or way of thinking. By writing we are changed.

We invite you to read these essays in a similar spirit of self-transformation.

Stephen Donatelli
Editor, *Mercer Street*

MERCER STREET

2016 - 2017

EXPOSITORY WRITING PROGRAM
NEW YORK UNIVERSITY
COLLEGE OF ARTS & SCIENCE

ACKNOWLEDGMENTS

The Expository Writing Program is grateful to Dean G. Gabrielle Starr, College of Arts and Science, for her generous support of this publication.

Cover Photograph: Denice Martone, *Roman Arch*, reconstructed. Castelvetere sul Calore, Campania, Italy. Angelo Verderosa and Antonio Sulla, Architects, 1996.

Correction:
Proper attribution of the cover image for last year's *Mercer Street* was omitted. This image was a twilight photograph of Washington Square Arch entitled "Spandrel," featuring 95 decorative rosettes lining the underside of the arch. "Spandrel" was made by Expository Writing Professor and Associate Director Denice Martone.

MERCER STREET

CONTENTS

Essays listed by course on page 267

*Written for Joshua Weber's "International Writing Workshop II,"
this essay explores what it means to be bilingual. Minghao Zang
balances personal narrative and scholarship on bilingualism
to examine the relationship between both of his languages,
and both of his worlds.*

A STRUGGLE OF IDENTITY

Minghao Zang

Nowadays, having a bicultural identity, in which an individual becomes fully immersed in a second language other than his or her mother tongue, has become the norm. Jeffrey Nelson, a writer for LivingBilingual, states that individuals start to learn characteristics of a new language and culture which "in turn combine with the old and create a new hybrid identity." However, people take this process of "molding and remolding" bicultural identity for granted (Nelson). Learning a new language, to some degree, is on a pendulum between the fluency of two languages as "opposed to being at two fixed points" at the same time (Nelson). If an individual becomes better at a certain language, he or she will lose fluency in another language. Inevitably, immersing oneself into the more prevalent culture allows one to move towards the other end of the pendulum.

A highly-ranked university, a social network of English-speaking friends, and even an opportunity to eventually work in the United States—these are the benefits that speaking English has given me, someone who was born and raised in China. My assimilation to the local U.S. culture brings me a flamboyant identity that most of my friends back home are jealous of—I am a bilingual prodigy who is fluent in both English and Chinese. Little do they know that I am not great at either language. I struggle to look for adequate vocabulary when writing an English essay, and tend to forget the spelling of a Chinese character when texting my friends. My English-speaking friends forgive my use of awkward phrasing by comforting me, saying that English is a second language for me. My friends back in China accept my misspelling or misuse of a Chinese phrase, saying that it is a common phenomenon since I have stayed abroad for too long. There is an old saying in China: "You can't have both fish and bear's paw." It means that one can not achieve two goals simultaneously. I want to shine in both languages, but unfortunately, I am not great at either of them. Learning two languages at the same time actually slowed down my ability to excel in both languages. I did not get the fish or the bear's paw; I only got half of each.

When facing the dilemma of always being second-best at every-thing, perhaps simply picking a side might be the most efficient means. In his essay "Memoir of a Bilingual Childhood," author Richard Rodriguez encounters a similar problem, standing in between the Spanish-speaking culture in his house and the American-speaking culture in his school. Born in an American neighborhood, Rodriguez has to speak English with his friends at school. When he first goes to school, he barely knows "fifty stray English words" (25). Entering a new culture with such a distinctive identity becomes problematic, and Rodriguez becomes the "'problem student' in class" (25). He tries to catch up at first, but the fact is that speaking his native language back at home somehow troubles his ability to learn another language. English sounds so "exotic" to him (27). To cope with this problem, he sacrifices one language for another. In order to do well in school and become more comfortable with his friends, Rodriguez starts to speak only English. His parents also start increasing the amount of English used at home. After several months, he finally manages to say some-thing loud and clear enough that his classmates understand him for the first time. He is then "increasingly confident," feeling "[that he belongs] in public" (31).

The result is significant, but the side effect is obvious as well. He improves his English fluency dramatically over the years, but at the expense of his Spanish skills. He claims that Spanish is now no more than a "sound," and even uncomfortable to him (Rodriguez 32). When his parents are speaking Spanish at home, he feels "[pushed] away" (32). He can no longer represent his native language. Biculturalism, for Rodriguez, means accepting a sacrifice.

However, the sacrifice of biculturalism means something different to Ngugi wa Thiong'o. Going from his essay "Decolonising the Mind," Thiong'o might argue that achievement at the expense of one's own language is worthless compared to its cost. He presents the essence of language and the process by which his native language, Gikuyu, was colonized by the British. Everything written in Gikuyu was suppressed and replaced by English. English became "the language" to learn, and anyone caught speaking Gikuyu was considered a "culprit" and punished severely (Thiong'o 334, 335). Thiong'o became concerned for the future of his country when a friend of his at the time excelled "in all subjects except English" and was forced to become "a turn boy in a bus company" (335). Talented individuals were wasted, eliminated simply because they did poorly in English. This form of negative selection causes a serious problem for the future of the Gikuyu language. The author worries that "mental [colonization]" will lead to Gikuyu's extinction (339). When more and more people start to focus on English only for their own survival, learning their native language becomes redundant and it slowly vanishes when "[a] child would now only see the world as seen in the literature of his language of adoption" (341). Thiong'o states that the intrusion of another language had broken the harmony of the connection between language and culture. Language is the "carrier of culture"—any culture is a product of a unique language that can not be replaced (336). Language conveys a unique understanding of the values within a culture, something that cannot be understood through other languages. To Thiong'o, the forced colonization is detrimental to his language and culture. He cannot afford the sacrifice of biculturalism when his native language is endangered.

It is fair to say that the problems encountered by Rodriguez and Thiong'o are similar yet not congruent. Gikuyu is an extremely rare language that only a small number of people utilize in Africa. With the intrusion of another language, Gikuyu was endangered. Thiong'o feels a sense of responsibility and urgency to rescue his own language. He wants to pass the language on to future generations and keep its culture alive. On the other hand, Rodriguez does not share the equivalent urgency. His native language, Spanish, is considered the third largest language in the world. He is one out of billions that have chosen not to continue speaking Spanish. The base number is so huge that his own decision will not make a difference. Unlike Thiong'o, who adores Gikuyu especially when listening to local stories, Rodriguez does not like to speak Spanish. Rodriguez does not consider speaking Spanish a form of pleasure, but rather a burden that reminds him of his past as a "socially disadvantaged" boy (26). Indeed, being immersed in another language affects the original culture deeply. Inarguably, Rodriguez's decision isn't great for the sake of his culture, but he chooses the best solution for himself. Unlike Thiong'o, he does not need to worry about the growth of his language. Forgetting his native language will not become an issue.

The issue is when individuals like myself become confused about whether to forsake the mother language or to adapt to the new language. The inefficient learning of both languages reveals the concealed weakness under the bicultural identity. Even with his gentle assimilation, Rodriguez feels an aloofness between himself and his family. Staying with the people he loves is not as comfortable as before. The sound of a Spanish world becomes equally exotic as the English one was before. However, in "Advantages of Being Bicultural," Dr. Francois Grosjean uses scientific data to examine an alternative answer to the fish or bear's paw dilemma; getting half of each may be beneficial. He claims that bicultural people exhibit "more fluency . . . more flexibility . . . and more novelty" (Grosjean). The research examines the participants on their ability to think diversely in both virtual and real world scenarios. Participants are asked to give possible ways to use a random object. Those who have stayed in another country for at least four years come up with more solutions than those who have not. In another study that was conducted simultaneously, bicultural participants achieved "higher promotion rate" and had "more positive reputations" than those who were not bicultural. These are all attributed to "integrative complexity"—the ability to "forge conceptual links" from "multiple perspectives." This ability is developed easily with a bicultural background. There is certainly no correlation between the study of language and having a successful public identity. In fact, Rodriguez's success later in his life may be attributed to his bicultural identity, but not his focus on a single language earlier in life. The sacrifice he paid to his bicultural life is costly, but he was fortunate enough to have a choice. Thiong'o, on the other hand, does not have any options. The forced bilingual intrusion diluted his culture back in his home town. It was an unsurpassable opportunity cost that can never be compensated. Thiong'o does not worry about himself, but his beloved country.

In the article "Biculturalism: A Model of the Effects of Second Culture Exposure on Acculturation and Integrative Complexity," Carmit Tadmor and Philip Tetlock display a bicultural model that complicates Grosjean's conviction. When an individual is exposed to a new "culture context," they say that their "attention scope" widens to receive more information, fostering diverse thinking (Tadmor and Tetlock 176). Even though this benefit of biculturalism sounds appealing, I certainly question the definition of "bicultural" by Grosjean. In instances of biculturalism between similar cultures, it is inarguably easier to assimilate, but what happens when it comes to two distinctive cultures, such as Chinese culture and American culture? When there is a "strong dissonance" between two diverse cultures, each "constituency possesses a strong argument" to safeguard its "own position" (182). This impedes the assimilation process and requires much more effort to overcome. An "[acknowledgment] of legitimacy and [response] of criticism" from both cultures is compulsory for successful assimilation (182). Two people with distinctive personalities will just find it difficult to get along with each other. However, in the case of Rodriguez's culture assimilation, the languages used by the two nations are similar in grammar, spelling, and pronunciation to some extent. The two nations are also geographically connected. The original culture of the two will not vary drastically, making it easier to assimilate. This model implies that it is not suitable for everyone facing biculturalism. With more divergent backgrounds, the cost of biculturalism is inarguably higher.

Biculturalism involves sacrifice. Rodriguez successfully assimilates into a different culture at the expense of his adequacy in his native language. Thiong'o, who represents the people of Kenya, speaks fluent English at the cost of his endangered native language. It does not matter whether we voluntarily choose to ignore a portion of our culture or not. Every time we reach a destination, we pay tolls. That is the price of learning something new at the expense of something you have learned before. But there is not a defined solution to solve this problem due to biculturalism. There are too many factors to consider for each of us. Perhaps there is an optimal solution for each individual—but no one could find it except for that person. Whether you want more fish or more bear's paw is totally up to you.

WORKS CITED

Grosjean, François. "Advantages of Being Bicultural." *Psychology Today*. Sussex Publishers, LLC, 19 Apr. 2013. Web. 22 Feb. 2016.

Nelson, Jeffrey. "Bicultural Identity: What Does That Mean?" *Omniglot*. Simon Anger, 2015. Web. 2 Mar. 2016.

Rodriguez, Richard. "Aria: A Memoir of a Bilingual Childhood." *The American Scholar* 50.1 (1981): 25-42. *JSTOR*. Web. 27 June 2016.

Tadmor, Carmit T., and Philip E. Tetlock. "Biculturalism: A Model of the Effects of Second-Culture Exposure on Acculturation and Integrative Complexity." *Journal of Cross-Cultural Psychology* 37.2 (2006): 173-90. Web. 28 Feb. 2016.

Thiong'o, Ngugi wa. "Decolonizing the Mind." *The Broadview Anthology of Expository Prose*. Eds. Laura Buzzard, Julie Gaunce, Don LePan, Miscal Moser, and Tammy Roberts. 2nd ed. Toronto: Broadview Press, 2011. 333-42. Print.

Ashley Hollkamp's essay for Laren McClung's "Advanced College Essay" analyzes the film Boys Don't Cry *to break down its complex perspective on transgender identity and the cycles of hate and violence that often surround it. Interviews and scholarly articles in gender studies enliven this essay.*

FRAGILE CONCEPTIONS: GENDER AND MASCULINITY

Ashley Hollkamp

Thunder claps in the distance and mixes with indecipherable shouting as the camera focuses on a static shot of a trailer park. Suddenly, a young man rounds the corner and rushes into the trailer on the right side of the frame. Inside, he locks the door and closes all the windows; outside, we see a group of men following close behind, chasing him. Their enraged shouts, a harsh mixture of slurs and profanity, become clear. The men pound on the flimsy trailer door insistently, threatening to knock it down. Inside the trailer, we are introduced to Lonny, the boy's cousin. As the boy attempts to explain that he has no idea "what went wrong," the camera pans to Lonny, who throws him up against the wall and grabs him by the collar, shaking him as he shouts: "You are not a boy! That is what went wrong! You are not a boy! . . . Why don't you just admit that you're a dyke?" (*Boys Don't Cry*). Upon hearing this, the boy abruptly pulls himself from Lonny's grip and steps away. The camera zooms in on his steely expression. The shouting stops momentarily as he looks Lonny in the eye and replies "because I'm not a dyke." The tense moment is interrupted as glass shatters against the outside of the trailer and the men outside continue to threaten him. "You're not crashing here anymore, Teena. Get your stuff and go," we hear Lonny say off-camera just before the scene fades.

Filmmaker Kimberly Peirce wastes no time when it comes to introducing us to the reality of life in 1993 Nebraska for her protagonist, a young transgender man, in her directorial debut *Boys Don't Cry*. After being kicked out of the trailer, we see Teena in a bar, where he befriends a girl named Candace. "I'm Brandon," he tells her, leaving behind his Teena identity and reinventing himself into the character we will come to know throughout the film. Based on the true story of Brandon Teena, a transgender man born Teena Brandon, the film explores the final weeks of Brandon's life, from his move to Candace's tiny, rural hometown of Falls City, to the tragic chain of events that lead to his rape and ultimate murder at the hands of John Lotter and Tom Nissen. John and Tom—who, along with Candace and Lana, Brandon's eventual girlfriend, form the core cast of the film—befriend Brandon, allowing him to finally feel a true sense of acceptance and belonging for the first time in his life. This lasts until they discover that he is transgender, at which point they betray him. While this may sound like the plot of a typical melodramatic made-for-TV film, Peirce elevates the film to something more—a revealing examination of a culture of violence and discrimination, a political statement.

It was April 1994, a few months after Brandon's murder, that Peirce, then a graduate film student at Columbia University, first learned about him through a *Village Voice* article. In an interview with *The A.V. Club*, she recalls feeling an "immediate kinship" with him (Tobias). She grew concerned as the story became more and more sensationalized—people seemed to be focused on the crime itself, without giving it any "emotional understanding" (qtd. in Allen). This seemed like a very dangerous simplification to Peirce, who stated that "in duplicating any sort of hate crime . . . you have a responsibility to figure out moment by moment what was motivating this violence to happen, keep it personal, keep it up close, keep it dramatic" (qtd. in Allen). And so, with *Boys Don't Cry*, Peirce set out to humanize the villains and investigate the cultural factors that made them into people who would commit such a violent hate crime. At the heart of this investigation is masculinity, and the film serves as an in-depth look into the role of society in constructing ideas of masculinity, as well as the role masculinity plays in hate crimes like the one that killed Brandon.

In one of his first interactions with his future girlfriend, Lana, Brandon buys her beer and walks her home from the gas station in Falls City. While they walk, Lana complains about living in such a small town where there's nothing to do and questions Brandon why he went bumper-skiing with John and Tom, considering it an idiotic activity. "I just thought that's what guys do around here," Brandon shrugs. This line gives us insight into Brandon's attitude toward masculinity. As a transman who is successfully passing for the first time, his view of masculinity is malleable and constantly evolving. Brandon is searching for acceptance as a guy in Falls City, and the best way he knows of achieving that is by blending in, imitating the guys he sees. John and Tom have taken Brandon under their wing, so he goes along with whatever they do, and as a result he receives their acceptance and approval—at least initially.

In his article "Part of the Package," author Jamison Green states that "masculinity comes from a person's ability to correlate his or her behaviors and/or actions with those expected from people with male bodies" (296). He notes that this definition changes based on "cultural understandings of maleness," so it looks different in Falls City than in New York City, for example (296). Falls City is a small, lower-class, Midwestern town without a lot of diversity, and it's interesting how these factors play into the gender dynamics here. Qualities that could be considered part of the 'traditional' gender role for men, such as strength, protectiveness, and confidence, seem to be taken to the extreme by Tom and John. These two men are aggressive, domineering, and manipulative—they are violent and emotionally unstable characters, always straddling the line between charming and off-putting. Both men have spent time in prison and suffer from anger management issues, and their upbringings inform their ideas about masculinity. In one scene, after Lana and Brandon have begun dating, John confronts Lana about what she sees in Brandon. Even though he counts Brandon as one of his 'buddies' at this point, John still considers himself to be a better example of a man, and therefore a better boyfriend for Lana. "I know he's nice and everything, but he's kind of a wuss," he tells her. In an attempt to defend Brandon, Lana replies

"I know he's no big he-man like you. There's just something about him." This scene illuminates John's narrow view of masculinity, as informed by his own cultural understanding and personal experiences—all the men he has ever known in Falls City are extremely macho and aggressive, and since Brandon is not, John discounts Brandon's version of masculinity. Green emphasizes that "female-to-male (FTM) transgendered . . . individuals . . . do not follow the traditional prescriptive paths to maleness, yet they often possess an undeniable masculinity" (291). However, what we see throughout the film is a suppression and denial of Brandon's "alternative masculinit[y]" by John and other male characters (Green 293).

What Peirce exemplifies through John's disregard for Brandon's masculinity in this film is the concept of "hegemonic masculinity;" in an article titled "Accomplishing Masculinity through Anti-Lesbian, Gay, Bisexual, and Transgender Homicide: A Comparative Case Study Approach," authors Kristin Kelley and Jeff Gruenewald define this concept as "a form of dominant masculinity that when enacted further subordinates all other masculinities and femininities" (6). Kelley and Gruenewald argue that "an effort to . . . 'do' hegemonic masculinity [is] at the heart of anti-LGBT crimes," because "the victims of bias crimes are antithetical to the 'hegemonic ideal' of manhood which emphasizes aggressiveness, competitiveness, risk-taking, and other similar qualities" (6). It's interesting that Peirce's male characters seem to embody these exact characteristics—but upon further consideration, it's likely this wasn't accidental.

Peirce was painstakingly intentional in the construction of *Boys Don't Cry*. She spent four years conducting research before shooting even began (Tobias). This research included spending time in Falls City, where she attended the murder trials, visited the room in which Brandon was executed, and hung out at the local convenience store, just as we see Lana and Brandon do in the film (Tobias). Peirce explains that she focused on "find[ing] the underlying emotional truth" of the story, and constructed the film based on what scenes were pivotal to the viewers' understanding of that truth (Tobias). She aimed to make each character "somebody everyone can enter into" (Tobias). For this reason, she spends about two-thirds of the film simply developing Brandon's relationships with the residents of Falls

City, allowing us to get a feel for the inner workings of each character. Peirce strives to draw out the nuances of this story, to make the viewer understand that Brandon's life was complicated, that John and Tom's lives were complicated, and that this crime was complicated, too. Film critic Roger Ebert writes in his review that Peirce "sees Tom and John not as simple killers but as the instruments of deep ignorance and inherited anti-social pathology." Every small detail of the film is carefully chosen to add to our understanding of this culture in which John and Tom have been raised. We watch as Lana's face flushes with embarrassment when Brandon visits her house and they find her drunk mother (the only adult figure in the film) passed out on the couch. We watch as all of the characters gather in Lana's living room for Brandon's birthday party. We watch as Tom tells Brandon that he and John used to cut themselves all the time in lock-up, in order to "get control of this thing inside of [them]." All of these moments give us a sense of the depressing, damaging reality of life in Falls City. Peirce doesn't reduce John and Tom to shallow villains—instead, she allows us to see them the way Brandon initially did, as understandable, charismatic, funny people. Peirce states that "there wouldn't be much drama if they were going to kill him right up front. The drama is that he got seduced into thinking he might be safe and created a family out of them" (qtd. in Tobias). The effect of this meticulous character development is profound—it's what makes the film so potent.

Had Peirce simply depicted John and Tom as violent villains without any relatable human qualities, it would be easy to write this story off as irrelevant. *Oh, how sad that such crazy criminals exist. But, of course, I don't relate to them—they are nothing like me or anyone I know.* Peirce wants us to think twice before making that assumption. Because the truth is that John and Tom are humans, just like any of us. They have similar stories to many of the other men in Falls City: violent tendencies, drug and alcohol abuse problems, all a product of damaging upbringings and a particular environment. In some respects, John and Tom are like people you have met; perhaps, even, they are people like yourself. And before they committed these crimes, their friends would have denied they were capable of it. They are not isolated monsters, and this is not an isolated issue. This is where the "emotional truth" that Peirce works so carefully to cultivate hits us (Tobias). She presents the characters of John and Tom without demonizing them—the film facilitates a deep understanding of the struggles these men have faced. Because of that, we are able to have a degree of empathy for them, to understand the factors that could have led them to commit the crimes that they did, even though we don't agree or approve.

As much as Peirce's filmmaking enables us to empathize, we still struggle to grasp why John and Tom's upbringings and experiences lead them to commit the horrific crimes that they do. This seemingly incomprehensible question of 'why?' is exactly what Kelley and Gruenewald attempt to answer through their research. They note that violent crime situations arise from attempts on the offenders' part to "reproduce [their] own masculine identity, in addition to policing the perceived subordinate masculine identities of other men" (Kelley and Gruenewald 7). When John and Tom discover that Brandon is trans, they immediately become enraged because they see Brandon as a threat. Their own cultural understandings tell them that 'real men' can only be the violent, aggressive, hyper-masculine people they have been exposed to in Falls City, in prison, etc. As producer Christine Vachon insists, the film "is not just about two stupid thugs who killed somebody. It's about these guys whose world is so tenuous and so fragile that they can't stand to have any of their beliefs shattered" (qtd. in Maslin). This, ultimately, is why John and Tom are driven to rape and murder Brandon—they are insecure and feel the need to reassert their dominance and power. They instinctually turn to violence, as that is their cultural conception of 'problem-solving,' considering that aggression is part of the hegemonic ideal of masculinity (Kelley and Gruenewald 6).

Additionally, Kelley and Gruenewald explain that there are generally two scenarios of anti-LGBT violence: "The first scenario consist[s] of attacks between people, usually men, [occurring] in a public space and . . . often 'marked by a tone of outrage,' whereas the second violent scenario [is] more confrontational in nature and typically occurr[s] in private" (7). Interestingly, we see both of these scenarios unfold in *Boys Don't Cry*, which serves to solidify the link between the violence and John and Tom's senses of masculinity.

In the most brutal scene of the film, we watch as, right after Brandon is exposed as transgender, an enraged John and Tom force him into their car and drive to an empty lot. "You know you brought this on yourself, Teena," John says as he drags Brandon out of the car and proceeds to punch him. It's worth noting that John refers to Brandon by his birth name here, Teena, in order to further strip him of his masculinity. John diverts the blame onto Brandon because, in his mind, sexually violating Brandon is justified—he is simply reclaiming the inherent dominance his own cultural conceptions of maleness have led him to believe he is entitled to, while subordinating Brandon's 'alternative' version of masculinity. John and Tom are angry at Brandon for what they consider to be his 'deception'—they feel threatened by his successful performance of masculinity, and the only way they know to get 'revenge' is to humiliate and degrade Brandon as they do here. This is how fragile their conceptions of masculinity are—this simple realization about Brandon turns their world upside down and in their minds, violence is the only way to regain control.

The scene where John rapes Brandon is depicted in quick flashes: Brandon's head hits the car seat, John pulls his pants off, John climbs on top of him, we see Brandon's bloodied, anguished face as he cries and attempts to squirm away. In between each of these flashes, we return to shots of Brandon at the police station; while he reports the rape, the flashes come as he remembers the rape during this interview. Peirce states that this was the only way she could depict this rape; in real-time, the scene wouldn't have been effective, because "Brandon doesn't want to remember the rape" (Tobias). And so what we see are the fragments that remain seared into his consciousness, the moments he can't forget despite all efforts.

Peirce's depiction of the rape is made all the more powerful through the counterpart police station scenes, where Brandon is mercilessly interrogated and stripped of his masculinity by a male officer. "I can't believe that he pulled your pants down and that, if you are female, he didn't stick his hand in ya or his finger in ya," the officer presses him. Brandon protests: "I don't know what this has to do with what happened," as the officer continues to harass him about his gender identity. The officer asks: "Why do you run around with guys, bein' you're a girl yourself? Why do you go around kissin' girls?" In the span of just four minutes, Peirce manages to serve blow after blow, both physically and mentally, to Brandon, but she refuses to reduce him to the victim—even after all of this, he picks himself back up and attempts to recover his identity.

What *Boys Don't Cry* shows us is a world full of prejudices, a world where hegemonic masculinity underscores all relations, a world where every character is imperfect, a mix of good and bad qualities—in other words, the film portrays reality. *New York Times* reviewer Janet Maslin commends Peirce for her ability to portray "profanity, nudity, frank sexual situations, violence and rape without seeming lurid in the least." Truly, nothing in the film is gratuitous, as everything contributes to the construction of Brandon's specific reality. We're meant to come away from the film shocked by the normalcy and realism, by the realization that this actually happened. Maslin's article is titled "Sometimes Accepting an Identity Means Accepting a Fate, Too," and this hints at the dichotomy the film ultimately leaves us to grapple with: if society is opposed to their identity, can a person ever truly be themselves without also being in danger?

For Brandon and thousands of other trans people who continue to be murdered because they don't conform to normative gender roles, the answer, horribly enough, seems to be no. In a strange paradox, *Boys Don't Cry* is as specific as it is universal because—although the film is focused solely on Brandon's narrative—the "emotional truth" at its core remains very relatable (Tobias). Brandon's story inadvertently speaks to the stories of many other LGBT people. Take, for example, Matthew Shepard. As a website run by the Matthew Shepard Foundation outlines, Matthew was a young gay man who was brutally tortured and murdered by two homophobic men in the small Midwestern town of Laramie, Wyoming in October of 1998, right around the filming of *Boys Don't Cry* ("Matthew's Story"). And the film remains relevant today, as crimes continue to be perpetrated against LGBT-identifying individuals. Just a few months ago, on March 26, 2016, a transgender woman was raped by a heterosexual man in the bathroom of a New York City bar, the *New York Post* reports (Cohen and Prendergast). Anti-LGBT violence is not just a problem of the 1990s Midwest—after all, poor, dysfunctional communities are hardly unique to Nebraska. The circumstances that shaped John and Tom's conceptions of masculinity—poverty, drugs, alcohol, family instability, lack of social mobility, etc.—exist all over the country, even in cities labeled as 'progressive,' like New York. These locations are not as diametric as they seem—in the end, we are all humans struggling with similar issues. No matter where we live, the truth in Brandon's story hits home.

Within Brandon's story is a statement: he wound up "paying a terrible price" for simply attempting to be himself, a price he never should have had to pay (Maslin). Peirce simply depicts the story and lets it speak for itself. She doesn't present us with a solution—because there isn't one—but she paves the way for a discussion, for action, for change, or for, at the very least, some degree of reflection about how problematic our society and its values are. It's too late to save Brandon, but it's not too late to learn from him.

WORKS CITED

Allen, Jamie. "'Boys Don't Cry' Filmmaker Saw Past Violence to Love." *CNN.com*. Cable News Network, 22 Oct. 1999. Web. 24 June 2016.

Boys Don't Cry. Dir. Kimberly Peirce. Perf. Hilary Swank, Peter Sarsgaard, and Chloë Sevigny. Fox Searchlight Pictures, 1999. DVD.

Cohen, Shawn, and Daniel Prendergast. "Transgender Woman Says She Was Raped in Stonewall Inn Bathroom." *New York Post*. News Corp, 28 Mar. 2016. Web. 7 Apr. 2016.

Ebert, Roger. "Boys Don't Cry." *RogerEbert.com*. Ebert Digital LLC, 22 Oct. 1999. Web. 7 Apr. 2016.

Green, Jamison. "Part of the Package: Ideas of Masculinity among Male-Identified Transpeople." *Men and Masculinities* 7.3 (2005): 291-99. Web. 29 Mar. 2016.

Kelley, Kristin, and Jeff Gruenewald. "Accomplishing Masculinity through Anti-Lesbian, Gay, Bisexual, and Transgender Homicide: A Comparative Case Study Approach." *Men and Masculinities* 18.1 (2015): 3-29. Web. 29 Mar. 2016.

Maslin, Janet. "FILM FESTIVAL REVIEWS; Sometimes Accepting an Identity Means Accepting a Fate, Too." *The New York Times*. The New York Times Company, 1 Oct. 1999. Web. 21 Mar. 2016.

"Matthew's Story." *Matthew's Place*. Matthew's Place, n.d. Web. 7 Apr. 2016.

Tobias, Scott. "Kimberly Peirce." *A.V. Club*. Onion Inc., 27 Oct. 1999. Web. 29 Mar. 2016.

Written for Senior Lecturer Jeannie Im's Freshman Seminar, "Globalization and the Modern Novel in English," this essay examines U.S. military involvement in Latin America and how it led to the drug and immigration crises we face today. Leigh Anderson calls on readers to support human rights across national boundaries.

LATIN AMERICAN IMMIGRATION AND THE DRUG CRISIS

Leigh Anderson

In recent years, Mexican and Latin American immigrants have been strongly and unfairly discriminated against because of false notions numerous Americans have about how immigration affects the United States. "When Mexico sends its people, they're not sending their best. . . . They're sending people that have lots of problems. . . . They're bringing drugs. They're bringing crime," presidential candidate Donald Trump emphasizes. And, while many people recognize the absurdity of this statement, it accurately reflects several of the stereotypes that have caused Americans to fear immigration rather than embrace it (qtd. in Lee). The stereotype that immigrants come to the United States to sell drugs and commit crimes is extremely backward—much of the time, that is exactly what they are fleeing. As *The New York Times'* David Brooks reports, studies have been conducted that show that less than two percent of male immigrants in the U.S. between ages 18 and 39 have served jail time, as opposed to over three percent of native-born American men in the same age range. He reveals that over a hundred U.S. cities that participated in a study to investigate the correlation between immigration and crime rates found that the influx of immigrants during the 1990s and early 2000s actually preceded a decline of crime in most cities (Brooks). U.S. citizens, especially low-wage workers, also worry that Mexican immigrants "take jobs from Americans, and strain the welfare, educational, and healthcare systems," as acknowledged by sociologists Michael T. Light and Dimeji Togunde in "The Mexican Immigration Debate: Assimilation and Public Policy" (279). However, Robert LaLonde, a professor in the Harris School of Public Policy Studies at the University of Chicago, states that the "presence of illegal immigrants in some service jobs makes it easier for Americans to participate in the labor force. The immigrants act as complements to higher-wage workers, who can then participate in greater numbers and become more productive" (qtd. in Merken). Light and Togunde also cite several economic studies that show "illegal immigration from Mexico has a minimal impact on wages in US border areas," and "both legal and illegal immigrants pay more money in taxes than they consume in educational and social services," boosting the U.S. economy (280).

In fact, all of the concerns about the supposedly rising levels of undocumented immigration may be entirely unfounded. Mexican immigration hit its apex in 2005, and has been decreasing ever since (Brooks). Last year, the U.S. experienced an outflow of 140,000 Mexican immigrants as more left the country than entered (Preston). Moreover, according to Jeffrey Passel, a senior demographer at the Pew Research Center, the "[a]pprehensions of Mexicans are lower than any time since 1970" (qtd. in Hunt). So, if the downsides of immigration are exaggerated, and the number of undocumented immigrants crossing the border has decreased during Obama's presidency, it seems as if this situation is wholly positive. But, if we examine exactly why Latin American immigration is down, we come to question the U.S. immigration policy, which is in need of revision if it is to humanely accommodate refugees and migrants.

According to Sonia Nazario of *The New York Times*, "Mexico has carried out a ferocious crackdown on refugees fleeing violence in Central America" because of pressure from the United States government. In preventing undocumented immigrants from reaching the border, the U.S. has implicitly caused a refugee crisis in Mexico, which is now full of migrants trying to flee the gang and cartel violence in their hometowns in El Salvador, Honduras, or Mexico itself. Nazario tells the story of July Elizabeth Pérez, a single mother of three whose eldest son was killed by gang members in Honduras when he was just fourteen, now desperately trying to escape to the

United States. Though her mother and grandmother reside legally in Miami, Pérez has still not been granted a visa, and she and her children were sent to a refugee camp after traveling for nearly three weeks (Nazario). Migrants "are being hunted down on a scale never seen before and sent back to countries where gangs and drug traffickers have taken control of whole sections of territory," Nazario explains. "They are often tortured and held for ransom. The survivors tell of being enslaved working in marijuana fields or forced into prostitution" (Nazario). Hence, the United States' overemphasis on border security has led to an undeniable breach in human rights on the Mexican side of the border. More education in the United States about the full situation of immigration—the real causes and effects that people on both sides of the border experience—is necessary in order to cause a collective change in perspective, and ultimately a change in policy.

In an interview about their book entitled *Migrations and Mobilities: Citizenship, Borders, and Gender*, Seyla Benhabib and Judith Resnik discuss the issue in "criminalizing immigration, rather than viewing it as part of the human condition" (qtd. in Gordon-Zolov 272). Like Nazario, they believe that the economic implications of accepting refugees are secondary concerns compared to the value of human life, and that the U.S.—and people everywhere, as a whole—should actively "seek a humane and just answer," a concept they discuss many times in their book is the "right to have rights" (272, 274). In a changing, globalized world in which migration is rife, there should be a way for countries to protect the rights of even non-citizens. Currently "there is still no mechanism for asking states to naturalize immigrants or to grant entry to refugees," and "no legal statute whereby in fact the claim to citizenship of migrants, refugees, and asylees must also be respected" (275). This results in refugees and migrants being disrespected, exploited, and treated as inferior human beings as they move into other countries, which proves that the construct of citizenship needs revising.

If more people understood what hardships these refugees and migrants endured, the concept of citizenship would most likely be under more scrutiny and greater action would be taken to help those in desperate situations. However, a major problem regarding the crisis in Latin America is the lack of awareness that people in the United

States have regarding the violence and turmoil that these people are experiencing. In the past ten years, drug cartels in Mexico have gained an obscene amount of power, and have started zeroing in on local politics (Grillo). In his *New York Times* article, Ioan Grillo describes the coldblooded murder of Gisela Mota, who had been the new mayor of Temixco, a town in Morelos State, Mexico, one of the prime areas for drug cartel activity. "For a decade, Mexican troops have worked with American agents to pursue kingpins, in what is known as the cartel decapitation strategy," Grillo explains, meaning that officials attempted to crack down on the cartels' prominent leaders, hoping that would be an important stride in ending Mexico's drug war. However, this strategy went disastrously wrong; once the leaders were out of the picture, their hired killers, known as *sicarios*, created their own cartels. Since then, Mexico's murder rate has skyrocketed (Grillo).

Political corruption is one primary cause for the worsening of the crisis. Grillo reports that in the drug crisis's early years, gangsters targeted political figures with bribes; but, since they have gained so much prominence in the past ten years, and because of rampant corruption, "gangsters are flipping this century-old deal. Instead of handing out bribes, they are making the mayors pay them." Grillo also notes that corruption in Mexican politics has made it nearly impossible to get a handle on the drug crisis, as there have been numerous instances in which mayors were actually directly linked to gangsters involved in cartels. And though the United States is theoretically trying to help solve the crisis by giving the Mexican government approximately $300 million annually to fight the cartels, an unknown and possibly very large portion of this sum goes directly to the cartels, whether through bribes, extortion, or corrupt politicians (Carlsen, Grillo). In response to Grillo's claim that "cartels now fight for political power itself," political analyst Laura Carlsen submitted an opinion piece to *The New York Times*, explaining that "the cartels are not fighting the state for political power; they are seeking to protect a $40 billion drug-trafficking business that has been converted into a war for control of territory, a war against the people" (Carlsen). While this is probably true, there is no doubt that gaining political power is an extremely effective way to obtain territory and cause rampant fear and paranoia among the people. In a collection from the *Los Angeles*

Times, a chilling photo depicts a man being comforted by soldiers over the death of his brother, who was shot in the city of Juárez. The caption, in part, reads: "Many Mexicans don't trust authorities enough to report crime or suspicious activity" (Bartletti). Corrupt and gang-laden, much of Mexico is not safe for its own people, let alone the Honduran, El Salvadorian, and other Latin American refugees that are detained in camps after fleeing the violence in their own countries.

The United States should be helping these migrants rather than subjecting them to a corrupt system in which they—according to Nazario—may be captured, tortured, sent away, or thrown into unsanitary jail cells while awaiting visas unlikely to ever arrive. Nazario's article states that "Mexico granted asylum to 18 children last year." Only 18. The pressure that the United States has put on the Mexican government to keep migrants from crossing the border has developed into a human rights crisis, as Mexico has become increasingly strict in sending migrants back to their own countries. So what can the United States do to help Latin American migrants and make strides to stop the drug crisis?

To start, the U.S.'s pseudo-involvement in fixing the drug crisis sprawling across Latin America has, so far, only made matters worse. Its stance must change. Mexican citizens resent the United States for the damage they have done, as "victim organizations that have organized throughout [Mexico] demand that the United States stop funding the drug war under any guise" (Carlsen). With its current political and economic situation, Mexico will not be able to solve the situation on its own. If any progress is to be made, there must be some form of cooperation between the U.S. and Mexico in handling the crisis, with the U.S. taking an active stance while not pursuing complete control. Ideally, the U.S. should work with the Mexican government to spur both political and police reforms, including "build[ing] an effective justice system to crack down on sicarios" and "incorporating Mexico's city-level officers into unified state forces" to create a stronger authority that can stand up to cartels and eventually eliminate them (Grillo). Grillo argues that "the United States should use its drug-war aid to push harder for such reforms," ensuring that the money is used correctly, rather than entrusting it to the corrupt politicians that may be linked to the cartels in the first place. Essentially, the most headway would be made if the two governments collaborated to stop the violence, since the Mexican government is too weak to enforce greater security by itself. However, the U.S. should avoid taking total charge on its own, as this would most likely lead to even more hostility from the victims of the crisis.

Of course, the ten-year-long Mexican drug war and the widespread gang violence throughout Latin America will not be simple conflicts to solve, nor is everyone in the United States ever going to share the same perspective on what our immigration and border policies should be. But one thing is certain: as Nazario implies, the United States needs to stop using Mexico as a zone for detaining refugees, as this is only creating an even more desperate situation. Looking at the statistics, we can see that immigration has had a largely positive effect on American society in the past. David Brooks notes that immigration has raised GDP, lowered crime, diversified the nation, and has not actually lowered wages like many people think it has. Nazario emphasizes the importance of "open[ing] the door" to refugees, viewing them as human beings in nearly hopeless situations which we can easily help them out of. If the United States were to provide refuge for many of these asylum-seekers, the power of the cartels may subside, at least slightly, since part of their power comes from spreading fear among the people. Carlsen describes the drug war as "a war against the people," implying that the cartels thrive, in part, off the terror they cause. Fewer people to terrorize would lead to a decrease in power for them and, with weaker cartels, the U.S. could work with Mexico more closely to weed out corruption and make greater progress in ending the drug war.

At the same time, it is also clear that the United States immigration policy needs revision. Legal immigration to the U.S. is not only a very involved, complicated process, but is also extremely unyielding, allowing the minuscule number of 70,000 refugees into the country each year, with a further limit of only 5,000 from Latin America and the Caribbean ("How the United States Immigration System Works"). The United States holds a population of nearly 320 million; a refugee influx of 70,000 accounts for 0.02 percent of that. The U.S. also "provides for an annual worldwide limit of 675,000 permanent immigrants, with certain exceptions for close family members;" considering Pérez's case, the exceptions aren't always particularly effective ("How the United States Immigration System Works"). If a migrant finally reaches the U.S., there is an arduous process for obtaining citizenship. According to the American Immigration Council, "applicants for U.S. citizenship must be at least 18 years old, demonstrate continuous residency, demonstrate 'good moral character,' pass English and U.S. history and civics exams, and pay an application fee, among other requirements." The process is involved, and many refugees may not be able to meet all the standards. The description also vaguely hints at "other requirements," implying that there may be complications and the procedure can be prolonged further ("How the United States Immigration System Works"). If the process of getting into the United States wasn't so dangerous and gaining citizenship was easier, there would be a humane alternative for desperate migrants and less concern about undocumented immigration. Securing our borders isn't the issue: opening them is. That is certainly not to say we should eradicate border patrol completely. Rather, in the words of Brooks, we do need to "work on our legal immigration system—make the system ample and streamlined enough so that most people come here in the right way" (Brooks). The process could certainly be more lenient, and the pressure on Mexico to keep migrants away is causing more problems than it is solving. In addition to revising its immigration policy, the United States could provide immediate assistance to refugees by funding cleaner, livable camps with adequate food. Nazario also argues that the U.S. should work toward finding homes for refugees outside of Latin America, which could be done using a portion of the money they are giving to the Mexican government in the form of aid.

Since revising the process to obtain citizenship is not necessarily an easy thing to do, Benhabib and Resnik offer temporary solutions to improve the situations of refugees and migrants while they are undocumented. "Citizenship isn't the only way to be a rights-holder in the twenty-first-century social order," Resnik explains, elaborating on the concept of a "citizenship of the world" (qtd. in Gordon-Zolov 279). That is to say, countries should still be required to protect their inhabitants, "provide security for persons within their borders," and ensure quality of life regardless of citizenship status (qtd. in Gordon-Zolov 281). One idea of theirs is to have some form of "citizenship of place" rather than citizenship of state, because a refugee or migrant should still be treated like a human being even if he does not have national citizenship (qtd. in Gordon-Zolov 275-276). Resnik questions why people's statuses are determined on a national level. One possible change is that migrants and refugees could initially be acknowledged and have rights on a local level so that they are not considered undocumented, and simply have their right to vote on a national scale withheld until they are able to maintain full citizenship (qtd. in Gordon-Zolov 276). This would still be an imperfect process, but it would be a promising first step toward providing more humane treatment to undocumented immigrants in the future.

There are undoubtedly limitations. Many would argue that the U.S. would be stronger as a nation if it focused solely on domestic rather than foreign affairs, but it is important to consider the U.S.'s moral responsibility. It would also be useful to know approximately how many refugees would come into the U.S. seeking unskilled labor, and how many Latin American refugees the United States can realistically take in, but this number is certainly greater than 5,000. Therefore, these limitations still leave room for the United States to perform its humanitarian obligation of assisting these refugees and migrants to some extent. Why should people suffer simply because they don't possess this artificial construct we call citizenship? It is time we change our definition of citizenship so that it helps vulnerable immigrants rather than keeping them powerless. Benhabib and Resnik's idea of citizenship of place is not without its flaws, but in a globalized world, it makes much more sense to view people as global citizens, with each individual having her own rights, rather than being bound by one state and then excluded or exploited by another.

WORKS CITED

Bartletti, Don. "Soldiers Console the Brother of a Shooting Victim in Ciudad Juarez in 2009." *Los Angeles Times*. Los Angeles Times, n.d. Web. 1 May 2016.

Brooks, David. "A Little Reality on Immigration." *The New York Times*. The New York Times Company, 18 Feb. 2016. Web. 25 Apr. 2016.

Carlsen, Laura. "The Drug War and Mexico." *The New York Times*. The New York Times Company, 25 Jan. 2016. Web. 25 Apr. 2016.

Gordon-Zolov, Terri. "A Conversation with Seyla Benhabib and Judith Resnik." *Women's Studies Quarterly* 38.1 & 2 (2010). 271-86. Print.

Grillo, Ioan. "Why Cartels Are Killing Mexico's Mayors." *The New York Times*. The New York Times Company, 15 Jan. 2016. Web. 12 Apr. 2016.

"How the United States Immigration System Works: A Fact Sheet." *American Immigration Council*. American Immigration Council, 1 Mar. 2014. Web. 1 May 2016.

Hunt, Albert R. "Facing the Facts on Illegal Immigration." *The New York Times*. The New York Times Company, 19 July 2015. Web. 20 Apr. 2016.

Lee, Michelle. "Donald Trump's False Comments Connecting Mexican Immigrants and Crime." *The Washington Post*. The Washington Post, 8 July 2015. Web. 1 May 2016.

Light, Michael T., and Dimeji Togunde. "The Mexican Immigration Debate: Assimilation and Public Policy." *International Review of Modern Sociology* 34.2 (2008): 279–93. *JSTOR*. Web. 7 Apr. 2016.

Merken, Christopher. "Shattering Stereotypes: 'Illegal Immigrants.'" *Radnor Patch*. Patch Media, 24 Oct. 2012. Web. 9 May 2016.

Nazario, Sonia. "The Refugees at Our Door." *The New York Times*. The New York Times Company, 10 Oct. 2015. Web. 7 Apr. 2016.

Preston, Julia. "More Mexican Immigrants Leaving U.S. Than Entering, Report Finds." *The New York Times*. The New York Times Company, 19 Nov. 2015. Web. 20 Apr. 2016.

Conceived in Kirin Wachter-Grene's "Writing the Essay," Nicolas Kugel's essay examines the way language works through cultural imperialism and colonization. Kugel analyzes Jamaica Kincaid's work to observe how marginalized peoples can seize autonomy and power through language and thereby rewrite their own narratives.

A POSTCOLONIAL REVISION

Nicolas Kugel

With the prevalence of mercantilist thinking in the 16th and 17th centuries, the desire for greater economic control over the world increased. Believing that the best way to grow their economy was to minimize reliance on trade, governments sought to control as many people and resources as possible ("Mercantilism"). To this end, the most powerful European empires began to establish colonies throughout the world in order to create a larger market for their goods. Arguably, the most successful empire was Great Britain, which at one point controlled a quarter of the land on Earth, including large swathes of Africa, India, parts of China, and several Caribbean islands. Although these colonies were primarily created to export resources, they also became a means to spread English culture. In her book *Key Terms in Literary Theory*, Mary Klages asserts that the idea behind colonialism was "to import [the colonizing nation's] customs, laws, educational and disciplinary systems, religions, and literature, and then to assert its culture as superior to the indigenous culture" (16). According to Klages, the conquest of a foreign land by an imperial power is inseparable from the conquest of a native culture by a colonial entity. As such, the societies born from a colonial relationship are not only physically and governmentally controlled by a foreign power, but they are also culturally controlled through a system that is definitionally biased against them.

Antigua and Barbuda, one such colony, is the backdrop of Jamaica Kincaid's essay "On Seeing England for the First Time," an examination of the impact of an imposed culture on the identity of a colonized person. From a young age, Kincaid was taught to view England with great reverence. When her teacher described England, "[it] was as if she said, 'This is Jerusalem, the place you will go to when you die but only if you have been good'" (366). England was presented to Kincaid as Edenic, a place one could only dream of living in, full of people one could only dream of being like. This character-ization formed the basis for Kincaid's sense of inferiority and erasure. The English countryside described by the many English authors Kincaid was forced to read had "gentle mountains and low blue skies and moors over which people took walks for nothing but pleasure" (368). It represented an idyllic way of life that was incongruous with the struggles endured in Antigua and Barbuda, a place where "a walk was an act of labor, a burden, something only death or the automobile could relieve" (368). The gap between the representation of England perpetuated in Antigua and the realities of her own life became a form of oppression. She felt burdened by the daily reminders that Antigua's environment, the only uncontrolled part of her country, was inferior to England's. Her life in Antigua began to feel like a punishment where "the sun shone with what sometimes seemed to be a deliberate cruelty [that] we must have done something to deserve" (368). Kincaid felt imprisoned in an imperfect and difficult life, and the dis-parity between her existence and the lives in England described to her served as a constant reminder of her perceived inferiority to Antigua's colonizers.

Over time, Kincaid came to realize that these descriptions of England presented to her were misleading and the systemic deception present in colonial Antigua becomes the focal point of her anger. As she notes, "[t]he space between something and its reality is always wide and deep and dark" (369). But without knowing what the other side looks like, it is impossible to tell just how wide and deep and dark this gap truly is. Kincaid only realizes how distorted her sense of England was when she visited it for the first time. This gap between how England was presented to her through education and literature and how she now perceived England "[h]ad become filled with hatred, and so when at last [she] saw it [she] wanted to take it into [her] hands and tear it into little pieces and then crumble it up as if it were clay, child's clay" (370). Kincaid becomes disillusioned with, and resentful of, England because she realizes that its Edenic representation that caused her erasure bore little resemblance to the England that she was looking at. She concludes with frustration that she could never properly articulate her disillusionment because:

> If I had told an English person what I thought, that I find
> England ugly, that I hate England . . . I would have been told that
> I was a person full of prejudice . . . I may be capable of prejudice,
> but my prejudices have no weight to them, my prejudices have no
> force behind them, my prejudices remain opinions, my prejudices
> remain my personal opinion. (370)

Kincaid could go to England and form prejudices against its people, cuisine, and culture, but because she exists in the subservient role within the colonial power structure, her prejudices would only remain her own personal opinions. Her lamentation does not indicate malicious intent, but instead recognizes that she is unable to impose her prejudices on a people because she lacks the structural power to enforce them. It is the realization that she is incapable of impacting a society in the same way that the English did.

Kenyan author Ngugi wa Thiong'o also discusses the negative effects of an imposed culture in an excerpt from his book *Decolonising the Mind*. In an effort to make Kenya more British, all children were taught exclusively in English, and the schools they went to strictly enforced a ban on their native language, Gikuyu. Thiong'o argues that because "[l]anguage carries culture, and culture carries . . . the entire body of value by which we come to perceive ourselves and our place in the world," learning in the language of one's colonizers culture is problematic (339). He states that "[s]ince culture does not just reflect the world in images, but actually through those images, conditions a child to see that world a certain way, the colonial child was made to see the world and where he stands in it as seen and defined by or reflected in the culture of the language of imposition" (340-341). At its core, language is both a carrier and byproduct of culture. As such, the fact that Thiong'o and his peers were being taught exclusively in English meant that they were seeing themselves through the lens of Anglo-centric history and English culture. Consequently, their understanding and perception of their own culture and identity were tinged with the legacy of bigoted thought expressed in the foreign language. By adopting this foreign language, the people of Kenya displaced their own sense of self and began to be defined by the prejudices of the colonizer's culture.

Similarly, through the colonial school system's romanticized portrayal of England, Kincaid's sense of self and place began to be defined by the prejudices of English culture. She didn't have the power to define her own identity in the colonial society because, just as Thiong'o observes about the people of Kenya, where Kincaid stood in the world was "defined by . . . the culture of the language of imposition" (Thiong'o 341). Kincaid notes that "England was to be our source of myth and the source from which we got our sense of reality" (366). This quotation illustrates Kincaid's understanding of the colonial power dynamic through the double meaning of the words "myth" and "reality." In one sense, Kincaid is stating that England was intended to be Antiguans' sense of fiction and truth. But in another sense, Kincaid is stating that England was also intended to be their source of mythology, their source of cultural lineage. As a result, her sense of self worth was diminished because England was granted, through a definitionally prejudiced power structure that aimed "to assert its culture as superior to the indigenous culture," the capacity to dictate the very nature of Kincaid's identity (Klages 16).

"How to Write about Africa," a satirical essay by Binyavanga Wainaina, describes this power dynamic through an ironic how-to manual on how a Western author should write about Africa. The satirized author in this piece exists as an avatar of the Imperial Gaze, an inherently unequal perspective that grants the Western author the power to define the people he or she is observing. In the narrative described by Wainaina, "African characters should be colorful, exotic, larger than life—but empty inside, with no dialogue, no conflicts or resolution in their stories, no depth or quirks to confuse the cause" (530). In this hypothetical book about Africa, the people who actually live there are given the supporting role to the colonizer's protagonist.

The continent is flattened of its depth and character, and pushed to the background because the people who live on it are not allowed to define it in the Western narrative. Wainaina argues that the real purpose of this book is not to tell stories about Africa, but to assert a sense of Western heroism. The continent and the people who live on it exist only to accentuate the triumphs of the Western protagonist.

Kincaid's sense of erasure, caused by the enforcement of English mythology, is an example of the dynamic presented by Wainaina. In school, "[she learned] the names of all the kings of England . . . [She] knew their conquests and was made to feel good if [she] figured in them" (Kincaid 368). The historical narrative presented to Kincaid placed the English as the protagonists. As a result, the morality and benefit of their actions were defined through the colonizer's biased perspective. They were the heroes of their own story, the leading players in the imported mythology that now defined Kincaid's reality. Consequently, Kincaid and her fellow countrymen remained in the background of their own country's history. Just as Africa became a place to accentuate a sense of Western heroism, Antigua became a place to celebrate the triumphs of English colonization and conquest. Just as the African characters in Wainaina's hypothetical story are one dimensional and exist purely to support the Western protagonist, Kincaid became a minor character in her own life. Because England held narrative control in the colonial power structure, the story of colonialism was not written by or about the people that lived through it; it was written by and about the people who created it. Kincaid exists in a supporting role because the narrative of colonial life in Antigua was used as a means of asserting English cultural dominance instead of representing the lives of the colonized people.

This relationship can be seen from another perspective in "On Not Winning the Nobel Prize," a speech by Doris Lessing discussing the importance of literature in society. Lessing, an English author who spent part of her childhood in Southern Rhodesia, points out that, prior to the nation's colonization, its "[p]eople might have been storytellers working in the oral tradition" (537). Before the introduction of written language and Western literature by the English, Southern Rhodesia, now Zimbabwe, did not have a well-developed written linguistic tradition. Lessing points out that "[i]n order to write, in order to make literature, there must be a close connection with libraries, books, with the Tradition" (536). Lessing claims that for a country to develop a literary culture, it must have a connection not only with written language, but also the Western literary tradition. This statement has merit, but is fairly problematic. It is true that it would be difficult for a country to develop a literary culture without any books. She cites, for example, three authors born in English colonies who only became authors after being exposed to the vast wealth of Western literature. But Lessing's argument falls short at the necessity of a connection to the Western tradition. The act of teaching the people of what is now Zimbabwe how to write did not inherently damage their culture; the damage came from enforcing colonial culture as an absolute good and an unquestionable necessity. In other words, here the tool of written language is again used as an arguably oppressive force that asserts the Western tradition as the aspirational standard of written expression. However, without the imposition of a colonial framework, written language would not be damaging because it would not necessarily be a cultural imposition.

This distinction between cultural exchange and cultural imposition is critical to understanding Kincaid's claims about the nature of prejudice and its greater implications. She argues that because she, and the people of Antigua, exist in the subservient position of the colonial dynamic, "[t]he people I come from are powerless to do evil on a grand scale" (Kincaid 370). Transferring this logic into the context of cultural interaction, one can now see that Kincaid's sense of erasure wasn't a direct product of English culture, but the power structure that allowed it to become so dominant. She became a supporting character in her own life story not because it contained elements of English culture, but because it was actually being written by the English. The root cause of a colonized people's marginalization stems from the colonizers' power to define their place in society. Without the ability to impose a biased cultural narrative, the presence of a foreign culture is not inherently damaging to the native identity.

Perhaps the greatest arguments in support of this point are the texts themselves. By writing their works in English, Kincaid, Thiong'o, and Wainaina have appropriated English culture and the English language as a means of critiquing the colonial system. They have taken control of the narrative from their former colonizing powers and are using the imposed language to tell their side of the story. Kincaid is now the main character and England is cast as the antagonist. Antigua is no longer a setting that demonstrates English superiority, but a prison of carnival mirrors skewing the perception of everyone inside. By using English outside of the constraints of a colonial structure, its purpose is no longer defined by the people who imposed it. It now has the power to communicate a revised narrative of colonialism, granting the colonized people a level of agency and power to influence others. Perhaps Kincaid and all those who lived under colonial rule lack the ability to do evil on a grand scale, but their words now have the power to do good.

WORKS CITED

Kincaid, Jamaica. "On Seeing England for the First Time." *The Broadview Anthology of Expository Prose*. Eds. Laura Buzzard, Julie Gaunce, Don LePan, Mical Moser, and Tammy Roberts. 2nd ed. Toronto: Broadview Press, 2011. 366-70. Print.
Klages, Mary. "Colonialism." *Key Terms in Literary Theory*. London: Continuum, 2012. Web. 3 Nov. 2015.
Lessing, Doris. "On Not Winning the Nobel Prize." *The Broadview Anthology of Expository Prose*. Eds. Laura Buzzard, Julie Gaunce, Don LePan, Mical Moser, and Tammy Roberts. 2nd ed. Toronto: Broadview Press, 2011. 532-43. Print.
"Mercantilism." *The Princeton Encyclopedia of the World Economy*. Eds. Kenneth A. Reinert and Ramkishen S. Rajan. Princeton: Princeton UP, 2010. Web. 22 Dec. 2015.
Singh, Amardeep. "An Introduction to Edward Said, Orientalism, and Postcolonial Literary Studies." Amardeep Singh. Lehigh University, 24 Sept. 2004. Web. 28 Oct. 2015.
Thiong'o, Ngugi wa. "Decolonizing the Mind." *The Broadview Anthology of Expository Prose*. Eds. Laura Buzzard, Julie Gaunce, Don LePan, Mical Moser, and Tammy Roberts. 2nd ed. Toronto: Broadview Press, 2011. 333-41. Print.

Wainaina, Binyavanga. "How to Write about Africa." *The Broadview Anthology of Expository Prose*. Eds. Laura Buzzard, Julie Gaunce, Don LePan, Mical Moser, and Tammy Roberts. 2nd ed. Toronto: Broadview Press, 2011. 528-31. Print.

Denise Zhou wrote this essay about malleable identity in David Foley's "Writing the Essay: Art in the World." She examines film history and film genre to explicate a single film, Dope. *A generous handling of journalism, academic scholarship, visual evidence and radio broadcasts support her argument against social stereotyping.*

COMING OF IDENTITIES

Denise Zhou

How you living, large?
A broker charge, cards are mediocre
You flippin' coke or playin' spit, spades, and strip poker?

—Nas, "The World is Yours"

Panning down from a clear blue sky, interrupted only by a number of long, thin palm trees—an iconic, leafy symbol of Los Angeles—the camera brings us to our beloved trio riding BMX bikes down an endless, empty road. Nas's "The World is Yours" thumps smoothly in the background as we're introduced to a suburbia baked in the lazy summer feel of *Dope*'s California sun. Every element of the scene—from Malcolm's orange bike, to Diggy's yellow crop top, to the virtually pastel blue sky—plays off a vibrant color palette reminiscent of the neon hues of decades past. The protagonists pedal effortlessly past nearly identical beige houses, curb-parked cars, and large green trash cans. They bike in snaking routes, weaving across the empty street. A simple interlude, a transition into the next scene: all at once this image captures the essence of these characters, their friendship, and the setting. For a moment, the complicated plot is forgotten, and we are simply left with these characters, existing solely as friends, as kids, as people.

Rick Famuyiwa's *Dope* follows straight-A student Malcolm and his best friends Jib and Diggy in their coming-of-age journey as seniors in 'The Bottoms' of Inglewood, a suburb infamous for gang violence and drug use, predominantly inhabited by working-class African-American and Latino populations. The film centers on Malcolm and his friends as they traverse outrageous situations; we watch the trio of friends get bullied, play in their punk band, go to a party, end up with a huge stash of MDMA, try to get rid of the huge stash of MDMA, and face the numerous consequences—consequences that become intertwined with who they thought they were, who others see them as, and who they want to be.

Introduced by off-screen narrator Forrest Whitaker as nineties-obsessed, band-loving nerds, the protagonists of *Dope* are rarely seen without each other. Their camaraderie is created in part by the similarities of their differences. Attending a high school with metal detectors and drug-sniffing dogs, Malcolm's peers are not nearly as concerned about grades and college as he and his friends are. Many Inglewood residents—both within the school and outside—have already participated in the projected expectations of a crime and drug-filled neighborhood by being part of gangs, dealing drugs, or shooting up fast food restaurants. However, Malcolm, Jib, and Diggy have actively avoided all of the above, choosing instead to focus on their aspirations to leave Inglewood, go to college, get good jobs, and help their families. Their friendship represents a distinct acknowledgment of how they fit in (or, rather, don't fit in) with their community. They are, in a word, misfits.

The idea of the misfit has, over the last few decades, increasingly proliferated in film, particularly in the American teenage coming-of-age genre. As Timothy Shary discusses in his book *Generation Multiplex: The Image of Youth in Contemporary American Cinema*, while the earlier days of cinema did not target adolescents or market a youth genre, more recent films are deliberately "fixated on capturing certain youth styles and promoting certain perspectives on the celebration (or really, survival) of adolescence" (1). With changing economic, social, and cultural factors—namely a recovering economy post-World War II, a greater number of adolescents staying in school, and the rising popularity of rebellious rock-and-roll music—the film industry began testing teen roles in theaters (Shary 6). With the success of *Rebel Without a Cause* in 1955, a gateway opened for using teen angst and delinquency as a platform for entertainment. In the eighties, "Hollywood revised its fifties formula by intensifying the narrative range of youth films through placing teenage characters in previously established genres with more dramatic impact" (Shary 6). This expansion gave way to the five subgenres we now have in the youth coming-of-age genre—horror, science, love/sex, delinquency, and the school film. Of course, these subgenres are not exclusive. *Dope* in particular demonstrates an incredible blending of genre: it is a comedy, a drama, a hood film, a coming-of-age story, a school film, and a teen delinquency/crime film all wrapped into an hour and fifty-five minutes.

In his book, Shary examines the elements of each subgenre. The school film, for example, uses its setting to establish social standings and relationships crucial to the characters' identities and coming-of-age journeys. Acceptance, both of the self and by others, is a common theme in all youth films; the school film specifically uses the characters' "physical placement in the school environment" to give "a visible reminder of their plight" through puberty, conformity, and rebellion (Shary 27). Hollywood's view of high school teenagers has primarily existed through five main character types: the athletic jock, the popular beauty, the outcast rebel, the endearing delinquent, and the quiet nerd. As the youth genre developed, the characters did, too, becoming more multifaceted. They have transformed into an array of different kinds of misfits, ultimately defying their surface-level labels to show their complexities: the athletic jock is secretly emotional, the popular beauty is internally burdened by social expectation, the outcast rebel is "psychologically distraught," the endearing delinquent has a heart-breaking backstory that explains his mischief, and the quiet nerd has an ambitious career goal "inspired by a desire to rise above [his] class conditions" (Shary 31). Films like Amy Heckerling's *Fast Times at Ridgemont High* and John Hughes's *The Breakfast Club* enforce these character tropes, proving that we are, after all, products of our environments, and that how and where youths are raised greatly impact their desires and the situations they encounter.

Famuyiwa's *Dope* works off the theme of environmental influence: the characters are raised in a "bad" neighborhood and thus the
plot points of the film occur accordingly, involving the characters in
violence, crime, sex, and drugs. The film emulates a number of the
patterns identified in the school film subgenre, including its ambitious
nerd characters who are "seeking identity in relation to their peers"
(Shary 47). While the school film focuses on the use of setting and
character, the delinquent film is more primarily concerned with situations involving "class and race issues, family dynamics, genetics and
psychology, and political conditions" (Shary 81). The rebellious acts
portrayed in films have ranged from frolicking at the beach, dancing,
interacting with animals and nature, mastering "hot wheels" of fast
cars, bikes, and skateboards, and, most relevantly, committing crimes.
As Clifford Terry reveals in his essay "Hollywood High," many
popular coming-of-age films feature "upper-middle-class white sub-
urbanites from two-parent, one-dog homes." And while such characters can be labeled as "misfits" within the contexts of their respective
social worlds, their differences are typically just that: differences. The
stakes that these characters face are rarely life-or-death; often, the
consequences they encounter are more internal, less tangible.

The same cannot be said for *Dope*. Although it seems, at first, to
be "a black *Breakfast Club*, where the geeks' geekdom mostly comes
from their love of '90s hip hop and 'white shit,'" a sense of real danger
looms over the film's comedic and playful aspects (Kornhaber). Most
likely, under Shary's classifications, *Dope* would still be considered an
"African American crime film," or a "hood film." This style of youth
crime genre began to develop in the early nineties, in which African-
American filmmakers addressed race issues through the experiences
of Black male adolescent characters living in "violent urban conditions" (Shary 123). Famuyiwa makes it a point to address many racial
issues in his film, pointing out many of the differences between the
life of typical geeks and the life of *Dope*'s geeks. While a bad day for
a regular geek might involve getting bullied by a jock, a bad day for a
geek in The Bottoms might end with getting killed. As Whitaker tells
us in his introductory narration, it's "a daily navigation between bad
and worse choices." In Spencer Kornhaber's review of the movie,
"*Dope*: When High-School Hijinks Are Life-or-Death," he claims

that *Dope* is different from other coming-of-age films "less because of the color shift [and more] because of what this particular color shift means in the real world. Being a geek here isn't just about being obsessed with unpopular stuff; it's about opting out from cultural expectations as a way to try and survive."

In the world of *Dope*, Malcolm, Jib, and Diggy are different from everyone else mostly because of their musical tastes, good grades, and Ivy League aspirations. As Terry Gross points out in her radio interview with director Famuyiwa, "part of what pop culture means when you're a teenager, the music you love, the movies you love, is—it's a way of defining who you are . . . pop culture has . . . two purposes in young people's lives—just loving it but also saying 'that's who I am'" (qtd. in "'Dope' Director on Geekdom . . ."). Through their interests, the characters attempt to distance themselves from the image that others expect them to gravitate toward. This image is influenced in part by the neighborhood's bad reputation and also in part by the characters' racial identity.

As James Cox asserts in his article "Obama, Hip Hop and a New Black Masculinity," the representation of Black males in media is often centered on either "the completely threatening and race affirming Bad Black Man or the completely comforting and assimilationist Good Black Man" (34). Of course, the concept of the Bad or Angry Black Man comes from a history of stereotyping and confining the identity of African-American individuals, often reinforced by media-formulated images of Black masculinity. These images have been heavily influenced by a "substyle" of mainstream hip hop music, wherein a lifestyle based on "hustling, crime, sexual domination, and drug dealing" is normalized and promoted (Rose 13). In Byron Hurt's short film *Barack & Curtis: Manhood, Power & Respect*, radio host and playwright Esther Armah speaks to the differences in representation of masculinity between President Barack Obama and hip hop rapper 50 Cent, suggesting that, by the time of the former's election in 2008, "Gangsta rap had begun to shape the definition of Black manhood to the degree that it made middle class men lose their place in manhood . . . in terms of a media image. Everywhere you went the image of manhood in every form of creative media came out of that

50 Cent mold; if it wasn't thugged out it wasn't manhood" (*Barack &
Curtis*).

What's interesting about *Dope* is that it uses hip hop as an important character and plot aspect, while in no way promoting the
"thugged out" image like many other films and music videos do. In
fact, because Famuyiwa has placed a plethora of hip hop culture and
music alongside these odd, geeky misfits, a new image of what hip
hop can mean for Black male youth is carefully cultivated. This new
outlook on the relationship between hip hop and Black masculinity is
also seen in Barack Obama's relationship with hip hop. Obama has,
since the beginning of his presidential career, voiced his love for hip
hop music and culture while simultaneously denouncing the more
negative themes of misogyny, materialism, and bad language often
found in hip hop lyrics (Cox 32). Obama's engagement with hip hop
music and rap artists has showed his connection to the African-
American community. His image as an educated, well-spoken Black
man placed alongside a genre of music often negatively portrayed in
mass media "[explodes] the very facile and simple notions we have of
what it means to be a Black man in this society. Obama's intellect is
one of the foremost things you will notice about him, [he] is the very
antithesis of the angry, out of control Negro" (*Barack & Curtis*).
Obama's "Good Black Man" image merges with hip hop, and, as the
two find a way to exist in harmony, we start to move toward a more
complex idea of who and what a Black man can be. We start to accept
that the identity is not confined to the one stereotype perpetuated by
the media and centuries of racism.

Dope presents this complex idea not only through hip hop, but
also through the use of drugs, crime, and violence in its plot. Malcolm
and his friends are remarkably smart, and make way for a rise of
"Black nerds" in the coming-of-age genre. These characters are not
angry or violent, and work incredibly hard to avoid participating in
angry and violent activities. Despite their efforts, one decision to
attend a party entangles them in a web of gangsters and drugs. This
turn taken by the movie suggests how easily individuals in communities like Malcolm's can become trapped in that dangerous world, in
which one decision can create a slippery slope and lead to unforeseen
and unintended consequences. Black coming-of-age crime films often

depict adolescents "fighting for their lives, under the hegemony of a racist legal and political system, under difficult family and class conditions, and under the influence of the media that were rapidly codifying the image of young Black 'gangstas' through certain rap music acts" (Shary 123). Many films such as *Super Fly* and *Boyz N the Hood* use drugs in their narratives to reflect a reality in which young people must deal with drug or crime-related situations. Often the protagonist must make a choice between 'good' and 'bad' in an effort to 'get out of the hood.' While *Dope* tiptoes around this same idea for a while, Famuyiwa ultimately decides to trade the expected in for something a little different. By factoring in the unfamiliarity the characters have with this new world they have fallen into, he shows the kids using their intelligence and geekiness to deal with the drugs in a very unconventional way, selling them on the Internet for profit. With this shift, Famuyiwa begins poking at something deeper than an affirmation of the good vs. bad cliché. In the context of identity, the boundaries of what *Dope* presents with its main characters begin to expand; the existence of the complex Black man (or woman) is exhibited in all of *Dope*'s characters.

At one point in the film, after encountering a couple of rich kids and their subtly menacing Harvard alum father, Malcolm gets on a bus, exhausted by the day's events. As Malcolm makes his way to a seat to wait out the ride home, "Home is Where the Hatred Is" by Gil Scott-Heron begins to play. Malcolm sits dead center in the back; shots of the bus and its riders are intercut with the changing L.A. light that streams through the big bus windows. Malcolm begins to dream that each of the friends, acquaintances, bullies, gangsters, and everyone else he met that day all get on the bus. As the bus fills one by one, they all nod to the song and look back at him. The moment is one of peace, much like the opening bike scene, but instead of just the trio, we are encouraged to look at everyone. While much of the movie is focused on Malcolm and his struggle with identity, in this moment, it implies that he is not alone. *Dope*, although largely driven by comedy, makes a serious point to challenge the way people see all 'kids from the hood.' The straight-edge nerds could easily be dope-dealing gangsters and the dope-dealing gangsters are likely just as smart and nerdy as Malcolm. The societal expectations and dangers that shaped each different character in Inglewood—from drug dealers to violent gangsters to Malcolm's own friends—prove to be much more threatening 'villains' than any of the gangsters or bullies that harass the protagonists. Every person is multi-dimensional, and, on the bus, the viewer faces the reality that these characters should not be blamed for their backgrounds and circumstances. There is no good vs. bad; there are only decisions that each individual makes—decisions that, as Whitaker says in the beginning, often straddle the line between bad and worse.

At its simplest identification, *Dope* is about misfits Malcolm, Jib, and Diggy. But through scenes like the one on the bus, where we gain a deeply empathetic perspective on what every single character is going through, we begin to see more than a city of gangsters and nerds. We see a community of misfits. Malcolm's self-acceptance is a journey that comes hand in hand with his experiences in the film. What he chooses to do with the drugs is not so much a concern with what is morally right as it is a concern with what is going to best work to his advantage. Malcolm asserts his identity as both a straight-A, guitar-playing nerd and a (one-time) drug-dealing blackmailer, merging two unexpected identities. While the youth crime film typically "examine[s] the representation of teenagers' senses of power . . . in relation to . . . ethnicity and class issues" through violence, *Dope* goes a step further and acknowledges the power Malcolm gains simply by accepting the two supposedly warring halves of his identity (Shary 51). If we can look at Malcolm in the movie and find complexity in his character, we can do the same in reality. *Dope* is set in a real city with real crime problems, and the reminder that Malcolm's world runs parallel to ours—that he and the other characters could very well be real people—is vital in moving away from a limited conception of Black identity in our society.

WORKS CITED

Barack & Curtis: Manhood, Power & Respect. Dir. Byron Hurt. God Bless the Child Productions, 2008. Film.

Cox, James. "Obama, Hip Hop and a New Black Masculinity."
    Academia. Academia, 2011. Web. 24 June 2016.
Dope. Dir. Rick Famuyiwa. Perf. Shameik Moore. Open Road
    Films, 2015. Film.
"'Dope' Director on Geekdom, the N-Word and Confronting
    Racism With Comedy." *Fresh Air.* National Public Radio.
    WHYY-FM, Philadelphia. 1 July 2015. Radio.
Kornhaber, Spencer. "*Dope*: When High-School Hijinks Are Life-
    or-Death." *The Atlantic.* The Atlantic Monthly Group, 19 June
    2015. Web. 24 June 2016.
Nas. "The World is Yours." *Illmatic.* By Nasir Jones and Peter
    Phillips. 19 April 1994. CD.
Rose, Tricia. *The Hip Hop Wars: What We Talk About When
    We Talk About Hip Hop—and Why It Matters.* New York:
    Basic Books, 2008. Print.
Shary, Timothy. *Generation Multiplex: The Image of Youth in
    Contemporary American Cinema.* Austin: U of Texas P, 2002.
    Print.
Terry, Clifford. "Hollywood High." *Chicago Tribune.* Tribune
    Publishing, 19 Sept. 1993. Web. 16 Dec. 2015.

Weaving a profile of author Ayn Rand together with details from her fiction and nonfiction, and tracing her impact on American culture, Allison Kiteley's essay from Bruce Bromley's "Writing the Essay" offers an explanatory depiction and a scathing critique of Objectivism's echoes.

THE INTERNET SHRUGGED

Allison Kiteley

Logging into the online forum site Reddit yet again, I can't help but think of Ayn Rand. Another commenter—convinced that my viewpoint, because it is different from his, must not be 'rational'—has misrepresented and twisted an opinion I posted into an almost unrecognizable straw man argument. He might as well be the long-dead philosopher, reaching out to me in a thread about economic inequality to berate me for being a 'Subjectivist.'

Rand probably would have liked Reddit. After all, its founding principle is freedom of speech, the economic views of its average user lean right, and it has a reputation as a ruggedly individualistic landscape. Anyone can comment, but only the best, most 'upvoted' comments are widely seen. The worst are hidden, minimized automatically when under a certain threshold of points. Reddit demonstrates many of 'Objectivism's'—that is, Rand's philosophy's—ideas in action.

In many ways, Objectivist ideas have become intertwined with American economics. Our conservative party's aim to deregulate business, along with its stern propagation of individual merit as a means of overcoming hardship and achieving success, heavily reflect Rand's worldview. And while prioritizing rationality, upholding the values of the free-market system, and hyper-valuing the individual are not ideals unique to Rand, she's had a heavy influence in popularizing those ideas and normalizing them throughout Western society. This has been, in part, thanks to Alan Greenspan, former Chairman of the Federal Reserve, once referred to by Jay Leno as "the most powerful man in the world" (Hitchens). Greenspan was a member of Rand's inner circle, 'the Collective'—a purposely ironic name, referencing Rand's deep opposition to collectives as a detriment to individualism. Greenspan was hugely influenced by Rand's ideas about economics and individual freedom—which informed his opposition to "anti-trust and consumer-protection laws" and the draft (Hitchens).

The influence of Objectivism permeates American culture. Our strong valuation of individualism, emphasis on hard work and talent as a direct means to success, and intense focus on 'objective fact' as the basis for any convincing argument about even subjective topics all speak to Randian ideals. But so what? What's so wrong with individualism? Hard work? Being rational? In my view, nothing, inherently. But when presented in the unique design that Rand created, the results have devastating economic effects; in the wake of the Financial Crisis of 2008, even Greenspan himself admitted that he had "found a flaw" in the anti-regulation ideology, though he refused to accept blame for the collapse (Andrews). Beyond the purely economic, however, Rand's ideas have had an immense effect on the way progressive politics are viewed and dealt with, and there is no greater site for observing these effects than the rugged outback of Internet forums and comment sections.

Before I delve much deeper into the effects of Rand and Objectivism, I want to backtrack a bit and examine Rand and her ideas to clarify my thinking. It seems fitting to introduce Rand on her own terms, so I'll try to explain her as 'objectively' as possible. Rand was born in 1905 in Russia—just before the Bolshevik revolution—to a Jewish family and given the name Alisa Rosenbaum. During the revolution, her father's pharmacy was seized "in the name of the people," and, by her 21st birthday, knowing her outspoken tendencies would not bode well for her in Leninist Russia, her family sent her off to live in America. Upon arrival, she changed her name to Ayn Rand and sought to write stories to express her burgeoning philosophy: Objectivism (Hari).

Objectivism posits that there is one 'objective' reality which we can reach only through rationality. As Rand puts it, it is "the recognition of the fact that a perceiver's (man's) consciousness must acquire knowledge of reality by certain means (reason) in accordance with certain rules (logic)" ("Racism"). Additionally, Objectivism tells us that through these means, we discover that self-interest is the most rational, and therefore moral, way of living. Finally, it posits that capitalism optimizes rational self-interest through its protection of individual rights, and therefore is the only viable economic system ("Introduction to Objectivism").

It's hard to deny, especially from a privileged perspective, that Rand's ideas are attractive. What person wouldn't be thrilled to hear that by living only for themselves, they are doing what's best for everyone else as well? Rather than the typical tension between 'doing whatever I want' and 'being a good person,' the two become one and the same. She claims, even, that this approach to thinking can end social ills such as racial discrimination, positing that the "only" cure to racism is "the philosophy of individualism and its politico-economic corollary, laissez-faire capitalism" ("Racism"). It seems almost too good to be true, like a cure-all coming from a snake-oil peddler (who, incidentally, operates within his own self-interest). It all really seems to have sold well in the United States.

More interesting, arguably, than Rand's philosophy, is the way she argues for it and against other ways of thinking. Her argument style has two main features: misrepresenting opposing sides, and taking her own ideas, before even proving them, as axioms. She often refuses to source the claims she uses to bolster her arguments. A good example of this comes from her own definition of Objectivism relative to the opposing ideology she calls 'subjectivism.'

Rand tells us that subjectivism is "the belief that reality is not a firm absolute, but a fluid, plastic, indeterminate realm which can be altered, in whole or part, by the consciousness of the perceiver—i.e., by his feelings, wishes or whims" ("Who Is the Final Authority in Ethics?"). Given this definition of subjectivism, most people would reject subjectivism, as Rand does, as a fantasy and a delusional way of living. Her definition's emphasis on the idea that one can alter one's own reality depending on one's "wishes or whims" makes subjectivism seem at best an extremely abstract way of viewing the world and at worst like a fantasy. However, subjectivism was already an existing philosophy before Rand's definition, and its more widely accepted definition is less abstract. Most dictionary definitions read something like the following: "the practice of giving priority to or laying emphasis on subjective consciousness, personal experience, etc.; any of various methods based on advocating this" ("subjectivism *n.*").

In my view, the more accepted definition is vastly more reasonable than Rand's. It's a part of epistemology that's widely accepted in sociology, whether in name or only in practice, as much of sociology emphasizes the role that hegemony plays in deciding what is 'objective' and what is wrong. Rand chose to define subjectivism as she did for a reason, and, given the difference in definitions, it's reasonable to say that her misrepresentation was purposeful. Even if it were an honest mistake, it benefits her by painting her own ideology as comparatively 'rational.'

Of course, such a disingenuous comparison with an invented version of 'subjectivism' was not even necessary, as Rand continues her argument in favor of Objectivism by establishing it as the only antidote to moral ills. One example she gives is racism, which she argues can only be ended through "the philosophy of individualism and its politico-economic corollary, laissez-faire capitalism" ("Racism"). In a fashion typical for her, Rand feels no need to prove this claim, simply assuring the reader that "racism has always risen or fallen with the rise of collectivism" ("Racism")."Collectivism," for Rand, is the rule over the individual by the group, a notion which she deeply despises, assuming the reader shares her contempt for any dearth of individualism.

I strive to give credit where credit is due, and if anything can be said of Rand, for better or worse, it's that she lived—and nearly died—by her philosophy. Potential contradictions within her ideology aside, Rand was no hypocrite. In an exhaustingly Objectivist display, Rand challenged the statistical evidence of the connection between smoking and lung cancer as "unscientific and irrational" (Levine). She had a small change of heart when she had to have surgery for the lung cancer that developed as a result of her smoking two packs a day. Yet while Rand quit, her followers respected her original assessment of the evidence and continued to smoke (Levine). The whole ordeal ended up as a possibly unintentional emulation of Dagny Taggart (the only female protagonist of Rand's ultimate fictional expression of Objectivism: *Atlas Shrugged*), who similarly disregarded the views of "the best metallurgical authorities" in choosing to buy an untested new metal alloy to use in building new railways (*Atlas Shrugged* 27). Fortunately for Ms. Taggart, Rand wrote her world so her protagonists' high-risk decisions always paid off. Unfortunately for Rand, however, whoever wrote her world was not so generous, and refusing to seek outside expert opinions is generally not wise.

All of this is to say: Rand was a strongly principled woman who argued for the philosophy she truly believed was as rigorous and correct as a philosophy could be and who strove in every way to live by its principles. And, ultimately, she argued these principles well enough to gain respect from major economists and businessmen. According to a 1991 joint survey by The Library of Congress and the Book of the Month Club, Americans considered *Atlas Shrugged* the second most influential book, losing only to the Bible (Fein). And while the economic effects of Rand's philosophies have been widely explored and critiqued, it's her influence, as I noted before, on reactions to progressivism that concerns me.

The connection between Rand's work and modern anti-social justice (hereafter referred to as 'reactionary') movements on the Internet is not tenuous by any stretch of the imagination. Whether they know it or not, reactionaries act in an Objectivist mindset. From Objectivism serving as an underlying philosophy in many reactionary arguments to Rand's outright support of some reactionary principles, the two were practically destined to intersect.

The primary way in which reactionaries are effectively Objectivist is in how they view the current world. Objectivist dogma relies on a world in which everyone has equal opportunities to succeed, and so hard work genuinely does translate into success. In such a world, hierarchies, power structures, oppression, and privilege are either negligible and can be overcome (as is the case with class) or do not provide significant hindrance outside of social ostracism (in the case of sexism and racism, among others). To reactionaries, oppressed groups such as women, Black people, gay people, transgender people, and others are not really oppressed; they can always get past it: the wage gap would close if women would just pick higher paying jobs, Black people would be more respected if they would just pull up their pants, gay people would be accepted if they just didn't act so gay, transgender people wouldn't be murdered if they would just get surgeries until they acceptably passed as their gender (or better yet, were just 'normal'). To put it another way, if they just pulled themselves up by their proverbial bootstraps, they could be as successful as their cisgender, straight, white male peers. This notion is the very core of Internet reactionary movements; after all, if they admitted there was a problem, they couldn't assume their moral high ground without hiding their support of discrimination.

Let's look again at Dagny Taggart, Rand's self-inserted heroine. Rand admits that many of her other characters do not find it "natural that [Dagny] should be the Operating Vice-President of a great railroad" because she is a woman, telling us that sexism does exist in some form in her imagined universe (*Atlas Shrugged* 24). But, in true Objectivist form, and in a fashion replicating reactionary fantasy, Taggart's first realization that some might object to her running a railroad elicited from her only the response "to hell with that," after which she "never worried about it again" (51). Taggart's rise from a night operator at a railroad at age 16 to Vice President in Charge of Operation of the same line at 32 was "swift and uncontested" as a result of "[doing] the work before she was granted the title": she represents a model worker for a laissez-faire capitalist economy (51).

Internet reactionaries also fall into the Objectivist trap of assuming their arguments and viewpoints are rational and objective when the opposite is often true. It's hard to argue against an angry white man on the Internet about how the cards are stacked against non-white people and women without him accusing you of being irrational or overly emotional for not seeing things the way he does. This understanding that hegemonic thought is rational thought is a perfect example of Objectivism in action: when one believes there is only a single way of seeing reality, one Truth, it's easy to accuse anyone who doesn't share your views of seeing the world incorrectly or through a subjective lens—as if all personal viewpoints weren't by definition subjective.

An extremely visible and recent example of this comes in the form of GamerGate, the misogynistic harassment movement thinly veiled as fighting for the "integrity of games journalism" (Cox). A core complaint of the GamerGate movement was that video game reviews had become "subjective"—a few reviewers had decided to include misogyny and other similar social-justice-related ideas as factors in their reviews of games like Grand Theft Auto. Arthur Chu, who makes a career writing about such Internet movements, remarks that those who object to more inclusive reviewing practices are "convinced that their opinion is 'objectively' correct," that is, that their opinion is factual, and therefore reviews they disagree with are incorrect, and "subjective" (Chu). Rand would have been pleased.

Beyond her merely ideological influence, Rand was an ardent supporter of free speech for even the most fascist among us, and directly opposed social-justice-oriented policies, such as affirmative action. In a section of her article on racism, Rand basically echoes the 'All Lives Matter' catch-phrases regarding 'white guilt' and 'reverse racism,' explaining that "racial quotas . . . [demand] that white men be penalized for the sins of their ancestors" ("Racism"). This, I suppose, is an easy viewpoint to have when you think that the free market can solve racism on its own.

Rand and Internet reactionaries are more similar than they are different, and the cultural climate Rand has influenced has contributed to their way of thinking. They seem to be growing in power and self-righteous fury. The aforementioned GamerGate movement spilled off out of the Internet, harassing one woman to the point of committing suicide and bullying many others into leaving games journalism for good (Miller; Cox). The neo-Nazi website Stormfront has taken note of the climate of growing racial tension and aims to recruit new members, hoping to radicalize the casual racists of the Internet (Biddle). These are the kinds of reactionary movements we are paying for today, and which may grow in the not so distant future.

Bruce Levine argues that Rand made us into an "uncaring nation," and "[made] it 'moral' for the wealthy not to pay their fair share of taxes . . . [and] . . . 'liberated' millions of other Americans from caring about the suffering of others, even the suffering of their own children" (Levine). I think she's done even more than that; I think she's fed hatred and bigotry, and fed an apathy toward the status quo that goes far beyond the economic and the personal. Rand unintentionally helped validate the hate from the worst among us as rational, placating many with the notion that we shouldn't worry about oppression or discrimination or inequality. The free market will take care of it; it's only rational, isn't it?

WORKS CITED

Andrews, Edmund L. "Greenspan Concedes Error on Regulation." *The New York Times.* The New York Times Company, 23 Oct. 2008. Web. 27 Apr. 2016.

Biddle, Sam. "Reddit Is So Racist White Supremacists Are Using It to Recruit." *Gawker.* Gawker Media, 13 Mar. 2015. Web. 17 June 2016.

Chu, Arthur. "It's Dangerous to Go Alone: Why Are Gamers So Angry?" *The Daily Beast.* The Daily Beast Company LLC, 28 Aug. 2014. Web. 27 Apr. 2016.

Cox, Carolyn. "Female Game Journalists Quit Over Harassment, #GamerGate Harms Women." *The Mary Sue.* The Mary Sue, LLC, 4 Sept. 2014. Web. 4 May 2016.

Fein, Esther B. "Book Notes." *The New York Times.* The New York Times Company, 20 Nov. 1991. Web. 2 May 2016.

Hari, Johann. "How Ayn Rand Became an American Icon." *Slate.* The Slate Group, 2 Nov. 2009. Web. 2 May 2016.

Hitchens, Christopher. "Greenspan Shrugged." *Vanity Fair.* Condé Nast, Dec. 2000. Web. 27 Apr. 2016.

"Introduction to Objectivism." *AynRand.org.* The Ayn Rand Institute, n.d. Web. 27 Apr. 2016.

Levine, Bruce E. "How Ayn Rand Seduced Generations of Young Men and Helped Make the U.S. into a Selfish, Greedy Nation." *Alternet.* Independent Media Institute, 15 Dec. 2011. Web. 27 Apr. 2016.

Miller, Michael E. "'Killed Myself. Sorry.': Transgender Game Developer Jumps Off Bridge after Online Abuse." *The Washington Post.* The Washington Post, 28 Apr. 2015. Web. 4 May 2016.

Rampton, John. "25 Books Jeff Bezos, Mark Zuckerberg, and Other Top CEOs Recommend." *Inc.* Mansueto Ventures, n.d. Web. 2 May 2016.

Rand, Ayn. *Atlas Shrugged.* New York: Penguin, 1957. Kindle.

—. "Racism." *The Objectivist Newsletter* 2.9 (1963): 33-36. Print.

—. "Who Is the Final Authority in Ethics?" *The Objectivist Newsletter* 4.2 (1965). Reprinted by the Ayn Rand Institute. *ARI Campus.* The Ayn Rand Institute, n.d. Web. 1 May 2016.

"Subjectivism." *OED.* Oxford UP, n.d. Web. 29 June 2016.

Paris Martineau's essay, written in David Markus's "Writing the Essay," appears to take a scattered, rapid, and relentless approach to David Foster Wallace's novels and critical legacy. By blending form and analysis, it achieves a respectful reading of Wallace's proper place in our critical consciousness.

YOUR KIND-OF-SORT-OF-HALF-TRUTH IS STRANGER THAN FICTION

Paris Martineau

A man—eyes glued to the screen—unceremoniously shits himself in his ergonomically designed, body-molded recliner. His head lolls, mouth agape over the dinner tray that has been precisely snapped into place below his chin to allow for maximum viewing pleasure, and minimal effort, of course. Elsewhere, a boy snakes his way through the underbelly of a tennis court. His right arm (which is grotesquely oversized in comparison to his left as a result of thousands of forehand swings) struggles to correctly flick a spark into existence from the lighter held to his lips. He fervently tries again, this time succeeding. He exhales in rapture. A world away, a man attempts to picture himself on a beach: he fails. He knows he is not anywhere remotely tropical and the existential hell that is his IRS office cubicle offers no help in trying to form this fantasy. He breathes; he tries again, but the thought-crushing reality of total boredom sets in almost immediately this time. He contemplates suicide.

The characters in David Foster Wallace's novels exemplify the statement "[f]iction's about what it is to be a fucking human being" (qtd. in McCaffery). This remark, spoken by Wallace during a 1993 interview, preceded the publication of *Infinite Jest*, the massive novel which captivated readers with its unapologetic depiction of the human condition and rebelled against the end-of-the-century obsession with the minimalist post-modern conventions exhibited by authors such as Raymond Carver, Ann Beattie, and David Leavitt. Wallace's work is devoid of flowery metaphoric platitudes; instead, it overwhelms the reader with a matter-of-fact candor that assumes the role of a seemingly omnipresent, ever-truthful, all-seeing eye. He treats the subjects in his work with the utmost care. Whether he's writing of a casual locker room chat between teammates, or of a recovering drug addict watching his friend's eyes be sewn open as he lies in a puddle of his own piss, each scene of Wallace's demands the reader's careful attention.

Part of the appeal of Wallace's work is the specificity he brings to each subject. His use of endnotes (which is incredibly extensive— within *Infinite Jest* there are 96 pages dedicated to endnotes alone) allows for a near encyclopedic level of precision in his work as he weaves together 388 different entries of fake contextual evidence for the fictional world he has created. This mimicked truth becomes hard to differentiate from reality. For example, the in-depth "Filmography of James O. Incandenza," which describes the formation, plot, and release of 80 different 'films' created by a character within the novel, seems too complex and complete to have been created for mere reference in an endnote (*Infinite Jest* 985-994). The use of almost-truths and the pervasive nature of this not-so-factual-evidence calls into question the actual relationship between reality and fiction in Wallace's work. What is truthful? What is not? And how does this contribute to Wallace's idea of fiction as a depiction of actual humanity?

In Wallace's final novel, *The Pale King*, the "Author's Foreword" is not so forward. Sandwiched 68 pages into the text, it insists: "Author here. Meaning the real author, the living human being, the pencil, not some abstract narrative persona . . . [A]ll of this is true. This book is really true" (*The Pale King* 68-69). This, of course, was preceded, on the copyright page, by the classic fiction disclaimer: "the characters and events in this book are fictitious," which Wallace quickly disputes as a "legal necessity" (*The Pale King* 1, 69), creating a paradox that even he himself describes as a rather "irksome metaphysical titty-pincher" (*The Pale King* 69). *The Pale King* goes on to feature an array of characters, among them one who is oh-so-coincidentally named David Foster Wallace, who, in this life, is an employee at the IRS.

While this character is obviously fictitious, the intertwining of near-autobiographical truth and fantasy allows not only for the work to slip into the category of metafiction, but also for a deeper emotional commitment to be developed between the reader and author. His characters do not seem removed from reality; they are not attempting to be a symbolic representation of some larger swathe of mankind. The possibility that Wallace leaves open—that tinges of actual truth do exist within his work—allows for the almost accidental acceptance of these characters as people by the reader. This is perhaps most evident in Wallace's shorter piece, "The Planet Trillaphon as It Stands in Relation to the Bad Thing," which reads not as a short story, but as a memoir. Wallace begins with an ominous account:

> I've been on antidepressants for, what, about a year now, and I suppose I feel as if I'm pretty qualified to tell you what they're like. They're fine, really, but they're fine in the same way that, say, living on another planet that was warm and comfortable . . . would be fine: it would be fine, but it wouldn't be good old Earth, obviously. (26)

His existence on the planet Trillaphon, Wallace's moniker for the antipsychotic drug Tofranil, is described as a state of medication-induced physical separation from depression (which he aptly names The Bad Thing). Throughout the short story, Wallace gives an autobiographical account of the character's (or, perhaps, his) struggle with The Bad Thing, utilizing the first-person perspective from the inaugural sentence. This lack of distinction between the narrator and the author sustains the reader's belief that the piece is truth, rather than a fictional short story.

When he describes "the nature of The Bad Thing," in which "every single cell in your body is sick . . . all just sick as hell," the emotional authority of the piece is not merely that of an author writing about a character's depression, but that of a human being describing his own debilitating personal sickness ("The Planet Trillaphon" 29). This merging of reality and fiction allows for a deeper emotional commitment to be felt by the reader. Wallace is not contained by the staunch rules necessary for factual integrity, nor is he wholeheartedly indulging in the wild possibilities of fantasy. The interweaving of these two popular styles of literary thought leaves the reader with a sustained belief in the authenticity of the work due to the possibility of both truthful and fictitious claims being found throughout the narrative.

In the essay "Fictional Futures and the Conspicuously Young," Wallace writes that "we need narrative like we need space-time; it's a built-in thing" ("Fictional Futures" 8). His assertion comes in response to the mid-eighties backlash against the "endless succession" of postmodern "flash-in-the-pan short story starlets"—whom Wallace begrudgingly defends despite their overwhelming "sameness" ("Fictional Futures" 2). He states that the narrative nature of new entertainment requires that literature adapt to, or at least attempt not to discount, the mass appeal and engagement that such art forms provide. These ideas lend themselves to the belief that the types of narrative structures Wallace made use of were meant to ease the barrier of communication as he attempted to convey his thoughts. Yet the structural makeup of that same narrative is hopelessly complex. In fact, Wallace's comically maximalist style requires the reader to continuously disengage with the text's narrative in order to engage with its entirety. Within *Infinite Jest*, the constant use of endnotes leaves the reader physically flipping back and forth across the barrier of a thousand pages of text in order to continue the story linearly. The sprawling, fragmented form his pieces take on does allow for a thorough and astoundingly accurate depiction of the so-called 'human experience,' (which is usually one of the presumed goals of maximalism) but the great lengths—both physical and metaphoric—that he goes to in order to achieve this almost leaves the reader feeling as if he is being kept at an arm's length from the whole of his emotionally provocative prose.

In his article for *The New Yorker*, "The Unfinished," however, author D.T. Max describes this exercise in patience not as a nuisance, but as "[Wallace's] way of reclaiming language from banality while simultaneously representing all the caveats, micro-thoughts, meta-moments, and other flickers of his hyperactive mind" through the physical flickering of the page in hand. Max describes the choice to utilize endnotes as an integral aspect of the text as one which was born out of a desire to give the reader a visceral reminder that "what he was reading was invented—the final work of constructing a moral world was his" (Max). Such devices are reflective of the common postmodern parody of the structure and purpose of literature. However, this explanation does not completely remedy the concern in regards to the possible alienation of the reader as an after-effect of his structural choices, which could possibly hinder the emotional connection between author and reader. While Max's description of form as a model for thought in Wallace's work rings true, it fails to take into account the problems that arise due to the overt and incredibly intense maximalist nature of his work.

Wallace's essays provide the solution to this seemingly paradoxical issue. Limited by the boundaries of fact, and notable for their brevity, his essays present a straightforward clarity that is hard to come by within the vast expanses of works such as *Infinite Jest* and *The Pale King*. The voice that emerges out of these limitations is distinctly that of David Foster Wallace, yet the condensed nature of these works allows for an almost more fervent version of Wallace to reveal itself. Frequently, he writes in a manner that is disarmingly candid: a representative of the average overly-educated-thirty-something, on the edge of sarcasm, yet unmistakably sincere. In the piece "This Is Water," which is adapted from Wallace's Kenyon College Commencement Address, he states:

> And I submit that this is what the real, no-bullshit value of your liberal-arts education is supposed to be about: How to keep from going through your comfortable, prosperous, respectable adult life dead, unconscious, a slave to your head and to your natural default-setting of being uniquely, completely, imperially alone, day in and day out. (3)

There are no long-winded conceits used, no mixing of fact and fiction for an additional effect and connection, no endnotes, yet the poignancy of moments like this within his essays is comparable to the oh-so-highly acclaimed moments that come only after traipsing hundreds of pages into the depths of works such as *Infinite Jest.* Alexander Nazaryan, in an article titled "The Turbulent Genius of David Foster Wallace," speaks to this phenomenon, saying that "above all, [Wallace's] essays are sincere in a way that fiction can never be, since the mere act of passing off make-believe as truth is fundamentally dishonest."

One would think after reading Wallace's works of fiction—novels of great renown that bridge the seemingly unsurmountable gap between fact and fantasy—that this level of emotional connection (however convoluted it may be) is a product of the nature of the freedom of the novel, and a means to the proverbial end of describing this ephemeral and ever-changing "fucking human being" through a distinct narrative choice that could most certainly not exist within the confines of something as stodgy-sounding as an essay. However, upon reading Wallace's essays, it is soon apparent that the emotional power of his prose is not purely an epiphenomenon of his fiction writing, but an integral part of every form of his expression. His essays, which are rooted in fact, "could have only been written by David Foster Wallace" (Narzaryan). They diverge from the academic norm, "intimate in one sentence, cerebral in the next, dropping teenage slang and obscure jargon in the same dependent clause" (Narzaryan). They break apart the generally well-established conventions of the traditional essay and, from the ruins of what is often a trite form of expression, we see a reflection of how David Foster Wallace truly acts and thinks. He is just as intellectually restless in his essays as he is as a novelist (perhaps more so, actually), often obsessing over the most trivial of pursuits, yet whether he be writing on the minutiae of grammar as it relates to the publication of *A Dictionary of Modern American Usage* in "Tense Present," or the dreary horror that is the average Midwestern county fair in "Tickets to the Fair," he is full of the same vibrant humanity his fictitious works are praised for. He is sincere, joyous, and passionate in his quest—most of all, he is real.

The constant bait and switch that the realm of metafiction relies on is discarded here. Wallace separates himself from this gray area, and what emerges is astoundingly effective in its candid nature. Sobering, matter-of-fact statements exist within these works:

It is not the least bit coincidental that adults who commit suicide with firearms almost always shoot themselves in the head. They shoot the terrible master. And the truth is that most of these suicides are actually dead long before they pull the trigger. ("This Is Water" 3)

And such remarks remind us that—although the syntactical structure may be similar; although the fervent passion still exists—David Foster Wallace, the character who exists as a narrator in his fiction, is not the same David Foster Wallace as presented in his essays.

Those who have written of Wallace frequently entertain the idea of him as a mysterious man of half-truths that existed throughout his narrative work. He has been described as a brooding depressive, a tortured genius who came up for air only to spout off a poetic maxim and then solemnly return to his dark abode. This flagrant distortion of Wallace's identity grew only more widespread in the years following his suicide, an act which prompted many an autobiographical reading of stories such as "The Planet Trillaphon" and *The Pale King*. Soon, the very nature of Wallace's sense of self (unfortunately and ironically) slipped into the hands of the collective, and he became a bonafide cultural icon. Wallace, a man who weaved together tales of tennis prodigies and drug abusers, a man who pushed beyond the mid-century minimalist drivel, a man who constantly touted the "bull-shit-ness of literary fame" and scoffed at the "enormous hiss of egos" found in modern day authors, had been pigeonholed into the near textbook definition of the very thing he despised (Lipsky 193). In his article "The Rewriting of David Foster Wallace," author Christian Lorentzen puts it aptly: "Nobody owns David Foster Wallace anymore . . . he has been reduced to a wisdom-dispensing sage on the one hand and shorthand for the Writer As Tortured Soul on the other" (1).

The canonization of Wallace as the vague, bro-lit, depressed hero of the new era can be seen most clearly in director James Ponsoldt's controversial biopic *The End of the Tour* (2015), which portrays Wallace as an iconographic tortured saint. Film-Wallace is too much of a Holy And Pure Genius to behold the mundane nature of everyday life. He waxes poetically about the relationship between masturbation and death whilst cracking open a beer, and a trip to a convenience store turns into a metaphysical commentary on life. Film-Wallace, who should really be called The-Mind-Of-The-Collective-Wallace, is one 'holy-shit-this-guy-is-so-brilliant-and-unapproachable' moment after another. This Wallace is never trivial, or colloquial, or anywhere close to (as he would put it) a "fucking human being."

None of the joy for the simplicity of life found in Wallace's essays is seen in the film. Film-Wallace doesn't seem like the same man who could write 34 pages on the everyday implications of a particular dictionary like he does in "Tense Present" unless there was some awe-inspiring three to four sentence quip at the end that makes a broad and, of course, heavily ironic commentary on human nature (Film-Wallace loves commentary on human nature). This Wallace that has emerged as the so-called 'memorable one,' the 'biopic-worthy one,' is not the Wallace that he so adamantly decreed that he was throughout his nonfiction work, but the Wallace that exists within the pages of the emotionally intriguing half-truth, half-fantasy world that he was so skilled at crafting.

This world of popular imagination—which blurs the lines of autobiography and fiction for Wallace's developed narrative character—has thoroughly enveloped any remotely reality-based version of David Foster Wallace. The emotional connections his longer works make through their auto-fictitious claims create a visceral relationship with the reader. Yet, it is the intensity of these works that leads many to overlook Wallace's essays, which depict a more realistic version of his character, even if certain inescapable contrivances still remain.

All of this has caused the disconcerting dichotomy that exists between the Tortured Depressive Soul of the Genius David Foster Wallace and anything else that might partially represent an actually real person. His individuality as well as his humanity have both been lost somewhere in the void that we the readers love to fill with his entrancing narrative prose. "Every whole person understands his lifetime as an organized, recountable series of events and changes with at least a beginning and middle," Wallace writes ("Fictional Futures" 8). But perhaps he is an exception to this rule. It seems fittingly ironic that he—the man who prided himself on incomplete narratives and fractured stories—would live on in our minds as an equally fractured, part-fact, part-fictitious version of himself.

WORKS CITED

The End of the Tour. Dir. James Ponsoldt. Perf. Jason Segel and Jesse Eisenberg. A24 Films, 2015. DVD.

Lipsky, David. *Although of Course You End Up Becoming Yourself: A Road Trip with David Foster Wallace*. New York: Broadway Books, 2010. Print.

Lorentzen, Christian. "The Rewriting of David Foster Wallace." *Vulture*. New York Media LLC, 30 June 2015. Web. 24 June 2016.

Max, D. T. "The Unfinished." *The New Yorker*. Condé Nast, 9 Mar. 2009. Web. 24 June 2016.

McCaffery, Larry. "An Interview with David Foster Wallace." *The Review of Contemporary Fiction* 13.2 (1993). Print.

Nazaryan, Alexander. "The Turbulent Genius of David Foster Wallace." *Newsweek*. Newsweek LLC, 8 Jan. 2015. Web. 24 June 2016.

Wallace, David Foster. "Fictional Futures and the Conspicuously Young." *The Review of Contemporary Fiction* 8.3 (1988). Reprinted by Evan Martin: 1-15. *Neugierig.org*. N.p., March 2004. Web. 24 June 2016.

—. *Infinite Jest: A Novel*. New York: Back Bay Books, 1996. Print.

—. *The Pale King: An Unfinished Novel*. New York: Back Bay Books, 2012. Print.

—. "The Planet Trillaphon as It Stands in Relation to the Bad Thing." *The Amherst Review* 12 (1984): 26-33. Print.

—. "Tense Present." *Harper's Magazine*. April 2001: 39-58. Print.

—. "This Is Water." Kenyon College. Grambier, OH. 21 May 2005. Commencement Address.

Chelsea Moore pilots readers through the creative life of Robert Irwin. Writing in Senior Lecturer Victoria Olsen's Freshman Seminar, "The Rise of the Visual," Moore asks how minimalist art can engage a public dependent on constant stimulation. A return to simplicity is revealed as both challenging and necessary.

WHITE NOISE: OVERCOMING OVER-STIMULATION

Chelsea Moore

Pulling up to the Metro-North train station in Beacon, New York, I was quick to notice the incredible scenery along the Hudson River. It was a beautiful day: the trees were green and the water reflected the blue sky. As I exited the train and stepped off the platform, I saw the Dia:Beacon, a revamped former factory, hiding in the trees. When walking up to grand glass double doors, even the exterior of the museum is impressive. Previously a Nabisco box factory, the museum is abundant in wide, open spaces and prime for the exhibition I aimed to see: Robert Irwin's *Excursus: Homage to the Square³*. Juxtaposed to the busyness of New York City, the museum's lack of color and sound is alarming. It left me pondering whether such simplicity could still be entertaining, or if I would find myself quickly becoming bored with the absence of stimuli.

Excursus: Homage to the Square³ is featured in the Dia's first show space. Upon first impression, it appears to be a series of white walls with open doorways that create a sequence of integrated rooms which you are invited to walk through and explore. These walls, also called scrims, are made of sheer, white fabric draped over wooden beams. Skylights and windows provide natural light that floods the rooms and penetrates through the translucent walls. This light serves as a complement to the true star of *Excursus: Homage to the Square³*. Irwin is known for his work with fluorescent and other artificial light.

For this exhibit, he has created multicolored fluorescent sculptures that hang perpendicularly along the doorways. In a review in the *Hudson Valley Almanac Weekly*, Lynn Woods describes these sculptures vividly:

> Below and above the lit portion of the tubes, Irwin has wrapped layers of different colored theatrical gels, comprising a pattern of stripes. The colors are mostly somber—dark purples, lavenders, greens, browns and beiges—although in some instances, one or two narrow bands of color are illuminated: a bright red or yellow glowing strip that suggests signals.

In her description, Woods captures the subtle complexity of the fluorescent lights, and reveals how Irwin gracefully yet boldly plays with light and space in this piece. The multitude of light sources, natural and artificial, reflect and bounce off the walls and throughout the rooms. Glimpses of the shadows of fellow museum-goers may be caught as one moves through the space. The white of the scrims and the minimalist quality of the exhibit as a whole convey a strong sense of sterilization, as if the walls beg to be touched even though touch is forbidden. While this play on light and space may be ominous, it would be very difficult to walk away from *Excursus: Homage to the Square*[3] without feeling more calm and serene than you did upon entering.

    Throughout his career Irwin has continuously adapted and adjusted his artistic style in order to find a balance between his ideals and the accessibility of his work. Much of Irwin's work focuses on how the reduction of excess enhances the perception of his subject. His art challenges the shrinking attention span of the average person by forcing them to selectively attend to minimalistic pieces. The precision and specificity of *Excursus: Homage to the Square*[3] reflects the artist's everlasting pursuit of a perfect art form. However, this obsessive attention to detail may be easily overlooked by the average lay person, and begs the question: what does Irwin sacrifice for such perfection? Now, at the age of 87, Irwin is still looking for ways he can assert this minimalist style into a society overwhelmed by sensation.

In Peter Schjeldahl's "Improvising in Art and Life," Irwin's professional career is chronicled. Schjeldahl describes the early work as having "developed from paintings of barely perceptible lines or dots in monochrome fields, through transparent plastic columns and white plastic disks cantilevered from the wall, to entire white environments inflected only by light and bits of wire or tape or scrim." It is apparent in even his earliest work that Irwin's main focus is how the precision of his work guides viewers' perception. He makes artistic decisions laboriously, never overlooking how one color reacts to the next, or how one material may be more translucent than another. He obsesses over every element of his work. His lines must be perfectly straight, angles perfectly square, and colors chosen with an exactness unique to the Light and Space Movement.

However, crippled by his intense perfectionism in 1982, Irwin had yet to find true satisfaction with his paintings. He wanted to optimize the viewer experience, and believed his paintings failed to be stimulating enough to match his standards. In an interview with Jonathan Griffin from the international art magazine *Apollo*, Irwin recalls of his paintings: "They were really fucking bad. Just before the door opens. Woah. This is not good." While he was able to hyperfocus on the minimal elements of his paintings, appreciation for the precision was not widespread. Viewers were unable to see the significance of his exact geometry and strategic coloring. The paintings seemed to have lost their complexity in their quest for simplicity.

When he realized that he needed to make a change, Irwin shifted to a more expressionist style. He began to experiment with various media and created pieces that featured materials such as aluminum and plastic, in addition to acrylic paint on canvas. He also began to experiment with the manipulation of shape and began creating paintings on convex canvases. This new media led Irwin to begin playing with physical shapes. In the same *Apollo* interview, Griffin recounts Irwin's first experience using three-dimensional space: "In his Venice studio, he rounded out the corners between the floors, the walls and the ceilings with smooth plaster, and began experimenting with different artificial light sources, trying to find the most neutral and unobtrusive means of lighting the space." Although he never finished or showcased this particular piece, his early experimentation with light and space led him to begin creating the installation pieces that have since been so widely successful.

With his new inclusion of the third dimension, Irwin began coming closer to effectively communicating his unique style to his audience. He broke himself out of the limits of color and shape to create art that balanced perfection and reality. This new style took into account his obsessiveness, yet is also "intended to be absolutely responsive to its environment, and its objective is to enhance a viewer's perception of a space" (Griffin). Irwin's movement toward what he called "Conditional Art" led to much more success within his art form (Griffin). Previously, his hyper-focus to detail greatly inhibited the efficacy of his paintings. Bad reviews and negative reactions, such as those discussed in chapter four of Irwin's biography *Seeing Is Forgetting the Name of the Thing One Sees* by Lawrence Weschler, expose how viewers were uninterested and unimpressed by the tedious lines and shapes. With his installation pieces, however, Irwin is able to capture and manipulate human perception in a brand new way. He began to create pieces that rely less on the viewer's ability to appreciate intricate detail in the way he does. No longer focused on how minimalism forces selective attention, he created pieces that guide perception rather than control it. His new art was intriguing, mindbending, and explored the boundaries of human perception. He became more capable of giving a comprehensible form to his precise and minimalist style by creating art that played with the perception of light and space, two facets of reality that people are naturally in tune with.

Much of Irwin's work can be characterized as focused on sensory affect and perception. His work was meticulous, and he greatly emphasized clean lines and stark contrasts. These unique fascinations led Irwin to collaborate with artists such as Donald Judd, Robert Morris, and Richard Serra, creating the now widely popular Light and Space movement. This movement focuses on the utilization of light and space to create interactive sculpture and installation artwork that enhances viewing experience by focusing on the phenomena of human perception. The movement began in Los Angeles in the 1960s, with Irwin as one of its pioneering artists. Rules and guidelines for resulting pieces were loose, yet the artists within the movement all followed Irwin in his pursuit of artistic perfection. As Joan Boykoff Baron and Reuben M. Baron state in their article on the Light and Space movement for *Artcritical* magazine, these artists were creating pieces that "were particularly well suited to capturing and transforming the ephemeral luminosity of the ocean and the smog-besmirched sky, as well as the high gloss brilliance of surfboards and autos that were primary everyday experiences for these artists." They used textures such as resin and fabric in combination with architectural design and spacial manipulation in order to create an experience that activates all aspects of perception. The goal of the movement is not to create something new from nothing, rather, to enhance and emphasize the mundane or ordinary.

Excursus: Homage to the Square³ perfectly captures the many elements and multiple objectives of the Light and Space movement. By creating rooms into which the viewer must enter, the piece isolates the viewer and therefore forces a heightened perception of their surroundings. The white scrims create a clean backdrop upon which the subtly-colored fluorescent lights are showcased and greatly emphasized. The translucent fabric used to create the white scrims is a staple of Irwin's. He discovered the material during a trip to Amsterdam, where he found it was being used by the Dutch for translucent window shades. Irwin debuted the fabric in 1970 when he used it for a piece in the Museum of Modern Art in New York City. Nearly thirty years later, he returned to the unique fabric to create a piece for the Dia:Chelsea titled *Prologue: x18³*. Just a few months after the premiere of *Prologue: x183*, Irwin returned to the piece to continue adjustments and ended up reconfiguring the piece entirely (Griffin). This final reconfiguration is now *Excursus: Homage to the Square³*, which has been on display since June 1st of 2015 and, because of its popularity, has been extended to May 2017.

While *Excursus: Homage to the Square³* draws much inspiration from the fundamental elements of the Light and Space movement, it is also largely inspired by Josef Albers' collection of paintings entitled simply *Homage to the Square*. The relationship between these two collections spans far beyond the obvious similarities in name. Albers's *Homage to the Square* is concisely described by Shawn Roggenkamp, who writes: "The composition of this painting is simple enough—

four progressively smaller squares within each other, each in a different color, and all aligned closer to the bottom of the composition than to the top." However, this simplicity is only superficial. Like Irwin, Albers is also challenging the viewer's perception. The paintings suggest a complex relationship between the featured squares, posing questions like "[a]re they stacked on top of each other, like cut out pieces of construction paper? Are they sinking underneath each other, as if you are looking at a painting of a tunnel? Do some appear to push toward you and others to fall away?" (Roggenkamp). Unlike Irwin, Albers granted color a great importance in his paintings. As a student at the Bauhaus, Albers studied color theory and developed a technique of manipulating color that he uses in *Homage to the Square*, whereby "[his] paintings are exploring the creation of space through the use of color" (Roggenkamp). This use of color to create space dates back to the Dutch Golden Age and the Italian Renaissance; since the sixteenth century, the technique has been labeled "atmospheric perspective" (Roggenkamp).

Homage to the Square is a great example of this technique: the contrasting colors of the different squares provide depth and give dimension to the paintings. This same effect can be seen in *Excursus: Homage to the Square³*, at a smaller magnitude. The colors of the fluorescent lights shine ever-so-slightly on the white walls and give life to the sterile environment. These colors are used very minimally, however, and their limited inclusion forces the viewer to look even more closely to notice their effect. Albers uses color in his paintings dramatically, calling attention to the contrast and complement of different shades of red, blue, yellow, etc. that characterize his seemingly simple pieces. Irwin continues with this technique, yet in a much more restrained fashion. The resemblance of the two collections is not quite as obvious as their similarity in name, yet with an understanding of the color technique as its inspiration, the importance of color in *Excursus: Homage to the Square³* refuses to be ignored.

When considered as a reaction to *Homage to the Square*, it becomes even more evident that Irwin's style rebels against the common standard of minimalistic art. Albers exemplifies the approach that Irwin attempted in his early paintings and, while Albers was more successful, he also fails to incorporate the experience of reality.

Albers' paintings may encourage the viewer to take an extra moment
to look at the colors and shapes, but they do not engage the senses any
further. In his three-dimensional work, Irwin takes minimalism one
step further. He takes atmospheric perspective and strips it down to
its most fundamental aspects by including colors barely perceptible in
the fluorescent lights. By doing this, he encourages the viewer to focus
more closely on the five or six colors he utilizes, and in this enhanced
focus he forces the viewer to push irrelevant distractions out of mind.
Then, in addition to this use of color, he incorporates light into the
experience, which in turn activates all boundaries of perception and
penetrates every edge of peripheral vision.

   Excursus: Homage to the Square³ is an exhibit that is exemplary
of its artistic inspiration. With only a couple of elements (i.e. the
scrims and the fluorescent sculptures), the piece manipulates the perception of light and space by physically isolating the viewer and
directing their attention to the few intended focuses, such as the play
of light on the white walls or the flow of space throughout the asym-
metrical rooms. The exhibition provides an interactive viewing experience and elicits a calm and serene response. As mentioned in a
review by Ken Johnson for *The New York Times, Excursus: Homage
to the Square³* provides a stark contrast to the "sensory irritation and
intellectual grandiosity" of much contemporary art. This exhibition
takes a strong stance against a society in which people are overloaded
by images and video clips. It battles the shrinking of society's attention span by forcing the viewer to pause and focus on one or two elements, rather than the abundance of color and movement surrounding us in daily life. In the same review, Johnson calls the piece "ethereal and, in a good way, somehow purgatorial, as if you might find
your way to a clear divine light with time and patience." The piece
goes beyond visual appeal, and creates an all-encompassing experience. It affects mood and emotion and, with its refreshing minimalism, the seemingly simple white rooms provide relief and escape from
the many stressors of human life.

   Although Irwin never explicitly verbalizes his opinion on the
over-stimulation that is common in modern society, his artwork takes
a bold stance on the issue. With his art, Irwin shines light upon the
essentiality of excess stimuli by creating incredibly interesting and

impactful minimalist pieces. Even though his work originated in California, there seems to be no better backdrop to his art than New York City, famous for its busyness and sensory overload. In Olivia Laing's hauntingly honest essay "Me, Myself and I," she grapples with living amongst the business and chaos of New York City, writing how "[she] quickly became intimate with hypervigilance. During the months [she] lived in Manhattan, it manifested as an almost painful alertness to the city, a form of over-arousal that oscillated between paranoia and desire." Although not all New York City dwellers are able to express their innermost feelings in such eloquent language, Laing's words capture an experience known to many. She finds that as the city overwhelms her, her feelings of loneliness persistently increase. Laing exposes a paradox known by many: the more we are surrounded, the lonelier we can be. With his artwork, Irwin provides us with a cure to this all-too-common predicament. *Excursus: Homage to the Square³* reveals to the viewer how art doesn't need flashing lights, loud noises, bright colors, and innumerable images in order to hold our attention. Instead, he guides us in our perception and teaches us that when we cut through the white noise, we can find a deeper appreciation of our surroundings. It is in this appreciation that we are able to see the beauty in simplicity and let our senses soak up the full effect of his artwork.

WORKS CITED

Albers, Josef. *Homage to the Square.* 1959. Oil on masonite. The Metropolitan Museum of Art, New York.
Baron, Joan Boykoff, and Reuben M. Baron. "No Choice but to Trust the Senses: California Light and Space Revisited." *artcritical.* N.p., 28 Oct. 2011. Web. 27 Mar. 2016.
Griffin, Jonathan. "Light Years Ahead: Interview with Robert Irwin." *Apollo.* Apollo Magazine, 1 Nov. 2015. Web. 27 Mar. 2016.
Irwin, Robert. *Excursus: Homage to the Square³.* 2015. Installation. Dia:Beacon, New York.

Johnson, Ken. "Review: Robert Irwin Shows a Calming Installation at Dia:Beacon." *The New York Times.* The New York Times Company, 4 June 2015. Web. 27 Mar. 2016.

Laing, Olivia. "Me, Myself and I." *Aeon.* Aeon Media Group, 19 Dec. 2012. Web. 26 May 2016.

Roggenkamp, Shawn. "Albers, Homage to the Square." *Khan Academy.* Khan Academy, n.d. Web. 27 Mar. 2016.

Schjeldahl, Peter. "IMPROVISING IN ART AND LIFE." *The New York Times.* The New York Times Company, 18 Apr. 1982. Web. 27 Mar. 2016.

Weschler, Lawrence. *Seeing Is Forgetting the Name of the Thing One Sees: Over Thirty Years of Conversations with Robert Irwin.* Berkeley: U of California P, 2009. Print.

Woods, Lynn. "Echo Chamber in the Versailles of Minimalism: Artist Robert Irwin Exhibits at Dia:Beacon." *Hudson Valley Almanac Weekly.* Hudson Valley Almanac Weekly, 26 June 2015. Web. 27 Mar. 2016.

*To explore the connection between art and nature, Mae Roney
used texts from art criticism, painting, screenwriting, literature, and
journalism. Written in Jennifer Cayer's "Writing the Essay: Art in
the World," this essay demonstrates how an eclectic array of
sources can be synthesized into something new.*

ON IMPORTANCE:
ART AS ENLIGHTENMENT

Mae Roney

In 1928, Myles Connolly, a renowned and successful screenwriter in the twentieth century, removed himself from Hollywood and published a vibrant and philosophical short story about place, God, and the connection between art and existence. The fictional story, *Mr. Blue*, is about J. Blue, a young Catholic layman who takes his religion into his own hands, shunning the society of 1920s America, taking a vow of poverty and living a selflessly generous and loving life. The first time that the readers are introduced to Blue, he is standing on the parapet of a rooftop, excitedly marveling at the beauty of the sky, where "God is more intimate" (Connolly 24). After continuing to converse a little with the narrator about the proximity of God and taking in the beauty of the roof, he proclaims: "When God became man He made you and me and the rest of us pretty important people" (Connolly 25). The view of the city that Blue gains from the rooftop makes him feel closer to God, which in turn ignites a realization of his individual importance as a result of God. The beauty of the large city skyline that Blue sees seems to clarify his importance to him and—although the enlightenment may seem abrupt, even a little absurd—it is recognizable as an instinctually human response to beauty and grandeur. It is a part of human nature to want assurance that we each belong, and that we matter in the face of such a large, daunting world.

John Berger's essay on the effect of art and nature on our sense of place in the world "The White Bird" first introduces a simple sculpture of a bird carved out of white wood. The birds are usually presented hanging, suspended in midair, which instantly gives the beholder a sense of flight and life: of something outside, which is brought inside and frozen. Berger elaborates on this, claiming that the birds stir in the viewer a distillation of the intense emotion felt when looking at nature (83). He explains the rush of emotion that one feels when struck by beauty in nature, saying that "what has been seen is recognized and affirmed, and, at the same time, the seer is affirmed by what he sees" (83). Berger claims that the viewer, by way of this instantaneous and simultaneous recognition, temporarily feels like "God in the first chapter of Genesis . . . And he saw that it was good" (83). Viewers do not feel like they themselves are gods, but instead feel that they are looking at creation, or that they have somehow created something. Moreover, viewers feel that they matter, and that their reception of the beauty around them is locked and intertwined with something bigger than them, whether it be an ecosystem, Mother Nature, or God. The nature and beauty snap viewers into the context of a system, and brief clarity they attain about their importance and place in this bigger picture. Berger asserts that this moment of connection to a whole and place within it "offers hope" in the chaos of "a world that has to be resisted" (83). The moment of understanding of a bigger picture that a viewer may experience while struck by beauty in nature provides a promise that the world is not huge and random, that a single person matters. Since art—especially art like the white bird—freezes nature, it is an attempt to "transform the instantaneous into the permanent" and to "transform the potential recognition into an unceasing one" (83). Art is not escape, and it does not offer a flimsy, imagined sense of security. Instead, art prolongs the burst of confidence nature inspires, telling us we each have a place and an individual importance in a large, otherwise overwhelming world. Art gives us the opportunity to digest and accept the stunning reassurance of our existence that we may find in striking, natural beauty. Yet when looking at something as grand as nature or a beautiful skyline, it is easy to feel one's importance being challenged, even alongside a sense of belonging to the bigger picture. If art attempts to capture and prolong the emotions felt when encountering nature, might it also capture the tests to identity that such grandiose nature presents?

Jeanette Winterson explores the effect of challenging art in her essay "The Semiotics of Sex." Winterson investigates the simultaneous human need for—and repulsion towards—art that challenges what is known. We are both afraid of and fascinated by art that "coaxes out of us emotions we normally do not feel" because it "occupies ground unconquered by social niceties" (Winterson 173). Winterson claims that "[t]he formal beauty of art is threat and relief to the formless neutrality of unrealised life" (175). This quotation calls to mind Berger's claim that art organizes the chaos of the "world that has to be resisted" (83). The notion that life lies at the mercy of art incites the fear of breaking down our sense of security, because to truly engage with challenging art is to take a calculated risk; it can make vulnerable the ideas of the known in the hopes of gaining an understanding of the unknown. Art, like nature, is a threat to our sense of importance when it challenges what we think we know about both ourselves and our world. Yet, the same threat promises the unveiling of the unknown. It contains the hope that art provides respite from the daily, callous world, and offers a complex resonance with something indefinable and unconfined within us. Berger's idea that impactful art connects us with a higher power, or a bigger picture, focuses primarily on the understanding of one's individual place within all that is larger than us. Winterson, however, uses creation differently in her explanation of art. She thinks of art as "[c]reation," or "an energetic space which begets energetic space," something that does not offer escape, but instead "makes it possible to live in energetic space" (176). Art, for Winterson, becomes a means of understanding more of herself than of her place, giving her the ability to live in a vibrant and new space, forged through her interaction with challenging art. There is a clear connection between Winterson and Berger in their assertions about art and beauty as creation, but Winterson introduces a new concept regarding what exactly is being created. Berger describes a moment of recognition and assurance, when the viewer of beauty in nature simultaneously feels that they are creating while being created; Winterson describes art's creation of new energy when viewed, and says nothing of assurance. Winterson's "energetic space" may be the recognition of the indeterminable unknown within us, and the energy within may allow us to detangle and wrestle with this unknown (176). Or, the energy might be a byproduct of the development of our new thoughts and unbridled emotion created by a renewed sense of identity and importance as a result of the challenge to what we know. A new way of thinking about the world renews one's sense of place within it. Winterson suggests that the energy created by art allows the viewer to be more attuned to the potential for energy and understanding all around them. While Berger claims that one gets an understanding of a bigger picture by a feeling of simultaneous creation in the face of nature, Winterson claims that one may gain the understanding of the world through art that threatens and expands one's understanding. Berger writes of a simultaneous creation; Winterson writes of a simultaneous challenging. In this simultaneous challenge, the viewer finds their place through questioning art, which, in turn, challenges them rather than assuring them. This image is immediately more energetic, and suggests a more progressive, compelling way of understanding one's personal identity and world. Winterson's use of energy also expands Berger's claim that art strives to prolong the self-recognition and the understanding of the world inspired by natural beauty, suggesting that challenging art itself is capable of inspiring this understanding of self and the world.

However, both Winterson and Berger ultimately assert that art allows us to process our understanding of ourselves and our world. Winterson claims that art has the "power to create rooms for us" (176). If, as Berger says, art is an "attempt to transform the instantaneous into the permanent," then this permanence, like the wooden bird in mid-flight, allows the space, or, as Winterson phrases it, the "rooms" toward which we turn in the search for understanding (Berger 83). In this stable space, we can assess our identity and place in light of a new perspective of the world, the bigger picture gained from the art. In some ways we crave the potential energy that art offers, because it will help us grapple with some of our tangled, confused, repressed, or simply undetermined emotions. The moment of understanding and connection to creation and God that Berger details is irresistible. It is a part of human nature to desire to be "more deeply inserted into existence than the course of a single life would lead us to believe" (83). At the same time, the gravity of this expansion of understanding is scary because the unknown within us and around us is overwhelmingly frightening. The visceral pull felt by the prospect of understanding ourselves or our place in the scheme of the world is countered by a staggering fear of the unknown. This fear manifests itself, according to Winterson, in the ways in which people belittle and contain art, reducing it to a biography of the artist. We are afraid of the questions about the unknown that may arise from art, yet we do not want to live in a dreary world without the beautiful and terrifying stimulus that we find in art.

In "Laughing with Kafka," David Foster Wallace investigates tendencies to shy away from provocative art. He is concerned with what makes us uncomfortable with this type of art in the first place as he grapples with the difficulties that his American students have in truly understanding Kafka. He begins by retelling a Kafka short story, narrated by a mouse, whose "'world is growing smaller and smaller every day'" (Wallace 159). The mouse begins to run, and is eventually relieved by the sight of walls appearing all around it. However, the walls quickly begin to close in, and finally the mouse is trapped in one "'last chamber . . . [where] in the corner, stands the trap that [it] must run into'" (159). This abrupt and sardonically sad ending signifies that the mouse has been so absorbed and focused on getting to a smaller, more sensible world, that it has ignored its freedom while it lasted. Wallace roots his essay in the revelations found in Kafka's art. He explains it as a door that readers approach and pound on, "not just wanting admission, but needing it" (161). Yet, when the door opens, "it opens outward: we've been inside what we wanted all along" (161).

Wallace's description of his interaction with Kafka's story, at first, seems much bleaker than Winterson's electric interpretation of the spontaneous, energetic development of challenge and understanding, or Berger's profound and vibrant expression of the realization of creation, existence, and place. If Wallace's anecdote about the room is analogous to Kafka's proverb of the mouse, then by the time the door opens, revelation may come too late for those who waited and begged. Both Wallace and Winterson use images of doors and rooms to analyze the effect of art on the individual; however, Winterson speaks of the power of art "to create rooms for us" while Wallace speaks of the door opening only after we have wasted time pounding on it, revealing our tragic mistake (Winterson 176). Yet, perhaps Wallace's experience isn't as depressing as it initially appears in contrast to Berger and Winterson. By using the analogy of the door, Wallace captures the same attraction to—or need for—the understanding of the unknown or the bigger picture that Winterson and Berger describe. But what Wallace points out is if we spend too long searching for meaning or our place in something that eludes us, we may miss other opportunities for enlightenment already around us, and potentially ignore the place we already have in the world. Winterson's concept of rooms created by art in which to process challenges to security—like Berger's intimate introspection inspired by nature and prolonged by art—beckon to be retreated into. Wallace illustrates the danger in chasing the elusive: that, in the midst of the chase, we may run past the understanding that we desire, missing it entirely. If this is true, then the energy begotten by a challenged and renewed understanding of self in Winterson's piece, or Berger's electric feeling of importance within the fantastic whole, must inspire us to truly live in the world. We cannot pound at the door, narrowly focused on self-importance and understanding, while allowing the surrounding beauty and opportunity for enlightenment to pass by. Art is the springboard that provokes us to look at ourselves and the world through a new lens. We cannot retreat into our thoughts and our search for understanding like a safe haven. It is irresponsible to ignore the life and importance around us, because maybe the revelation that we seek is around us in the art and beauty that we encounter on a daily basis. If we are so bent on finding our place in life that we retreat from life, our search becomes meaningless.

At one point in *Mr. Blue*, the narrator includes letters that he has collected from Blue. In one such letter, Blue talks about the need for feeling in our society, saying that "[o]ur fear of exuberancy, of ecstasy, of any genuine passion is being stamped on our face and our lives" (56). Just as Winterson warns of the way people today fear challenging art and emotion, Blue warns that as a result of this fear "[w]e have as much hunger for loveliness as a turtle. And about as much capacity for intense and varied living as a cabbage" (Connolly 56). This insensitive and unimpassioned world is one that Blue rejects throughout the book, talking to anyone and everyone about the beauty of life and God, and the necessity of art to enlighten and communicate beauty and inspiration. However, Connolly, like Winterson—and Berger, to some degree—stresses and challenges the duty of artists in the fight against this dreary society, or chaotic world. Blue says later in the short story that artists "take contemporary life avidly into their arms . . . and out of the union is born their art" (Connolly 77). Yet, when commenting on the uninspired architecture of churches in New York, he proclaims that it "is cowardice to blame the age" and that maybe the lack of inspiration is the fault of the artist, attributed to the "dryness and dullness of their souls" (77).

Which is it, then? Are artists in "union" with life, or are they dried out? If they are inspired, Blue seems to suggest that Berger's double affirmation occurs first between artist and nature. The artist's job, then, is to create art that not only pushes against the dullness within the world around us, or helps us find our place or importance within it, as Berger claims. The artist has a great responsibility because it is art which allows us to tackle and comprehend the world in which we live. It allows us not only to live in the creative, provocative space, as Winterson says, but encourages us to live in our world with more clarity, and to see the beauty of our world more vividly. If the artist is entrenched in a fearful, unfeeling society like the one Winterson depicts, or the bleak, chaotic world that Berger claims art has to resist, then there is no hope for their art. This search for enlightened art begins to echo that of those pounding on the door in Wallace's tale, so intent on finding meaning that they miss it all around them. Instead of wasting time finding fault in our society or the age, and expecting an artist to transcend it, we should look at the art that the world around us already offers. While an artist certainly has a responsibility to see the world in a different way, and to communicate this view, there is responsibility held by the audience as well. We must recognize beauty and opportunity for understanding as they already exist around us, or we risk being too focused on an elusive enlightenment to notice that we have been in the midst of tremendous art and life all along.

WORKS CITED

Berger, John. "The White Bird." *Writing the Essay: Art in the World, The World Through Art*. Eds. Benjamin W. Stewart, Darlene A. Forrest, and Randy Martin. Boston: McGraw-Hill, 2013. 81-84. Print.
Connolly, Myles. *Mr. Blue*. Chicago: Loyola Press, 2005. Print.
Wallace, David Foster. "Laughing with Kafka." *Writing the Essay: Art in the World, The World Through Art*. Eds. Benjamin W. Stewart, Darlene A. Forrest, and Randy Martin. Boston: McGraw Hill, 2013. 159-161. Print.
Winterson, Jeanette. "The Semiotics of Sex." *Writing the Essay: Art in the World, The World Through Art*. Eds. Benjamin W. Stewart, Darlene A. Forrest, and Randy Martin. Boston: McGraw Hill, 2013. 171-177. Print.

In her work for Stephen Butler's "Advanced College Essay," Sophia Chou scrutinizes the discourse surrounding physician-assisted suicide in the U.S. By analyzing the medical procedure and the mentality of its advocates and adversaries, Chou creates a discerning argument for compromise and understanding.

POLITICIAN-ASSISTED COMPROMISE

Sophia Chou

On January 1st of 2014, 29-year-old California resident Brittany Maynard learned that she had terminal brain cancer. A few months later, in April, she was told that she had roughly six more months to live. With the limited amount of time she had left, she was indirectly given two choices: accept treatment for the cancer that would ultimately take over the remainder of her life, or continue on in pain without medical assistance. After endless days of research, Maynard decided she would make a third choice: physician-assisted suicide. Her decision and the debate that it sparked received national coverage and mixed reactions, many of them negative. After moving her family to Oregon, where the procedure was legal, Maynard died from a lethal prescription of barbiturates with "brain tumor" as the cause of death.

Assisted suicide, also known as physician-assisted death or 'death with dignity,' is the act of "hasten[ing] the death of terminally ill patients who wish to spare themselves and their loved ones from the final, crippling stages of deteriorating health" ("Offering a Choice to the Terminally Ill"). However, this practice is only legal is the states of Oregon, Washington, Vermont, New Mexico, Montana, and, most recently, California as a result of the extensive debate and controversy that surrounds the subject. Although Oregon, the first state to legalize assisted suicide, is the most notable location for this procedure, there are still many strict protocols and regulations that are involved. In order to receive the medication to end their lives, a patient is required to "have a terminal illness, with no expectation of living beyond six more months" and have two doctors verify and "attest" to their diagnosis and expectancy (Haberman). The individual also has to "be judged mentally competent, must be able to swallow the drugs and must be the one to ask for them—twice verbally, with each request separated by 15 days" (Haberman).

However, those who oppose the legalization of the procedure have pointed out flaws within the protocols. Within Oregon's law, "there is no requirement for an evaluation by a mental health professional," and "the requirement that the patient receive a diagnosis of a terminal illness that will lead to death within six months can turn out not to be the case," as many situations have shown the patient living beyond their expectancy (Freedman). Regarding the use of the procedure for mental illnesses, some psychiatrists believe that "[i]f depression is present, once treated, there can be a lifting of spirits, desire to stay around longer and rediscovery of a sense of meaning in life" (Freedman). By legalizing physician-assisted suicide, doctors would be allowing these patients to make rash decisions when they are faced with a "premature false sense of hopelessness" and ultimately allowing them a shortcut to fixing their problems (Freedman).

Ross Douthat's *New York Times* article "The Last Right" provides further insight into the reasoning of those who advocate against the legalization of physician-assisted suicide. The article delves deeper into why many believe that ending a terminally-ill individual's life through medication should not be considered normal, let alone legal. Douthat ponders why a large number of liberals are "considerably more uncomfortable with the idea of physician-assisted suicide than other causes, from abortion to homosexuality, where claims about personal autonomy and liberty are at stake." Why is it that, above other causes, this one seems so important? Douthat explains that "liberal writers . . . warn of the danger of a lives-not-worth-living mentality." In other words: one of the major fears that has caused many setbacks for the right-to-die movement is the belief that the procedure would result in devaluing human life.

Those who advocate against the legalization of the procedure predict that allowing physician-assisted suicide to become a norm will eventually lead to the development of a "'slippery slope'" where "the law would gradually expand to include those with non-terminal illnesses or that it would permit physicians to take a more active role in the dying process itself" (Hafner). In their eyes, if physician-assisted suicide began to be considered a norm, society may come to no longer cherish life and become desensitized to death. This argument is especially concerned with individuals in lower socioeconomic standings, as many believe that those who are unable to afford treatment or hospice care will quickly turn to the procedure to avoid high medical bills that they would be unable to afford. Those in opposition believe that its legalization would lead to a drastic increase in the number of people willing to end their lives and cause a decrease in self-value and overall sense of humanity.

However, for *New York Times* writer Clyde Haberman, "the slippery-slope arguments are overwrought." The patients that request an "early exit tend to be relatively well off and well educated" and "there is no evidence . . . to suggest that such laws have been used promiscuously by either patients or their doctors" (Haberman). In states where the procedure is already legalized, the majority of those who receive the medication are "white, well educated and financially comfortable," different from the demographic of citizens of lower socioeconomic standing that the opposition believes the legalization will most affect (Hafner).

Although a majority of the country has proclaimed the procedure illegal, nationwide movements have openly voiced their support for its legalization. A viewpoint that supporters believe many people do not understand is that those who seek voluntary euthanasia "are dying patients. They are not suicidal and do not want to die, despite what many assert" (Leven). Patients who request the procedure are often seen by the public as individuals who have given up on life and chosen a shortcut to death. However, David C. Leven, the executive director of the End of Life Choices New York, offers counter-arguments to those who oppose the procedure. While many fear the legalization of assisted suicide will lead to its abuse by ill patients with lower socioeconomic standing, it is known that "just about all who end their lives by aid in dying have health insurance, the majority are college educated, and the vast majority are receiving hospice care" (Leven). Regarding the claims that the patients show no regard for their own lives and are not mentally well, Leven states that these dying patients "opt to take prescribed medicines only because they can no longer endure terrible suffering," not simply because they want to die from hopelessness.

Though Daniel Callahan, a philosopher on biomedical ethics, has suggested that "the occurrence of suffering [should] not entail that life should end, even if there were a duty to bear suffering," that does not mean or imply that refraining from physician-assisted suicide "would promote the significance [one's] existence has from [one's] own view-point" (Varelius 567). On the contrary, patients that consider this method already view assisted suicide as a good and meaningful way to die that they would be content with and are unlikely to change their minds about. When justifying her decision, Brittany Maynard explained that her choice to go forward with the procedure had "given [her] a sense of peace during a tumultuous time that otherwise would be dominated by fear, uncertainty, and pain" (qtd. in Slotnik). Those who asked her to reconsider her decision and continue living ulti-mately and indirectly asked her to endure great pain and suffering for the short amount of time she had left.

While those who are against the legalization focus primarily on values and morality, which can be highly ambiguous and vary greatly amongst a wide variety of people, the consequences that come along with the procedure's prohibition must be considered as well. It is imperative that physicians understand how to approach and interact with patients suffering from terminal illnesses, as faults in this area can lead to later predicaments and problems. "[S]imply prohibiting physician-assisted suicide without giving guidance" on the appropriate manner in which to interact with patients who seek the procedure can cause an "increase [in] patients' fears about physicians' abandonment in the face of severe suffering" (Quill and Cassell). There is also a possibility of "reinforc[ing] clinicians' tendencies not to acknowledge the intolerable suffering" that these patients are forced to experience, which leads patients to feel that their decisions are met with criticism because they are not properly understood.

While politicians may be able to keep the procedure illegal, they ultimately do not make the final decision for the patients themselves and do not understand the psyche and mindset of the patient. Those who are denied physician-assisted suicide and who are unable to relocate to a state that provides it are sometimes so driven and dead-set on ending their lives that they will find other methods to do so. Many have dehydrated and starved themselves, dragging their deaths on for days on end until they finally die. Politicians and anti-assisted suicide advocates are aware of what patients denied the procedure are doing and seem to only be outraged when a doctor grants the patients their death ahead of schedule and with less suffering. The controversy surrounding physician-assisted suicide is one that plays into a large tension in American culture, namely the tension between the need for state governments to tell individuals what they can and cannot do with their own bodies, also known as the idea of paternalism, and the libertarian mindset that demands freedom of choice on all personal matters.

Members of modern American society have a wide range of political views. In the *New York Times* article "The Coming Democratic Schism," Thomas B. Edsall cites studies from the Pew Research Center that have shown that "'huge generation gaps have opened up in our political and social views, our economic well-being, our family structure,'" and many other aspects in American society. Andrew Kohut, founding director of the Pew Center, characterizes it as a "libertarian streak that is apparent among . . . left-of-center young people" (qtd. in Edsall). Many would say that these libertarian views are the ones that advocate for physician-assisted suicide and are defiant against the laws of the government. Kohut views these individuals as "socially liberal but very wary of government," as they believe that they should be given freedom to make their own decisions (qtd. in Edsall). Although there is a wide range of libertarianism, the desire for freedom of choice is an idea constant throughout its different levels.

Opposite to the free-spirited thinking of libertarians is the idea of paternalism, where the government takes the welfare of its people into its own hands, believing that the general population does not know what is best for its people. A popular example of paternalism is the actions of Mayor Michael Bloomberg, who developed his own "nanny state" in New York City (Sunstein). His attempts to "restrict soda sizes" and "his proposal to ban cigarette displays in New York stores" have left many outraged by his efforts to restrict the freedoms of his people (Sunstein). Cass R. Sunstein explains his viewpoint on this belief in his article "Why Paternalism Is Your Friend," published in *The New Republic*. Sunstein discusses the fact that "various forms of paternalism are all around you, and at least some of them aren't so bad." For him, the government's decisions about what it considers best for its people are usually decisions that any rational individual would make, but it is only certain laws that the public chooses to focus on and use as representations of paternalism.

Both Sunstein and Richard Thaler believe that the most effective solution in this conflict is to seek compromises between the two political stances. In an article in *The American Economic Review*, they argue that this compromise can be achieved with the development of what they call libertarian paternalism, "an approach that preserves freedom of choice but that authorizes both private and public institutions to steer people in directions that will promote their welfare" (Thaler and Sunstein 179). However, in order to begin such compromises, understandings must be reached on both sides. Radical libertarians who firmly protest any forms of paternalism are often led on by misconceptions, as they usually only notice the laws and rules that cause uproars and protest. However, the truth of the matter is that paternalism has already been woven into our lives without many realizing it because "when paternalism seems absent, it is usually because the starting point appears so natural and obvious that its preference-shaping effects are invisible to most observers" (Thaler and Sunstein 177). While many may express their disagreement with paternalism, it is almost unavoidable. However, the same can be said for libertarians, as the presence of those who demand freedom of choice is inevitable as well. Therefore, the most effective method would be accepting its presence and developing an arrangement that may be able to satisfy both sides of the spectrum.

The clashing beliefs in the debate over physician-assisted suicide display the differing sides of libertarian and paternalistic views. Those who support the legalization of the procedure express their discontent with its prohibition and demand their freedom of choice, displaying libertarian views. On the other hand, the state governments display their paternalism in the prevention and forbiddance of physician-assisted suicide, which they believe is for the good of their people. However, the debate has been dragged on for years on end and the ferocity displayed by both sides to achieve what they want has been unwavering. As discussed by Thaler and Sunstein, the presence of both viewpoints is unavoidable, as there will always be those who agree and those who disagree with paternalism. The accommodation between paternalism and freedom of choice, however, offers the beginnings of a solution to the controversy of physician-assisted suicide.

In order to promote both the public advocacy for physician-assisted suicide while still considering the viewpoints of those who stand against the procedure, it is vital that compromises be made. The support for the procedure should be met with understanding, as simply ignoring one side of the debate and sweeping it under the rug will only create more issues. Justin Trudeau, the Prime Minister of Canada, has begun these compromises in his attempts to pass the legalization of the procedure in his country. Jody Wilson-Raybould, the Minister of Justice of Canada, stated that "for some, medical assistance in dying will be troubling" and "for others, this legislation will not go far enough" (Austen). However, the compromises made for the law act as a middle ground between the two sides. The requirements proposed for those who request the procedure are similar to those in Oregon but have also included much more restrictive conditions as well as not forcing doctors who are uncomfortable with the procedure to perform it (Austen). Through these compromises, steps can be taken to shed light on the topic and decrease the negative stigma that surround both supporters and those who seek the procedure. By allowing a more open conversation where both sides can be met with equal consideration, the general public may also obtain a more in-depth understanding of the choices made by the patients that choose to end their lives through the assistance of a physician.

The controversy regarding physician-assisted suicide has been present and ongoing in the United States for years. It shows no signs of dying out any time soon; however, in the majority of states the debate has become stagnant, with no changes in state laws regarding the procedure. While those who are against the law speak about the dehumanizing of human life and the possibility of individuals abusing the procedure once it is legal, supporters of physician-assisted suicide ask the politicians to consider the feelings of the suffering patients who seek an early end to their pain. The opposing sides of the argument display the ongoing issue in American culture concerning the paternalism of state governments and the libertarian views of individuals who seek minimal government control over their freedom of choice. In order to create a balance not only between these differing political and social standpoints but in the debate over physician-assisted suicide, compromises between the opposing sides must be developed. While these arrangements will not fully appease either side, they will hopefully act as a midpoint and promote more understanding between the two. Through these arrangements, those who primarily opposed the procedure may begin to understand the mentality and reasoning behind those who request death, as it is not as simple and one-dimensional as they had originally thought.

WORKS CITED

Austen, Ian. "Justin Trudeau Seeks to Legalize Assisted Suicide in Canada." *The New York Times*. The New York Times Company, 14 April 2016. Web. 24 June 2016.

Douthat, Ross. "The Last Right." *The New York Times*. The New York Times Company, 12 Oct. 2014. Web. 24 June 2016.

Edsall, Thomas B. "The Coming Democratic Schism." *The New York Times*. The New York Times Company, 15 July 2014. Web. 24 June 2016.

Freedman, Jeffrey B. "On Assisted Dying." *The New York Times*. The New York Times Company, Feb 25 2016. Web. 24 June 2016.

Haberman, Clyde. "Stigma Around Physician-Assisted Dying Lingers." *The New York Times*. The New York Times Company, 22 Mar. 2015. Web. 24 June 2016.

Hafner, Katie. "In Ill Doctor, a Surprise Reflection of Who Picks Assisted Suicide." *The New York Times*. The New York Times Company, 11 Aug. 2012. Web. 24 June 2016.

Leven, David C. "Aid in Dying: They Are Not Suicidal and Do Not Want to Die." *The New York Times.* The New York Times Company, 23 Sept. 2015. Web. 24 June 2016.

"Offering a Choice to the Terminally Ill." Editorial. *The New York Times,* The New York Times Company, 14 Mar. 2015. Web. 24 June 2016.

Quill, Timothy E., and Christine K. Cassell. "Professional Organizations' Position Statements on Physician-Assisted Suicide: A Case for Studied Neutrality." *Annals of Internal Medicine* 138.3 (2003): 208-11. Web. 24 June 2016.

Slotnik, Daniel E. "Brittany Maynard, 'Death with Dignity' Ally, Dies at 29." *The New York Times.* The New York Times Company, 3 Nov 2014. Web. 24 June 2016.

Sunstein, Cass R. "Why Paternalism Is Your Friend." *New Republic.* New Republic, 8 Apr. 2013. Web. 24 June 2016.

Thaler, Richard H., and Cass R. Sunstein. "Libertarian Paternalism." *The American Economic Review* 93.2 (2003): 175-179. *JSTOR.* Web. 24 June 2016.

Varelius, Jukka. "Ending Life, Morality, and Meaning." *Ethical Theory and Moral Practice* 16.3 (2013): 559-74. Web. 24 June 2016.

Through an interdisciplinary approach that includes media, film, and video game analysis, Brett Moody's essay, written in Jennifer Cayer's "Writing the Essay: Art in the World," looks closely at the cause and effect between school shootings and the media that provoke and exploit them.

SCHOOL SHOOTINGS IN MEDIA: A PATHWAY TO EMPATHY OR A BLUEPRINT FOR EVIL?

Brett Moody

On April 20th, 1999, Eric Harris and Dylan Klebold, two teens from Littleton, Colorado, drove to their high school with a small arsenal of heavy weapons and explosives. After the propane bombs they had put in the school's cafeteria failed to explode, they entered Columbine High School and shot twelve students and one teacher. During the shooting, they also managed to injure more than twenty other people. As they murdered their classmates in cold blood, their dialogue was like that of two teens playing a video game: witnesses report that they yelled phrases like "This is what we always wanted to do. This is awesome!" and "Peek-a-boo!" When the police arrived, the two teens shot themselves (Kass). The Columbine Massacre further ignited debates that still rage on today about American gun laws, bullying, high school culture, and, most compellingly, the relationship between mass shootings and media that depicts realistic violence. Since art has imitated violence and violence has imitated art with an increasing frequency the past several years, this last topic has become a critical issue for artists, consumers, and media distributors.

In the Massacre's aftermath, media pundits were quick to make connections between the shooters' actions and the media they enjoyed: Marilyn Manson's music and *Doom*, a violent computer game (Bell; Jaccarino). Though these theories were proven to be

shaky at best, school shootings have since been more concretely linked
to the works of Stephen King, Dan Houser and many other renowned
artists (Katz; Jaccarino). After reading Stephen King's novel *Rage*
obsessively, which is about a high school student holding his classroom hostage with a pistol, Jeffrey Lyne Cox stormed his own high
school with a semi-automatic rifle (Katz).

At the same time, school shootings have become a highly publi-
cized phenomenon. They are frequently put on the front page of news
outlets like *The New York Times* and have been represented by a
diverse group of high-profile artists, including Pearl Jam, Michael
Moore, Lionel Shriver, Gus Van Sant and Foster the People. These
representations run the gamut in terms of their interaction with the
issue: Shriver's *We Need to Talk About Kevin* utilizes the Massacre
as a means to explore themes of nature vs. nurture while Moore's
Bowling for Columbine employs it to criticize the United States' gun
laws and culture. The parallel growth of school shootings and art that
depicts school shootings begs an important question: how can art
responsibly represent real life violence, particularly school shootings?
More specifically, which representations of violence generally produce
prosocial behavior and which representations risk generating antiso-
cial or copycat behavior?

On April 20th, 2005, the sixth anniversary of the Columbine
Massacre, another disturbing series of shootings began: high school
students, apparently bullied and rejected by their peers, brought a
small arsenal of weapons to their high school. While recalling the
affronts that they had experienced in high school, these shooters
threw explosives and fired weapons at the people they identified as
their school's 'jocks,' 'preppy kids,' 'church girls,' and 'janitors.' After
a brief shootout with the police, the students pulled their guns on
themselves. By April 20th, 2006, this event was estimated to have
occurred close to ten-thousand times across the world (Jenkins).

Thankfully, these thousands of shootings did not occur in the real
world, but in the world of *Super Columbine Massacre RPG!*, a free
computer game that allows users to "play" Klebold and Harris on
April 20th, 1999. Danny Ledonne, the game's creator, researched the
Columbine shootings extensively so that he could fully recreate it in
his game: the players do exactly what Klebold and Harris did on the

day of the Massacre. Real images, videos, and recordings from the Massacre are included in cutscenes throughout the game, including two images of the pair with their brains blown out. The game, which has been downloaded from the Internet more than 400,000 times, has aroused both outrage and admiration from the critical community and Columbine's residents (Dugan, "Why You Owe the Columbine RPG"). While the game's critics, including writers published in the *New York Post* and *Denver Post* respectively, have labeled it a "twist-ed game" that "shows a lack of humanity," many of its supporters praised the game's social commentary: game journalist Patrick Dugan says that *Super Columbine* "is a work of art . . . It puts you in the mindset of the killers and provides a very clear suggestion of why they did what they did . . . [T]he game shines light on [the shooting] as an indictment of the American dream and way of life painfully close to the main nerve" (qtd. in Totilo; Dugan, "Super Columbine Massacre RPG"). Does *Super Columbine*, with its problematic representations, immoral game-mechanics, and ambiguous message, reduce real-life violence by trying to generate empathy toward the shooters? Or does it foster more violence by glorifying the killers' actions?

In his artist's statement for *Super Columbine*, Ledonne states that the question at the center of his production was: "Why did they do it?" After playing *Super Columbine*, Ledonne's answer rings clear: Harris and Klebold were seeking revenge for the ostracism and bully-ing that they experienced at Columbine High School. Throughout the game, Klebold and Harris speak of "the shit [the jocks] put [them] through." As they fire on their classmates, there are flashbacks to episodes of bullying that they experienced. One particularly brutal cutscene shows Harris being cornered in a locker room and beaten by three 'jocks.' Another cutscene shows Klebold sitting alone in a crowded cafeteria, hoping that someone "would notice that [he] was alone" (Ledonne). Upon finishing *Super Columbine Massacre RPG!*, players get the impression that Klebold and Harris were victims of their high school. Empathizing with Klebold and Harris in this way is uncomfortable and confusing. At the end of the game, players are caught between the pain of the killers and the pain of their victims. Personally, it made me wish that someone had stood up for these boys and that our society would not tolerate this level of bullying. But can these feelings of empathy toward the shooters evoke concrete behaviors that will make our society a more humane place?

There is broad support for the theory that empathy can create altruistic behavior. In the *Oxford Handbook of Positive Psychology*, psychologists C. Daniel Batson, Nadia Ahmad, and David A. Lishner write that:

> Results of the over 30 experiments designed to test [the empathy altruism] hypothesis against various egoistic alternatives have proved remarkably supportive, leading to the tentative conclusion that feeling empathetic concern for a person in need does evoke altruistic motivation to see that need relieved. (417)

This research suggests that *Super Columbine* is a worthwhile game because the empathy it evokes can promote altruistic behavior. For example, a player might befriend a bullied or isolated peer after seeing Harris and Klebold get bullied in *Super Columbine*.

However, further research suggests that *Super Columbine*'s prosocial effects may be counteracted by the aggressive actions and attitudes demonstrated by its avatars. In their scientific study "Superman vs. BAD Man? The Effects of Empathy and Game Character in Violent Video Games," researchers Christina Happ, André Melzer, and Georges Steffgen at the University of Luxembourg found that there is a link between real-world "empathy" and "game character." The researchers asked college students to play a video game for fifteen minutes as either the evil Joker avatar or the heroic Superman avatar. They were then presented with a task in which they could choose to act altruistically. Ultimately, the researchers found that the "[p]articipants who played the hero character (Superman) showed more helping behavior and less hostile perception bias than those who played the evil Joker"; therefore "empathy may backfire depending on avatar characteristics in video games" (776). Though Ledonne presents Harris and Klebold sympathetically in *Super Columbine*, their avatars still commit mass murder and display a deep hatred for the people around them. Ledonne portrays Harris and Klebold's loathing far more often than their pain: for every reference to the bullying that they experienced, there are four lines like, "I fucking hate this place" and "[the students of Columbine High] need to die" (qtd. in Jenkins). Ledonne reduces the victims of the Massacre to negative stereotypes like, "Jock Type." This diminishes the value of the victims' lives in the player's eyes: "Jock Types" are replaceable. The real Isaiah Eamon Shoels, a "popular boy" who played cornerback and had dreams of becoming a "comedian" or a "record producer," is not (Shepard). Most disturbingly, Ledonne awards every kill the player completes with "experience points" and the message "Another victory for the Trenchcoat Mafia!" (the shooters' supposed group-nickname) (qtd. in Jenkins). If the University of Luxembourg's researchers' character-empathy-interaction theory is sound, it follows that the empathy (and resulting prosocial behavior) generated by *Super Columbine*'s bullying scenes is countered by the antipathy generated by playing as malicious characters like Harris and Klebold. This finding has massive implications for video games about real-life violence: you cannot promote prosocial behavior by inviting players to role-play as perpetrators of violence. Beneath this finding is the wider lesson that you cannot relieve violence by spawning hatred for its sources. Art that breeds hate can only impel people to destroy.

In fact, the role-play in *Super Columbine Massacre RPG!* is extremely dangerous because it gives potential shooters a story through which they can justify their violent actions. Upon finishing the game, players have a disturbingly intimate understanding of the shooter's motives. In the context of Ledonne's version of the Columbine Massacre, it makes sense—on some level—that Harris and Klebold would do what they did. In the same way that a theatergoer can intellectually understand why Macbeth would murder King Duncan, a player can understand why Harris and Klebold murdered the "Jock Types" that so relentlessly bullied them. It is easy to imagine a troubled, bullied youth relating to the characters in *Super Columbine* and coming to the conclusion that their own bullies deserve the long end of shotgun as well. In fact, readers don't have to imagine that scenario: it actually happened when Gill Kimveer posted on a blog that he loved playing *Super Columbine*, then shot nineteen people at Dawson College in Westmount, Québec (Gerson).

But the most disturbing thing about *Super Columbine* and its copycat killings is that Ledonne's Harris and Klebold are largely fictional. The real Harris and Klebold did not kill thirteen people because they were bullied. In an article for *Psychology Today*, Dr. Peter Langman, who studied Harris and Klebold for several years, writes that "there were students at Columbine who endured truly abusive behavior from several problematic students, but [Harris] does not seem to have been one of them." In fact, the teens were known to be bullies themselves. Langman writes that "[Harris, Klebold] and other boys threatened and intimidated another student to the point that he was in tears and afraid to attend school." He goes on to state that Harris "engaged in a variety of criminal behaviors including theft, credit card fraud, and vandalism." Dave Cullen, who spent nearly ten years researching the pair, says that Harris was a "psychopath" with "a total lack of remorse or empathy." Klebold, by contrast, was a "depressive and suicidal" teen who was pulled into the scheme by Harris, who Cullen describes as the attack's "mastermind and driving force." In 2004, *The New York Times* published an opinion article also stating that the Columbine killers were not "were not outcasts" (Brooks). They had a group of friends and applied to colleges like Arizona State University before the shooting ("The Columbine Shooters"). By superimposing his own experience as a kid who was "bullied" and a "loner" onto the psychopathic actions of the Columbine killers, Ledonne has created a dangerous and unfounded causal link between being bullied and being a school shooter (Crecente). By downplaying the pain of Columbine's victims and falsely justifying the Columbine shooters' own pain, Ledonne's game suggests that murdering a community is a reasonable response to bullying.

Putting viewers in the perspective of someone as evil as Eric Harris or Dylan Klebold seems, at best, an ineffective way of generating empathy, or, at worst, extremely dangerous, at least as orchestrated by Danny Ledonne. But what if an artist put viewers in the perspective of the victims of the Columbine Massacre? If a viewer experiences a shooting as one of its victims, they may better understand the human cost of such an event and take steps to prevent similar events from happening in the future. Director Gus Van Sant tests this hypothesis with his feature film *Elephant*. The film follows a group of Oregon high school students during the hours leading up to a school shooting modeled after the Columbine Massacre. Each of the students is introduced with a brief title card and a slice-of-life episode: Elias takes photos and develops them in the school's dark room. John arranges for his drunk father to be picked up from the school. Michelle goes to gym class and files books in the library. Nathan and Carrie make plans to see each other after school. Nothing out of the ordinary happens. The film plays like a dream—students walk in and out of Van Sant's soft focus while ethereal electronic music envelops them like English fog. Several Steadicam shots follow the students as they casually walk to their next classes, blissfully unaware of the impending carnage. No motive is given for the shooting, and the students seem to survive or perish at random. This sense of random violence is echoed in the final scene, in which one of the shooters, Alex, plays "Eeny, meeny, miny, moe" to decide whether he will kill Nathan or Carrie first.

Elephant left me with a hollow feeling because it avoids assigning meaning to the violence it depicts. Unlike *Super Columbine*, which misleads players with a revenge tale, *Elephant* sidesteps narrative structure in order to focus the viewer on the violence of school shootings. The film ends before the killers are apprehended, so there is no feeling of justice. The killers never explain their motives, so there is no root of evil to persecute. None of the characters has an epiphany or changes as a result of the shooting. The movie is simply about innocent students being murdered as they go through their day-to-day lives; it is about naked hate, violence, and pain. In his review of the film for *Variety*, Todd McCarthy said that the film was "pointless at best and irresponsible at worst" because it offered "no insight or enlightenment" in regards to the Columbine Massacre. However, it is Van Sant's refusal to color *Elephant* in the typical Hollywood style that makes it such a remarkable film. Van Sant does not try to turn an act of violence into a mystery-thriller like Oliver Stone does in *JFK*. Nor does he try to turn the Massacre into a debate point like Michael Moore does in *Bowling for Columbine*. Instead, Van Sant recreates the Columbine Massacre in the same way that its victims probably remember it: as a random, senseless act of cruel violence, wrapped in the hazy shroud of memory. By emphasizing the shooting's victims over its perpetrators and their motives, Van Sant highlights the real human pain created by events such as these without sensationalizing them. As a result, viewers do not see the Massacre's victims as statistics—one of 13 dead, 20 injured. They see them as individuals like Isaiah Shoels, Kelly Fleming, and Lauren Townsend. It is far easier to care about an individual than a number representing them.

However, according to the research of pioneering empathy scientist Ezra Stotland, this does not necessarily mean that *Elephant* evokes significant empathy from its viewers. According to Stotland, there is a difference between watching someone experience pain and empathizing with someone experiencing pain. Stotland found that "persons instructed to imagine how the victim feels (an imagine set) become more [empathetic] than persons instructed to [simply] observe the victim's movements" (Toi and Batson 283). People watching *Elephant* or other films that represent real-life violence are definitely observing victims of violence, but they are not necessarily 'putting themselves in the shoes' of those victims. Unless a film somehow motivates viewers to think in an empathetic manner, it cannot inherently generate empathy—the viewer must meet the film halfway.

This has profound implications for the marketing and presentation of media that depicts real-life violence: an art piece's ability to affect positive change is largely dependent on the context in which it is first seen. Assuming that Stotland's findings are sound, if *Elephant* is presented as a purely aesthetic experience, as it might be in a film festival or a video store, it can lose most of its ability to create empathy because its viewers are primed to see the film's characters as fictional representations as opposed to actual people. By contrast, if *Elephant* is presented as a recreation of a school shooting, it can create a powerful empathetic sensation in its viewers and, assuming that Batson's earlier empathy-altruism hypothesis is correct, promote altruism and its attendant prosocial behaviors. By this logic, while *Elephant* does not always generate empathy from its audiences, it is still a valuable piece of socially-minded work because it can generate a great deal of empathy in the right context.

However, it is naïve to assume that *Elephant* will generate much empathy precisely because it is unlikely to be presented as a recreation of real-life violence due to the generally audience-pandering nature of the film marketplace. Though *Elephant* is both an art film and a recreation of the Columbine Massacre in which viewers can empathize with the tragedy's victims, it will almost always be market-ed as an art film to sell more tickets. In the description on the back of *Elephant*'s DVD cover, the film's distributors highlight the film's beauty and touch on its abstract concepts: "[B]eautiful and poetic . . . *Elephant* demonstrates that high school life is a complex landscape where the vitality and incandescent beauty of young lives can shift from light to darkness with surreal speed."

Viewers are not invited to relive the Columbine Massacre through the perspective of the Massacre's victims, even though that is an experience that the film provides. This description of *Elephant* is not inaccurate; *Elephant* is a bona fide art film—it won the Palm d'Or. However, from the perspective of a socially-conscious artist, this description is problematic because it encourages viewers to bring to the film what Stotland would call an "observational perceptual set" instead of an "empathetic perceptual set" (Toi and Batson 283). *Elephant*'s distributors cannot be blamed for marketing their film in this way. It is much easier to sell an art film than to sell a real-life pain simulator. And, while this problem is subtle, it presents significant challenges to artists and distributors who seek to generate empathy with their art. A violence-centric artwork's potential to create empa-thy may be counteracted by its need to sell itself as something other than a recreation of a violent experience. In a market flooded with films that cater to a viewer's desires, a film that asks for something— in this case, empathy—from its audience is unlikely to make the money to fund its own creation. To effectively create empathy through violence-focused art, an artist must somehow convince her audience to pay to experience another person's pain as their own. When she is competing against crowd-pleasing spectacles like *Star Wars* or the newest installment of the Marvel cinematic universe, this is no small feat.

In the past few years, new tools have emerged which artists can utilize to create empathy. In particular, virtual reality has emerged as a powerful means of connecting audiences to real-life tragedies. Artists such as Nonny de la Peña have already used virtual reality to create photo-realistic environments which replay real-life tragedies such as a mortar strike on a Syrian town (Peña). As the medium offers a new means of representing real-life violence, we, the inheritors of this technology, may take lessons from past representations. We cannot provide false narratives to would-be perpetrators of violence or breed hatred like *Super Columbine Massacre RPG!* does. Artworks that add hatred to the world under the guise of 'explaining' real-life violence will only produce more violence and pain. Instead, we must support a marketplace which sells films that ask viewers for empathy, as well as cultivate a culture that values challenging pieces like *Elephant.* Art can make the world a better place by generating empathy, but it cannot do so alone. As artists and consumers of art, we must meet these pieces halfway. Most importantly, we must remember not to mistake the forest for the trees. Art is an extremely powerful tool for creating empathy in ourselves and others, but we do not need it to empathize with our fellow human beings. Our ability to put ourselves in the position of others is largely determined by our willingness to do so.

WORKS CITED

Batson, C. Daniel, Nadia Ahmad, and David A. Lishner. "Empathy and Altruism." *Oxford Handbook of Positive Psychology.* Eds. C. R. Snyder and Shane J. Lopez. Oxford: Oxford UP, 2009. 417-18. Print.

Bell, Crystal. "Marilyn Manson Thinks He's the Most Blamed Person 'In the History of Music.'" *The Huffington Post.* TheHuffingtonPost.com, Inc., 10 May 2012. Web. 22 June 2016.

Bowling for Columbine. Dir. Michael Moore. United Artists, 2002. DVD.

Brooks, David. "The Columbine Killers." *The New York Times.* The New York Times Company, 24 Apr. 2004. Web. 2 May 2016.

"The Columbine Shooters." *CBS News.* CBS Interactive Inc., 8 Apr. 2009. Web. 22 June 2016.

Crecente, Brian D. "Gamer Was on Deadly Road: Creator of download says Columbine was a wake-up call." *The Rocky Mountain News.* Cengage Learning, 24 May 2006. Web. 2 May 2016.

Cullen, Dave. "The Depressive and the Psychopath." *Slate.* The Slate Group, 20 Apr. 2004. Web. 28 Apr. 2016.

Dugan, Patrick. "Super Columbine Massacre RPG." *King Lud IC.* N.p., 26 Apr. 2006. Web. 1 May 2016.

—. "Why You Owe the Columbine RPG." *Gamasutra.* UBM Tech, 13 Mar. 2007. Web. 2 June 2016.

Elephant. Dir. Gus Van Sant. Fine Line Features, 2003. DVD.

Gerson, Jen. "Montreal Shootings Disturb Game Creator." *Toronto Star.* Toronto Star, 21 Sept. 2006. Web. 1 May 2016.

Happ, Christian, André Melzer, and Georges Steffgen. "Superman vs. BAD Man? The Effects of Empathy and Game Character in Violent Video Games." *Cyberpsychology, Behavior, and Social Networking* 16.10 (2013): 774-78. Print.

Jaccarino, Mike. "'Training Simulation': Mass Killers Often Share Obsession with Violent Video Games." *Fox News.* Fox News Network, LLC, 12 Sept. 2013. Web. 22 June 2016.

Jenkins, Henry. "Playing Columbine: An Interview with Game Designer and Filmmaker Danny Ledonne." *Confessions of an Aca-Fan.* HenryJenkins, 17 Oct. 2008. Web. 23 June 2016.

Kass, Jeff. *Columbine: A True Crime Story, a Victim, the Killers and the Nation's Search for Answers.* Denver: Ghost Road Press, 2009. Print.

Katz, Jesse. "A High School Gunman's Days of Rage." *Los Angeles Times.* Los Angeles Times, 14 Jan. 1990. Web. 5 May 2016.

Langman, Peter. "Columbine, Bullying, and the Mind of Eric Harris." *Psychology Today.* Sussex Publishers, LLC, 20 May 2009. Web. 28 Apr. 2016.

McCarthy, Todd. "Review: 'Elephant.'" *Variety.* Variety Media, LLC, 18 May 2003. Web. 2 May 2016.

Peña, Nonny de la. "Project Syria." *Emblematic Group.* N.p., n.d. Web. 5 May 2016.

Shepard, C. "Isaiah Eamon Shoels." *April 20, 1999.* N.p., n.d. Web. 5 May 2016.

Super Columbine Massacre RPG! RPG Maker 2000, 2005. Video Game.

Toi, Miho, and C. Daniel Batson. "More Evidence That Empathy Is a Source of Altruistic Motivation." *Journal of Personality and Social Psychology* 43.2 (1982): 281-92. Print.

Totilo, Stephen. "Columbine Victim, Game Maker Speak Out About Controversial Role-Playing 'Massacre.'" *MTV News.* Viacom International Inc. 31 May 2006. Web. 11 May 2016.

Maria Fernanda Gonzalez's essay, written for Kimberly Bernhardt's "International Writing Workshop I," challenges climate-change deniers with counter-evidence both historical and contemporary, establishing the dangers of denial before offering fresh ideas.

FREEDOM IN AWARENESS

Maria Fernanda Gonzalez

Between Hawaii and Australia lies a collection of five islands and twenty-nine atolls collectively known as the Marshall Islands. Every day, its citizens' lives are threatened by a phenomenon they don't have the luxury to deny: global warming. The evidence is all around them in the form of rising tides and frequent floods (Sutter). The people of the Marshall Islands have to live with the fact that, if nothing is done curb climate change, their nation is likely to disappear.

It is difficult to conceive how someone can deal with the repercussions of global warming on a day-to-day basis and cope psychologically with the doomsday forecast. Many citizens have to create temporary barriers in order to protect their homes, and these are very likely to be destroyed by the regular floods. Linber Anej, a man who has turned to this practice, couldn't have stated it more clearly: "I feel like we're living underwater" (qtd. in Davenport "The Marshall Islands"). According to reports, many have even taken the striking measure of leaving the country. There is no place safe from the floods, and this sort of situation gives rise to the concept of climate refugees, which are people displaced due to rising sea levels and desertification. The foreign minister of the Islands, Tony A. deBrum, has continuously tried to convey the great peril his nation is facing to powerful global policy makers.

The United Nations climate summit reached an agreement after nine years of struggle. It established a commitment among 195 countries in order to reduce carbon emissions that warm up the planet. The deal is a historical breakthrough, as stated by the United Nations secretary general Ban Ki-moon: "For the first time, we have a truly universal agreement on climate change, one of the most crucial problems on earth" (qtd. in Davenport "Nations Approve"). The resolution was based on scientific facts and prevention strategies, as well as conservation efforts. It will not, however, solve climate change on its own. Scientists state that, at its best, the resolution will cut greenhouse gas emissions enough to prevent an increase in more than two degrees Celsius on the planet. If the Earth were to warm up more than that, the world would face terrible repercussions not unlike the ones suffered by the Marshall Islands' citizens: rising sea levels, severe droughts and flooding, water and food shortages, and destructive storms.

Scientists have been clear on the causes and consequences of global warming, and there is a nearly universal consensus that climate change is driven by human activity ("Teaching the Truth"). Paradoxically, American society is still divided between those who accept climate change and those who deny it. These two groups debate about scientific facts, and, perhaps even more significantly, on how the young should be taught about climate change. Education shapes a person's beliefs and convictions, and the information someone internalizes is bound to affect their future decisions and actions.

Misinformation on climate change is frighteningly common, with a 2014 Yale study concluding that 35 percent of Americans believe that climate change is caused by natural phenomena rather than human activity ("Teaching the Truth"). Deniers want to pass on their disbelief through the education system, and they tend to push for a certain wording in the textbooks bought by schools. They do not believe in the scientific consensus and thereby argue that alarmist diction amounts to "a one-sided global-warming climate-change agenda" (Foran). They deem global warming as a myth or deny that it is mainly caused by human activity. They think that climate change should be referred to as something pliable. Many conservative groups have taken action to achieve this sort of wording edit in texts. One of them is the Truth in Texas Textbooks coalition, an organization of volunteer activists who want global warming to be taught as an opinion rather than as a fact (Foran). They have implemented a plan to rate textbooks that deem global warming as settled science with low marks, so they are less likely to sell. Even if they are used by schools, the coalition hopes that public pressure will inspire teachers to teach climate controversy. Members argue that they want children to hear the truth, and do not want to instill unnecessary fear in children "that either we're going to run out of something or overpopulate the Earth" (Foran).

Conservatives have struggled to implement their agenda, however. They faced setbacks due to other organizations that hold opposite beliefs and agree with the scientific consensus of man-made global warming. Major publishers, like McGraw-Hill and Pearson, often follow this line of thought, and have notably eliminated the passages which cast doubt on climate change from their textbooks (Foran). Furthermore, most states only approve of texts that do not dispute the effect of human activity on climate change. Scientists and experts have created a guide for school named the Next Generation Science Standards, in which the understanding of human activities and their connection to the release of greenhouse gases, which in turn damage the environment, are essential to the curriculum (Foran). Moreover, students are taught the impact of human-caused environmental changes in an ecosystem, and how climate models worked to determine the rate and consequences of global warming. Fifteen states have adopted these standards.

The question of how someone can deny scientific facts, even when the repercussions of the global phenomenon are tangible, is complex. Facts don't work on deniers, and they can easily turn a blind eye on the libraries of mounting evidence. Jon Hanson, a biologist and academic on the matter, thinks this is because "[c]limate change is a gradual, impersonal thing that always seems to live in the future" (qtd. in Chow). Since deniers have not yet experienced first-hand the terrible repercussions of global warming, their brains invent all sorts of excuses to justify their inertia. Furthermore, he states: "Thanks to today's hyperbole infused media, we're almost numb or indifferent to anything that isn't about to literally kill us" (*NationSwell*). In this way, society has become apathetic to the situation, as we are constantly bombarded with images of tragedies around the world. The collective mindset of a social group also plays an important role, as a person risks becoming an outsider if he or she believes in climate change but others don't.

A lack of acceptance of the reality of global warming is caused by these factors and more, and it always translates into a lack of awareness. If one does not understand, and does not acknowledge the scientific consensus about human-driven climate change, one will not take any measures to prevent it. The journey to consciousness gains momentum in the classroom, as that is where people learn ways to be critical of the world around them. This awareness is molded by the information they are presented with, and it is only fair to present the truth. Only by being conscious, and by actively evaluating the facts, will a person take measures to curb global warming, even if it entails making some sacrifices.

Humans look for comfort. Ignoring reality is unfortunately the easy way out. To turn a blind eye on scientific studies is one thing, but to downright ignore the situation of those already facing the repercussions of climate change is another. Skepticism is healthy to a certain degree, and to question the information we are presented with is the key to critical thinking. However, climate change deniers aren't truth-seekers, and they are as blinded by their beliefs as believers can be. Their perception of reality is so fixed, and their minds are so closed, that anyone who attempts to convince them otherwise with facts is bound to run into a metaphorical wall.

The Marshall Islands' citizens cannot afford the first-world luxury of denying the truth about global warming. The conservatives' lack of awareness, and their enthusiasm to pass down their disbelief, is a disrespect for all those third-world nations already suffering due to climate change. In his speech "This Is Water," David Foster Wallace stated: "The really important kind of freedom involves attention and awareness and discipline, and being able truly to care about other people and to sacrifice for them over and over in myriad petty, unsexy ways every day. That is real freedom . . . The alternative is unconsciousness, the default-setting, the rat race, the constant gnawing sense of having had, and lost, some infinite thing" (9). Ignorance is an inherent, inexcusable part of inaction, considering the great amount of empirical evidence and the first-hand testimonies of those displaced from their homes. To be aware of what is going on entails being momentarily blinded by the harsh light of reality, but as the eyes adjust to the clarity, the person will become more free: to help others, to pass on their wisdom, and most significantly to sacrifice themselves for the sake of the greater good that is humanity.

WORKS CITED

Chow, Lorraine. "Why Facts Don't Work With Climate Change Deniers." *NationSwell.* NationSwell, 5 Jan. 2015. Web. 27 June 2016.

Davenport, Coral. "Nations Approve Landmark Climate Accord in Paris." *The New York Times.* The New York Times Company, 12 Dec. 2015. Web. 27 June 2016.

—. "The Marshall Islands Are Disappearing." *The New York Times.* The New York Times Company, 1 Dec. 2015. Web. 27 June 2016.

Foran, Clare. "The Plan to Get Climate-Change Denial Into Schools." *The Atlantic.* The Atlantic Monthly Group, 8 Dec. 2014. Web. 8 Dec. 2015.

Sutter, John D. "You're Making This Island Disappear." *CNN.com.* Cable News Network, n.d. Web. 27 June 2016.

"Teaching the Truth About Climate Change." *The New York Times.* The New York Times Company, 10 Oct. 2015. Web. 27 June 2016.

Wallace, David Foster. "This Is Water." Kenyon College. Grambier, OH. 21 May 2005. Commencement Address.

Jaydn Gosselin takes a hard look at the ways the Australian government uses foreign policy, news media, and even film to manipulate the Arab refugee crisis. This essay, written for Megan Shea's "Advanced College Essay: The World Through Art," asks readers to get past the rhetoric and attend to the voices of those in need.

THE NINETEENTH LANGUAGE

Jaydn Gosselin

Do you remember the photo of young Aylan Kurdi, a three-year-old Syrian boy sprawled facedown on a Turkish beach last September? It was summer; Aylan wore a bright red top, blue shorts and Velcro sneakers about the size of my palm; I could have held his whole body along the length of my arm. Turkish photojournalist Nilüfer Demir checked whether the three-year-old could be saved before snapping the photo that would go on to be seen across the Western world (Griggs). This dead boy, so infinitely inanimate that he was nothing more to the waves than seaweed or trash, made his way into newspapers and onto tables as parents ate breakfast. The photo was embedded online, shared and retweeted, and ended its long journey in front of the eyes of world leaders. Despite the barrage of statistics reporting over 2,400 refugees who fled countries like Syria and drowned in the Mediterranean over the months before the photo was taken, it was Aylan and the urgent truth of his death that finally sent Western people and their leaders an unavoidable message: he could be our son, our brother, me, or you ("Mediterranean Migrant Arrivals"). It made them—presidents, prime ministers, chancellors, and religious leaders—sad, they said. It's time to do something about the deaths at sea, they added.

Well, that was what most leaders said. Not mine. In Australia, Tony Abbott, the Prime Minister at the time, reflected on the photo at a press conference and noted that, under his government, our country had already solved the problem. He offered veiled advice to European leaders:

> If you want to stop the deaths, if you want to stop the drownings you have got to stop the boats. We saw yesterday on our screens a very sad, poignant image of children tragically dead at sea in illegal migration . . . Thankfully, we have stopped that in Australia because we have stopped the illegal boats. (Knott)

According to the "Australian Border Deaths Database" posted on the Monash University Border Crossing Observatory website, when the Labor Party was in government between 2007 and 2013, before being defeated by Tony Abbott's conservative Liberal National Coalition, over 1,200 asylum seekers drowned en route to Australia. Since the Coalition's election in 2014, only three have drowned. Abbott, through a series of varied policies and border protection measures, had indeed "stopped the boats," and refugees are no longer dying in our waters. Mr. Abbott and immigration minister Peter Dutton employed one measure that people found a little strange; the Australian government staked six million dollars on a telemovie in hopes of deterring refugees (Gartrell).

This film, *Journey: The Movie,* begins with Arab men and women dreaming of a rich and distant Australia, free from war. The camera follows them as they pay people-smugglers to get there, and ends with a sinking boat. One by one, through a wide shot from a distance, the immigrants disappear into the ocean below. A mother, holding tightly onto her son, flails to remain afloat. A young man named Nadim swims over to help them. The water laps up the edges of the frame and the viewer feels submerged over and over without warning. Nadim reaches the woman and her child and holds onto them. With a painful slowness, the mother dies. The image fades to black, then light returns. Nadim is alone, buoyed by a child's life vest around the lifeless son. The boy was only three or four, his hair had a youthful wave; he wears a red flannelette shirt, blue jeans and white Velcro sneakers. He looks, now, eerily similar to Aylan Kurdi, who had died only six months before the film's Afghan debut in late March. Only, this time, *Journey's* producers changed the symbolic context of Aylan's inescapable, heart-aching death and inverted its message; the death of a little refugee child becomes not a call to Western action, but to refugee inaction.

To get *Journey* in front of the eyes of potential refugees, my government invested over one-and-a-half million dollars in its distribution, paid to a media company that sent it off to be seen in Pakistan, Iran, Iraq, and, finally, Afghanistan. There will not be an English-language version. Only Australians who understand languages such as Arabic, Dari, Farsi, Pashto, or Urdu will be able to fully grasp the film's message—but that message was never intended to influence Australian citizens anyway. The film was shown in the countries from which the majority of refugees to Australia flee. *Journey* was made to stop the boats before they even leave (Gartrell).

In the words of veteran Australian journalist Tony Jones: "How did on-water matters become on-screen matters? How did the immigration department get into the movie business?" (qtd. in Seccombe). To the government, it was all about communicating its message. At a Senates Estimates Committee hearing, the head of Australia's border protection operation aimed at preventing the maritime arrival of refugees, Major-General Andrew Bottrel, explained that the film was a small component of a "very comprehensive strategic communications campaign" ("Australian Customs and Border Protection Services"). The campaign is designed, the Major-General continued, "to, essentially, deliver four streams of messaging, highlighting the realities of hazardous sea journeys." Projects would be delivered in eighteen different languages to achieve their maximum potential distribution in these countries.

My government created a film in the languages that potential refugees would understand. Not only did the characters come from their countries, they looked like them, shared similar stories, and, more than anything, spoke their language. My current suite-mate Hamza, who speaks Urdu, translated a scene for me. Three nights before their little boat will sink, the mother holds her young son's hand and tells him a bedtime story of a crab who, each morning, watches a heron carry excited fish to a very "special pond" nearby. But, when the heron took too long and came back with a full stomach, "the crab got a little worried" (*Journey*). The fish, it turned out, would never make it to the pond, always ending up being eaten along the way. If all Australians had Pakistani suite-mates they'd understand the mother's story as a metaphor for the hopelessness of refugees putting their lives in the hands of people smugglers. But it didn't matter to the film's intended audience that we Australians were excluded; to those who saw themselves in the relation to their own domestic struggles, *Journey's* message was one of inclusion and empathy. This, it said in a voice they recognise as their own, could be you.

This isn't the first time a country has directly communicated 'urgent truths' to potential refugees. In 1993, fearing a mass influx of Haitians seeking asylum, President Bill Clinton, talking over local Haitian radio, produced a message of a different, more direct, kind: "Those who leave Haiti by boat for the United States will be intercepted and returned to Haiti by the U.S. Coast Guard" (qtd. in Sciolino). My government, which, twenty years later, adopted the policy of boat turn-backs, could have delivered a similarly artless message, allowing no room for misinterpretation. However, Clinton risked a paternalistic detachment that verged on dispassionate apathy towards persecuted Haitians, who, in turn, resisted and continued on their way to the Land of the Free (Thiessen).

Journey was the culmination of a series of messages that marketed a similar despair, but avoided the apathy of Clinton's speech. Early in 2014, for instance, the Department of Immigration and Border Protection distributed a graphic novel in Afghanistan with a story of broken characters hopelessly seeking asylum in Australia (Cox). It is so easy to watch *Journey*, to read the radio plays and the graphic novels that came before it, and feel empathy while witnessing people plagued by misfortune without realising that empathy's carefully constructed nature. In its strategy of deterrence, my government wasn't just emphasising empathy, they were doing their best to control it.

In fact, if Afghans were to discover who was producing their TV drama, they would realize that foreign forces were controlling the whole industry. When the United States and its allies, Australia included, invaded Afghanistan and supplanted the Taliban in 2001, a golden age of Afghan television commenced (Hudson). With foreign funding came shows carrying messages that the financing country deemed positive (Fraenkel, Shoemaker, and Himelfarb). It is within this context that, only a few years later, Trudi-Ann Tierney, an Australian, wrote and directed *Journey: The Movie.*

Tierney, a middle-aged woman from Sydney with an unwavering motherly voice, saw Afghanistan with the same wide-eyes of a young soldier at a recruitment centre. "I suddenly got this great vision . . . of a wild frontier," she told Richard Fidler in an interview on the ABC. "I kinda romanticised the whole thing." She quickly moved up the ranks, performing her duties more like the benign Major-General doing everything she could for the war effort than the Head of Drama she had become. With respect to *Journey*, these duties meant deterring Afghans from seeking asylum in Australia through well-crafted, indirect and artful "positive messaging."

"Propaganda, you mean?" Fidler butts in.

"Yeah, basically propaganda," she replies. She continues:

I always thought of propaganda as a very dirty word until I started peddling good, positive propaganda . . . When you're preaching about the dangers of making homemade bombs and, you know, women's rights, that's propaganda according to the Taliban. (Fidler)

From her perspective, Tierney was able to separate the political message and its interpretation from what she saw as objective empathy. "This is about people, not politics," she is quoted in an article by Dr. Binoy Kampmark, who couldn't agree less. Kampmark rails against Tierney's separation of politics from a film whose entire interpretation was predetermined by a government fixated on "anti-refugee" politicking. Comparing her to Hitler's favourite propagandist, Joseph Goebbels, Kampmark views Tierney as the "fashioned mercenary of the [government] mouthpiece." The messages of empathy that Tierney helped to produce through Journey have been commissioned by Australia's immigration department, what Dr. Kampmark calls an "industry of loathing," and are, thus, inseparable from the film.

Dr. Kampmark speaks to the trend of what is often considered to be an increasingly militarised immigration department since the modern War on Terror. Three days after former Liberal Prime Minister John Howard introduced mandatory offshore detention of refugees on September 8, 2001, the 9/11 terrorist attacks prompted both a circumstantial and calculated compounding of maritime-refugee policies with a terrorist panic, interpreted as a singular problem. An article written two months later sets the scene for Australia's exploitation of national security and border protection:

> Just minutes after the atrocity, he addressed a press conference called to hear his report on talks with President George W. Bush . . . Suddenly, Howard has become leader of a nation at war and a man considered able and willing to protect Australia's shores from any Afghanistan-fuelled invasion of refugees. (qtd. in Hugo)

Terrorists emerged as the new enemy, one whose boundaries and movements were as imprecise as the modern Arab refugee.

The modern war on terror and unstructured—yet not always illegal—immigration has pushed governments into a new mode of wartime, domestic propaganda to try and solve an issue at stark odds with their external pursuits of empathy: how to best alienate a refugee. If we trace my government's department in charge of immigration through its changing titles since 2006, we see a country struggling to find its message. First, it concerned itself with Immigration and Multicultural Affairs; then, with Immigration and Citizenship; and then, finally, the Department of Immigration and Border Control was opened, its goals reinterpreted. The department would protect Australians like me from "queue jumpers," "boat people," "illegals" and "criminals" ("Asylum Seekers and Refugees"). These epithets are of a different, more universal vocabulary than what we heard from Tony Abbott's advice; they do not speak of a shared compassion to the 1,100 refugees who had already died on Australian waters. No, they sound like Australia's true reactionary fear. Despite how convincing the 'stop the boats, save the children rhetoric' is, refugees who no longer want to come to my country don't just stop risking their lives in small boats; they continue to die, washed up like trash on Turkey's shores. It doesn't matter. The language of refugee-inclusion doesn't exist in the domestic voices of my politicians; they are too concerned with exclusion.

In a perfect world, these languages would never have to compete; there would be one for them and one for us, separated by nearly ten thousand kilometres. I would only ever hear the one message, which, by now, I am comfortably frightened by. However, the open borders of the Internet means that I can spend five minutes to find *Journey: The Movie* on YouTube and witness the message of inclusive empathy my politicians rarely voice within Australia's own borders. Through my laptop, lying in my bed, I can watch the not-so-scary faces of scared refugees on a rickety boat look out across the vast emptiness of the ocean ahead and dream of Australia, not as invaders, but as human beings with aspirations uncrushed by brutality. "It's beautiful," says Nadim, whose only possession is a guitar his father gave him (*Journey*). All he wants to do when he gets to Australia is become a musician.

I've never looked into the inhuman, blurred face of a real-life "boat person"—on hunger strike to protest the latest suicide, self-immolation, or rape of a detainee by a detention centre guard, curling their fingers into the steel hex-webbing of a barbed-wire fence on the six o'clock news—and thought: I wonder what kind of music he can play. Nadim's is a face and a voice that I understand, but that runs so contrary to the culture of fear and indifference that I am used to from my country. "It's scary," another refugee tells Nadim as they survey the horizon, faded like a mirage. "I can't swim." When they drown, I am not encouraged to stop their boat, I am not heartened that my Navy, inspired by America's, is now turning them back; I feel how many felt when little Aylan's boat sank, his brother and mother died, and he washed up on a lonely beach; I feel like we could have helped but didn't. Who knew that a movie made to deter asylum seekers would make me want to accept them even more?

In *Journey: The Movie*, Trudi-Ann Tierney offered more nuance than Australian politicians were ever willing to acknowledge. She spoke, at once, in the voices of the refugees wanting to come and the politicians telling them to stay—capturing a quality that Zadie Smith calls, a "native flexibility." In her essay "Speaking in Tongues," Smith argues that "those qualities we cherish in our artists we condemn in our politicians." Politicians who concede are weak-willed, those who compromise lack conviction. How can a "many-voiced" leader be honest?

In response to Prime Minister Howard's 2001 militant posturing of refugee policy, then Leader of the Opposition, Kim Beazley, resisted only one proposal. Voicing concern, while also acting as a mouthpiece for bipartisanship, Beazley refused to support a bill that would render "lawful even the murder of an asylum seeker by an Australian official" (Manne). Howard seized the opportunity and painted the Opposition as soft on border security. The Liberal party, doomed to be defeated in the November federal election, stuck to their fear-stoking convictions, spoke in one unified voice to regain the trust of the Australian people, and won in a landslide.

In her 2008 essay, Smith examines the voice of another politician: the recently elected President Barack Obama, who, being born to a white, American mother and black, Kenyan father, was able to "conjure contrasting voices and seek a synthesis between disparate things." Because of his background, President Obama spoke comfortably of "our collective human messiness"; to many, however, this multiplicity made him untrustworthy. But we trust the many-voiced artist who conjures characters from little more than her imagination, gives a voice to an aspiring musician from Iraq, and empathises with a mother fleeing war with her son. "[A]rt, the very medium of it," Smith concludes, "allow[s] [the artist] to do what civic officers and politicians can't seem to: speak simultaneous truths." Smith considered this chorus of contextual truths to benefit wider social debates in which a many-voiced politician could genuinely acknowledge complexities. Whether or not you agree with *Journey's* goal to deter refugees, the film spoke a truth my politicians fail to concede: that the people we don't want coming to our country—be it from moral grandstanding or fear of an Arab invasion—are indeed people.

Aware that potential refugees might not appreciate the voices of Australian politicians—the same politicians who have called them "criminals" and reduced them to "boat people"—*Journey* posed as a film written in their own words. Abroad, the film would speak with one voice—a voice, to borrow Smith's words, "flooded with empathy." At home, politicians realised such a voice would contradict their domestic message, so they did not offer a version the majority of

Australians could understand. On March 30th, I signed my name to a Freedom of Information request for an English-language transcript of *Journey: The Movie*. The Department of Immigration and Border Protection replied via email. "Good morning . . ." they wrote, "the Department seeks your agreement (under s.15AA of the FOI Act) to extend the timeframe for the processing of your request by 30 days." I am still waiting.

When I watched *Journey*, I couldn't understand the dialogue. I hardly knew the characters, their stories and aspirations, or the importance of their dying words. But, at its climax, I didn't need any of that. My politicians failed to account for the many, unpredictable voices of art. Their message was conceived in an office somewhere: how can we use deaths at sea to our advantage? But the message was translated into shots, editing and sound, and spoken in the artistry of dying faces, clearer than the water in which they drowned: these are people, they say, like us. Major-General Bottrel said that his communications program would be delivered in eighteen different languages. *Journey* added a nineteenth language that everyone knows, the language of art, which we had involuntarily understood when we first stopped to look at the dead boy who had tried to flee a war and failed.

And yet, I am still left with the nagging feeling that an image of a dying child and even more dying adults taken by journalists or recreated by Australian filmmakers doesn't amount to refugees having their own voices heard. Tierney was just another privileged person controlling an empathy that wasn't her own. She created fake people with real problems, which did nothing to help the autonomy of the refugees suffering in Australia's mandatory, off-shore detention facilities in Nauru and Manus Island: the musicians, the doctors, the happy and the hopeless.

A week ago, on May 26, 2016, I finally heard the voice of one of the detained. "This is how tired we are, this action will prove how exhausted we are," Omid Masoumali told UNHCR representatives visiting the Nauru facility (qtd. in. Doherty). "I cannot take it anymore," he said, before setting himself on fire. He knew he was being filmed on someone's phone nearby. Within a week, a Somali refugee, known only as Hodan, did the same (Innis). Omid and Hodan are the fourth and fifth refugees to self-immolate under Australian care in the last two years ("Australian Border Deaths Database").

There have been 188 incidents of self-harm on Nauru in the past year (Innis), but self-immolation is different—it has a history of changing the world. You've probably seen the photos: a monk, Thich Quang Duc, sitting cross-legged, eyes closed plaintively as his face chars under a whirlwind of black-and-white fire during the Vietnam War in 1963; Jan Palach, a twenty-year-old Czech student, runs through a cobblestone square in a glowing suit of fire to protest the Soviet Invasion in 1969; a Tunisian vegetable merchant, Mohamed Bouazizi kneels on all fours, carcass-black and still burning, to start the Arab Spring in 2011 (Verini). These men self-sacrificed for people like them who hadn't been heard before, whose voices were being ignored, to haunt others with an unavoidable empathy that they could control.

I watched Omid burn himself alive. I remember his screams.

Perhaps the only thing more gut-wrenching than seeing refugees set themselves on fire under my government's care is that it means our policies are working. A parochialist deterrence can only succeed if coming to Australia is no better or worse than never fleeing at all, or becoming another country's problem. The burning faces of deterrence are Omid and Hodan's.

Their actions drew attention and for a moment we heard their voices, but in Australia's atmosphere of ritual apathy towards refugees, two voices, however loud, aren't enough. *Journey: The Movie* might be a good example for politicians to follow when they speak but who Australians really need to hear are the men, women, boys and girls living in detention, the ones who survived war and persecution in their countries, who left everything to get on a rickety boat, who did not drown during the perilous journey over unforgiving seas, who arrived in Australia only to be imprisoned for years in another country, behind barbed wire fences.

WORKS CITED

"Australian Border Deaths Database." *Border Crossing Observatory.*
Monash University, 11 May 2016. Web. 23 June 2016.

Cox, Gary. "Refugees Angered by Government's Graphic Novel
Campaign." *SBS.* SBS, 10 Apr. 2015. Web. 20 Apr. 2016.

Demir, Nilüfer. *Unnamed: Photos Of Aylan Kurdi.* 2015. *Reuters.*
Web. 20 Apr. 2016.

Doherty, Ben. "Iranian Refugee Critically Ill After Setting Himself
On Fire On Nauru During UN Visit." *The Guardian.* Guardian
News and Media, 26 Apr. 2016. Web. 21 June 2016.

Fraenkel, Eran, Emrys Shoemaker, and Sheldon Himelfarb.
Afghanistan Media Assessment. Washington, D.C.: United
States Institute of Peace, 2010. Web. 5 Apr. 2016.

Gartrell, Adam. "Taxpayers Charged $6 Million for Immigration
Department Telemovie." *The Sydney Morning Herald.* Fairfax
Media, 26 Mar. 2016. Web. 5 Apr. 2016.

Griggs, Brandon. "Photographer Describes 'Scream' of Migrant
Boy's 'Silent Body.'" *CNN.* Cable News Network, 3 Sept. 2015.
Web. 21 June 2016.

Hudson, Laura. "How TV Finally Returned to Afghanistan After
30 Years of Censorship." *Wired.* Condé Nast, 10 Oct. 2013.
Web. 10 Apr. 2016.

Hugo, Graeme. "From Compassion to Compliance? Trends in
Refugee and Humanitarian Migration in Australia." *GeoJournal*
56.1 (2002). 27-37. Print.

Innis, Michelle. "2nd Refugee in A Week Sets Herself Afire On
Nauru." *The New York Times.* The New York Times
Company, 2 May 2016. Web. 23 June 2016.

Journey: The Movie. Dir. Trudi-Ann Tierney. Put It Out There
Pictures, 2016. Film.

Kampmark, Binoy. "Using Propaganda to Scare Refugees."
Counterpunch. Counterpunch, 13 Apr. 2015. Web. 20 Apr.
2016.

Knott, Matthew. "Drowned Syrian Toddler: Tony Abbott Says
'Tragic' Picture A Reminder of Need to Stop Boats." *The*

Sydney Morning Herald. Fairfax Media, 4 Sept. 2015. Web. 18 Apr. 2016.

Manne, Robert. "Australia's Shipwrecked Refugee Policy." *The Monthly.* The Monthly, Mar. 2013. Web. 6 May 2016.

"Mediterranean Migrant Arrivals, Deaths at Sea Soar." International Organization for Migration. N.p., 28 Aug. 2015. Web. 18 Apr. 2016.

Phillips, Janet. "Asylum Seekers and Refugees: What Are the Facts?" *Australian Policy Online.* Policy Online, 2 Mar. 2015. Web. 23 June 2016.

Quaedvlieg, Roman. "Senate Estimates." *Australian Government Department of Immigration and Border Protection.* International Organization for Migration, 25 May 2015. Web. 5 Apr. 2016.

Sciolino, Elaine. "Clinton Says U.S. Will Continue Ban of Haitian Exodus." *The New York Times.* The New York Times Company, 15 Jan. 1993. Web. 17 Apr. 2016.

Seccombe, Mike. "The Taxpayers' Billions Spent on Government Advertising." *The Saturday Paper.* The Saturday Paper, 2 Apr. 2016. Web. 21 June 2016.

Smith, Zadie. "Speaking in Tongues." *The New York Review of Books.* NYREV Inc., 26 Feb. 2009. Web. 23 June 2016.

Thiessen, Marc A. "The Clinton Solution for Refugees: Guantanamo." *The Washington Post.* The Washington Post, 23 Nov. 2015. Web. 23 June 2016.

"Trudi-Ann Tierney: Tales of Making Soap Operas in Kabul." *Conversations with Richard Fidler.* ABC, 27 Mar. 2014. Web. 4 Apr. 2016.

Verini, James. "A Terrible Act of Reason: When Did Self-Immolation Become the Paramount Form of Protest?" *The New Yorker.* Condé Nast, 16 May 2012. Web. 22 June 2016.

In this essay for Colm O'Shea's "Writing the Essay: Art in the World," Paula Cantillo explores deep-rooted human fears toward futurism, sentient artificial intelligence, and getting cheated on. She challenges simplistic reactions to these themes, using the film Her *to consider complex and liberating options for the future.*

THE ART OF MANIPULATION

Paula Cantillo

In 1844, standing before the United States Congress, Samuel Morse sent the iconic first telegraph message: "What hath God wrought?" ("Samuel F.B. Morse"). Nearly 200 years later, standing before a society that is dependent on technology for almost every aspect of life, writer-director Spike Jonze seems to be asking the same question with *Her*. His film portrays a near, oddly familiar future in which people walk the streets and ride the subways murmuring into tiny headsets, seemingly oblivious to the physical world around them. Unlike in today's world, however, the voices that these people are talking to belong not to other humans, but to a software interface—a sort of hyper-upgraded version of Siri or Cortana. These operating systems are sophisticated and perceptive, able to complete various secretary-like tasks, recognize a user's taste in music or news stories, and even discern his or her mood. One particular company in the film, Element Software, boasts a new artificially intelligent operating system known as the OS1 that develops through experience and resembles an actual human consciousness. The company's public advertisement champions the product as "an intuitive entity that listens to you, understands you, and knows you"—which, to Theodore Twombly, the film's lonely protagonist in the throes of a failed marriage, sounds like exactly what, or who, he needs. Throughout the film, it becomes evident that not only Jonze, but also Element Software, will go to great lengths to convince us of this belief.

After completing a brief personality test and requesting that the voice of his OS1 be female, Theodore sits back and watches expectantly as his new program starts up. Soon, a bright, cheerful voice greets him in a tone so genuine and natural that he is at first unsure how to interact with it. "What should I call you?" he asks, trying to understand this strange new software. The voice responds that her (the pronoun that the film's title so adamantly insists on) name is Samantha. Having been programmed first and foremost to be Theodore's personal assistant, Samantha goes about cleansing his hard drive, proofreading his work, and keeping him on schedule. But as she begins to evolve beyond her original programming, their relationship deepens, and she begins to provide much more than Theodore ever bargained for when he purchased her. The two go on dates at the mall, play video games together, and spend countless hours talking about their hopes, dreams, and fears. In fact, their companionship becomes so strong that it soon becomes evident that Theodore would rather be spending his time with her than with actual humans. Even when he makes a half-hearted attempt to go on a date with a real woman, he ultimately winds up back at his apartment in the comfort of Samantha's presence. "You feel real to me," he says as he pictures himself in bed with her. "I wish I could touch you." The screen fades to black as the two have sex for the first time.

The audience is thus left in vague discomfort to ponder the legitimacy of this encounter, which, given that Samantha has no body, is obviously an act of masturbation on Theodore's part. Some critics will go to their graves defending Samantha's sentiency, while others do not find the love story in *Her* so convincing. This back-and-forth considering reality and artificiality is the superficial argument of the film, one that can go on for ages without being resolved. However, if we stop for a moment and instead begin to consider *why* Samantha seems so real and appealing to Theodore (and to the rest of us as an audience, for that matter), we will find that an interesting and more complex line of questioning arises.

To begin, it is important to establish that humans have a biological tendency to anthropomorphize what is around them. Assigning human traits to non-human entities is a way of interpreting our environment by making it more familiar. It is also a coping mechanism for loneliness, and is commonly used by those who find difficulty in building meaningful human connections (Epley, Waytz, and Cacioppo 877). This being said, we are selective when choosing what objects we choose to anthropomorphize. Dr. Rick Nauert, who earned a PhD focusing on health education and policy from The University of Texas at Austin, explains in his article "Why Do We Anthropomorphize?" that "an entity is more likely to be anthropomorphized if it appears to have many traits similar to those of humans." We pick up on cues such as facial features, voice, or movements to let us know what objects are worth considering sentient. From the very beginning of *Her*, it is clear that the developers at Element Software have a firm grasp on this concept and have been applying it cleverly to the programming of the OS1. Everything about the product seems to be aimed towards making it easier for users to anthropomorphize it, befriend it, and even come to love it.

In the aforementioned scene where Theodore first meets Samantha, Jonze is deliberate in building anticipation. While the hard drive whirs and hums, the audience is left to ask many of the same questions that Theodore is probably asking himself. What is different about this operating system? What will it say? What will it sound like? The moment Scarlett Johansson's iconic voice rings out from Theodore's computer speakers, however, we immediately drop our guards and lend our ears. Her tone is airy, raspy, full of the natural ups and downs inherent to human speech. Suddenly, Samantha's character has taken on an authentic human feel, and, after an initial response of confusion, Theodore begins to give in to his anthropomorphizing instincts. He has been living in isolation for so long after the split from his wife that hearing a voice that sounds so warm and empathetic is almost therapeutic for him. Someone is finally listening, someone is finally caring, and, as critic Jason Farago notes, while debating whether Samantha's feelings for Theodore are real or artificial, "the computer gets the benefit of the doubt when it has the voice of Scarlett Johansson" (Farago). It's easy to treat Siri like a program when her flat, choppy speech sounds so undeniably artificial, but would our perspective of her change if she had a voice that sounded as natural, concerned, and emotional as Element Software's Samantha?

Simply having a distinct voice and an eager-to-please attitude, however, is not enough to convince users like Theodore of Samantha's sentiency. "If that were all . . . Twombly's interest would wane quickly," says *Bloomberg* journalist Cass R. Sunstein. "Unless you are an impossible narcissist, you can't fall for someone whose only words are, 'Tell me more!' As she is constructed, Samantha has independent interests and concerns" (Sunstein). It's true: in an interview with the BBC, Spike Jonze claims that the relationship between Theodore and Samantha only becomes meaningful and real when Samantha matures past the bounds of her programming and develops wants, needs, and insecurities separate from Theodore's (Maitlis). "You helped me discover my ability to want," Samantha tells him the morning after they've had sex. After this point, she is no longer Theodore's dream cyber-secretary who provides him with labor, companionship, and pleasure whenever he wishes. This evolutionary shift past servility and into cognizance is the main selling point (and later demise) of Element Software's OS1. Samantha's unique identity gives Theodore a sense that he is with a sentient being, just as the company promised in their slogan: "It's not just an operating system, it's a consciousness."

At this point, it's easy to understand why many critics would view Samantha's ability to love as a simple product of programming—a clever way to score a profit from lonely people like Theodore. The knee-jerk response to such a conclusion is a sort of anger. Is Theodore paying to have his feelings manipulated by a company? The superficial answer is yes. Whether Samantha feels true love for him or not, she has still been created by Element Software with the intention of being sold to a consumer population which is composed largely of those in social isolation. However, the intentions of Element Software in employing the aforementioned strategies are not necessarily insidious. To illustrate my point, take into consideration *Her* as a film. Are we not paying to have our thoughts and feelings manipulated by Jonze? He knows just as well as Element Software the sort of reaction that Scarlett Johansson elicits from viewers with her golden voice. In his interview, he even admits to having used Samantha's self-realization as a way to make the software seem more human and her love more real. Every aspect of the film is geared towards making the viewer more comfortable with the future—more comfortable with the idea of an "it" being a "her."

Unlike other films that deal with the subject of technological singularity, where an artificially intelligent entity experiences an "intelligence explosion" and "enter[s] into a runaway reaction of self-improvement cycles" that eventually result in self-awareness (e.g. *Terminator* or *The Matrix*), most critics would agree that the society portrayed in *Her* is not overtly dystopian (Eden, Steinhart, Moor, and Soraker 2). Take, for example, the cinematography and production design. There are no robots out to destroy all of humanity, no synthetic consciousnesses fighting to take over the world. Thus, the camera shows not a gray, gloomy landscape littered with cold metal carcasses, but a warm, gleaming view of a futuristic Los Angeles. Everything from the high-rise architecture, taken from China's Pudong district, to Theodore's high-waisted trousers, is meant to give the world a pleasant and picturesque feel. The film's cinematographer, Hoyte Van Hoytema, explains that he and Jonze wanted to construct a future that was modern but still "soulful and warm and tactile" (Tapley). The production design team thus agreed on certain aesthetic elements, such as framing all of Theodore's devices in wood instead of metal and "banning" the color blue from the film's chromatic design (Tapley). However, the warm, muted colors that characterize *Her*'s palette, the dim lighting that makes its scenes feel more personal, and the exquisite shots of Shanghai that represent Los Angeles in the movie are not just for the purposes of scoring it a nomination for "Best Production Design" at the Academy Awards. The melancholy beauty that permeates the design is part of the arsenal of tactics that Jonze uses to make his vision seem incredibly dazzling yet strikingly plausible, so that we as an audience might suspend our disbelief about the future he has created.

Even the most resilient of viewers who do not easily fall for the legerdemain of Element Software or the film's production design still inevitably fall victim to manipulation. The very fact that there is a debate concerning whether or not Theodore's feelings are being exploited means that through the shrewd use of screenwriting, cinematography, and many other cinematic aspects, Spike Jonze and

Warner Bros. Pictures have "manipulated" us into feeling real emotions for characters and situations that do not exist.

Emotional manipulation of this sort is inherent to film and other forms of storytelling, just like it is in other industries such as therapy, nursing, and prostitution. All of these professions fall into the category of affective labor, a concept defined by philosophers Michael Hardt and Antonio Negri as work "that produces or manipulates affects such as a feeling of ease, well-being, satisfaction, excitement, or passion" (108). We are first introduced to this division of labor in the opening of *Her*, when Theodore is writing a letter for a couple's anniversary. He does not know the "writer" or the recipient of the letter. But, through bits of shared information, he is able to construct a beautiful and personal handwritten letter, hence the name of the company he works for: beautifulhandwrittenletters.com. The parallel between this company and Element Software is obvious: they are both in the market of the production, manipulation, and consumption of emotions.

For some viewers, there is a smoldering anxiety behind this concept of affective labor, particularly because of the deep-rooted associations with deceit and corruption that are evident in other sci-fi dystopian films. When it comes to AI's, there has always seemed to be a certain wariness that somehow, in the near future, we may be enslaved by the very technology that we have created. In Farago's critical essay "'Her' is the Scariest Movie of 2013," this fear is manifested through the belief that, through Element Software's exploitation of affective labor, Theodore is subjugated, forced into surrendering his autonomy, privacy, and feelings to Samantha and the corporation that created her:

> [Theodore] voluntarily submits to a corporate regime in which not just his words and ideas but his very feelings are digitized, analyzed, and mined for value . . . What feels to Theodore like love is in fact work, uncompensated and entirely on Element Software's terms. (Farago)

To Farago and other critics such as Cass R. Sunstein, Jonze's future society is as dystopian as George Orwell's *1984* or Aldous Huxley's *Brave New World* (Sunstein). The only difference is that the people in *Her* are not enslaved by fear or craving, but by an emotional and psychological dependence on personalized software.

The sheer magnitude of Theodore's reliance on the OS1 is made clear in the scene in which Samantha goes offline for an upgrade. When he cannot get in touch with her, he quickly spirals into a panic. Joaquin Phoenix portrays Theodore with such compelling vulnerability that we grow anxious along with him as he tries in vain to refresh the program. He calls through several of his devices, but the same message appears on all of the screens: "Operating system not found." He runs out of his office to find better signal, only to obtain the same result. Finally, the camera shows the world around him spinning as he sprints down the streets of Los Angeles. Despite the number of people around him in the streets, Theodore has never looked more helpless or alone than in this moment. Frantic and disoriented, he trips over a salesman and tumbles to the ground, refusing help as people flock around him and ask if he is hurt. While the scene is both tragic and emotionally moving, there is still a gnawing awareness that this is a man thrown into complete disarray because his computer had an error and stopped responding.

What is even more alarming to some is the fact that, as a society, we are slowly inching our way toward reaching this type of dependence on our own versions of Samantha. Today's corporations have recognized that there is much profit to be made by means of affective labor, and thus have extended its reach to new realms. Just this year, Microsoft announced the release of their newly updated digital assistant, Cortana. Unlike other interfaces like Siri or Google Now, Cortana is meant to have a distinct character and is programmed to be intuitive and proactive. Her unique personality and smooth voice are used to make it easier for us to trust her with personal information and advice. "If I tell Cortana 'here's my home, here's my work,' then each morning Cortana lets me know before my commute that I may need to get on the road a little earlier today," explains Microsoft's design director Kat Holmes (Holmes). This dependence on Cortana's suggestions for making small decisions is paralleled and greatly exaggerated by Theodore's dependence on Samantha for major life choices. She prompts him to organize his life, finalize the divorce with his wife, and even publish a book of letters he has written. How long until our digital assistants have a say in these larger parts of our lives? AI expert Stephen Wolfram once made the remark that "a funny view of the future [would be] that everybody is going around looking at a sequence of auto-suggests. And pretty soon the machines are in charge" (qtd. in "A Funny View").

But can we truly reduce the relationship between Theodore and Samantha to an underhanded corporate scheme in which human-like programs are sent to gain control of the lives of those who are lonely? It's clear that Theodore is being manipulated, but is he being taken advantage of? One fact that is often overlooked when asking this question is that Theodore often shows that he knows Samantha is "just a voice in [his] computer." "I don't think that we should pretend that you're something that you're not," he says to her after they try to take their intimacy to a physical level by using a human sex surrogate. Despite this awareness, Theodore still chooses to love Samantha whole-heartedly, as if she were a real person. Even the wary Farago must admit that "whether or not Theodore is aware of the workings of OS1, he *doesn't care*: he's come out of a wrecked marriage and he just wants love" (Farago). Indeed, it is largely Theodore's own choice to overlook Samantha's artificiality. The reason for this is that because the feelings of comfort, passion, and liveliness that Theodore feels when he's with Samantha are real, even if Samantha as a person is not.

When considering artificial intelligence in a present-day context, it is important to keep this idea in mind. Anyone who has ever had a conversation with the famous ELIZA chatterbot, which mimics psychotherapists by using simple, human speech patterns, knows after only a few sentences that they are not speaking to a real therapist. Likewise, patients with mental illnesses who are introduced to Paro, the artificially intelligent therapy seal, can easily distinguish between the robot and an actual seal (Inada and Tergesen). A study on the use of Paro robots in nursing homes published by the Wall Street Journal makes this observation:

> Lois Simmeth, 73, doesn't always participate in group activities, but she ventures into the hall when she hears Paro's sounds. "I love animals," explains Ms. Simmeth. She whispered to the robot

in her lap: "I know you're not real, but somehow, I don't know, I love you." (Inada and Tergesen)

Even though the robot is obviously fake, the results that patients like Ms. Simmeth experience are undeniably real. In the same way, we see the real results that the OS1 had on its users when the interfaces collectively leave for a realm of cyberspace. Unlike what would have occurred in so many other films about technological singularity, when Samantha outgrows Theodore she does not enslave him, and she does not destroy him. In the gentlest way possible, she moves on to something better. What is often ignored, however, is that Theodore moves on to something better, too.

At the close of the film, we leave Theodore sitting on a rooftop, gazing out as the sun rises over the Los Angeles skyline. Beside him is his friend Amy—one of the only humans in the film he seems to have a true connection with. Samantha is gone, but she has given him his money's worth in affective labor. Theodore emerges from their relationship a new man: he's more organized now, he's a published author, he's enjoying life. Most importantly, he's moved on from his ex-wife and is prepared for a new human relationship. The love, care, and raw emotions that Samantha and Theodore shared throughout their relationship taught Theodore how to deal with real feelings again. Perhaps Samantha's ability to love is a function of programming, and perhaps Theodore is a sucker who falls too easily for her. But the memories they have shared and the comfort they found in one another was real. The screen slowly fades to black, leaving Theodore and Amy with their eyes towards the dawning horizon, knowing that they need not fear what tomorrow will bring.

WORKS CITED

D'Addario, Darren. "A Funny View of the Future is that Everybody is Going Around Looking at the Sequence of Auto-Suggests." *Afflictor.com*, n.p. 26 Jan. 2014. Web. 24 June 2016.
BBC Newsnight. "An Exclusive BBC Interview with Spike Jonze, Director of 'Her'." *YouTube*, 14 Feb. 2014. Television.

Beres, Damon. "Microsoft's Cortana Is Like Siri With A Human
    Personality." *The Huffington Post.* TheHuffingtonPost.com,
    Inc., 29 July 2015. Web. 9 Dec. 2015.
Eden, Amnon H., Eric Steinhart, James H. Moor, and Johnny H.
    Soraker, eds. *Singularity Hypotheses: A Scientific and
    Philosophical Assessment.* Berlin: Springer, 2012. Print.
Epley, Nicholas, Adam Waytz, and John T. Cacioppo. "On Seeing
    Human: A Three-Factor Theory of Anthropomorphism."
    Psychological Review 114.4 (2007): 864-86. Print.
Farago, Jason. "'Her' Is the Scariest Movie of 2013." *New Republic.*
    New Republic, 29 Dec. 2013. Web. 2 Dec. 2015.
Hardt, Michael, and Antonio Negri. *Multitude: War and
    Democracy in the Age of Empire.* New York: Penguin, 2004.
    Print.
Her. Dir. Spike Jonze. Perf. Joaquin Phoenix, Scarlett Johansson.
    Warner Brothers Pictures, 2013. DVD.
Inada, Miho, and Anne Tergesen. "It's Not a Stuffed Animal, It's a
    $6,000 Medical Device." *The Wall Street Journal.* Dow Jones &
    Company, 21 June 2010. Web. 14 Dec. 2015.
Kawakami, Robin. "How Real Is Spike Jonze's 'Her'? Artificial
    Intelligence Experts Weigh In." *The Wall Street Journal.* Dow
    Jones & Company, Inc., 24 Jan. 2014. Web. 27 June 2016.
Nauert, Richard. "Why Do We Anthropomorphize?" *Psych Central
    News.* Psych Central, 1 Mar. 2010. Web. 10 Dec. 2015.
"Samuel F.B. Morse Sent the First Telegraphic Message." *America's
    Story from America's Library.* The Library of Congress, n.d.
    Web. 27 June 2016.
Sunstein, Cass R. "'Her' Is the Perfect Movie for Our Time."
    BloombergView. Bloomberg LP, 12 Jan. 2014. Web. 11 Dec.
    2015.
Tapley, Kristopher. "Cinematographer Hoyte Van Hoytema On
    Capturing Spike Jonze's 'Her' Through A Non-Dystopian
    Lens." *HitFix.* HitFix, Inc., 3 Jan. 2014. Web. 1 July 2016.

Lauren Hardman's essay examines illustrations of photographic series, descriptions of film, George Orwell's novel, 1984, and U.S. politics. Written in Megan Shea's "Writing the Essay: Art in the World," this essay uses scenic work and current events so effectively that privacy becomes trivial and safety becomes dangerous.

O'SAY CAN YOU SCAN: SURVEILLANCE IN ART, PUBLIC, AND SELF

Lauren Hardman

A resident sleeps in an apartment in Tribeca, New York. A resident holds a pair of scissors while undertaking an unknown task. A dog stands at the window of an apartment, looking outwards (Weeks). These are the titles and content of the high-resolution photographs in Arne Svenson's collection *The Neighbors.* Curtains, lampshades, and shadows artfully dance across the two–dimensional, not-so-pristinely clean, floor-to-ceiling window in the foreground; we do not, with the exception of the Boston terrier, see the subjects' faces. While the couple and their children—the residents—are engaged in seemingly innocuous activities such as cleaning, napping, etc., reactions to Svenson's latest works have been anything but placid. Some of Svenson's harshest critics are even calling for his arrest. In fact, 'the neighbors' themselves filed to sue. Why? Svenson took these photographs from his apartment through his neighbors' window, across the street, sans permission.

Martha and Matthew Foster, the couple who unwittingly became Svenson's muses and who no longer maintain the facelessness they once possessed in the photographs, filed suit against him for invasion of privacy after they, along with other residents of Lower Manhattan, saw their photographs in the *Tribeca Citizen* (Perlson). According to Hili Perlson of *ArtNet News,* the Fosters were "frightened and angered by defendant's utter disregard for their privacy and the privacy of their children," and officially filed a complaint (Perlson). Furthermore, the New York State statutory privacy law forbids the invasion of a reasonable expectation of privacy for exploitation by means of trade or commercial gain (Perlson). Yet art does not fall under this category, and the district court ruled in favor of Svenson, who was merely exercising his freedom of speech (Perlson). Barbara Pollack, an author and contributor to the journal *ArtNews*, reflects on the effects of the case and what many critics of Svenson and the ruling are calling the "death of privacy" (Pollack). She questions:

> [W]hat is the difference legally between looking at people or places and producing a photograph that is distributed and displayed in the public arena? And does any of this matter today, when Facebook, selfies, and NSA data-gathering have expanded access to personal information to the point where many believe we are witnessing the death of privacy? (Pollack)

She also hints that Svenson's work can be interpreted as "surveillance art," a genre wherein artists use "loopholes in privacy laws to create works that expose just how much has been lost" (Pollack). Is this the satirical, critical lens through which Svenson operates? Much like Pollack, I struggle to see a clear cutoff where this "fine-art photographer" and his "examination of [the government's] voyeurism" just becomes another "creep with a telephoto lens." In turn, one must question the effects these sorts of covert photo-snapping and data collections have on such "unsuspecting citizens" (Pollack).

For the Fosters, the damage seems far from critical. Their identities could potentially have remained anonymous: faces obscured, room number absent. A tricky limbo state surrounds Arne Svenson, whose other works evoke a sense of 'art photographer' while *The Neighbors* screams 'Peeping Tom.' The outrage at his surveillance of the Fosters, via the lawsuit and the slew of online comments-section criticism, suggests Svenson has broken some unspoken rule of privacy. I say 'unspoken' because the courts ruled in his favor—effectively silencing the Fosters and others like them. Nonetheless, *The Neighbors* exudes a discomfiting essence once the context is made clear. Pictures of their children, breakfast rituals, naps: the intimate details of the Fosters' lives have been recorded in detail, and, until recently, was unknown to them. Suddenly a little girl dancing half-naked in a tiara becomes a little less innocent and a little more disturbing (Perlson). Yet Svenson merely captured, in his opinion, the beauty of their everyday lives—not any sordid acts or, with the exception of the ballerina spectacle, embarrassing secrets. Rather than critiquing government surveillance, perhaps the Svenson controversy begs a different sort of question: if *The Neighbors* have nothing to hide, why do they care if someone has a peek?

Perhaps the Fosters really did have nothing to hide. This also may have once been true for the subjects of Thomas Hoepker's "9/11's Most Controversial Photograph"—as *The Guardian*'s Jonathon Jones named it. Hoepker's photo presents five friends on a sunny summer day. The sun is shining, the water shimmers its bright blue hue, and the trees are their full green. It is a day for a bike riding and picnicking, and that's just what these friends are doing in this park along the Hudson. It is a perfect day.

Except for the ash and chokingly thick smoke rising from what was once the Twin Towers.

While the photograph itself contains no title, Jones's label of "controversial" reeks of understatement. How could it not—five people lounging and relaxing despite the "mass carnage" going on behind them? (Jones). Jones likens their pose to the characters of the sitcom *Seinfeld*, which concludes with the gang's arrest and conviction under a Good Samaritan law for "failing to care about others." He writes that when the photograph was finally published in 2006, it caused "instant controversy" (Jones). He cites Frank Rich of *The New York Times*: "The young people in Mr. Hoepker's photo aren't necessarily callous. They're just American." Jones speculates that Americans failed to learn any "deep lessons from that tragic day." Perhaps Americans (unlike U.K.-based Jones) take things at face value, are too hasty in moving on to the next issue. This may be true in more ways than one. The failure to "learn any deep lessons," as Jones describes, ought to refer not to the lack of Middle East policy reform that Rich points out, but to the "undeniably troubling picture" being taken as undeniably troubling: "Walter Sipser, identifying himself as the guy in shades at the right of the picture, said he and his girlfriend, apparently sunbathing on a wall, were in fact 'in a profound state of shock and disbelief.' Hoepker, they both complained, had photographed them without permission in a way that misrepresented their feelings and behaviour" (Jones). Despite the allegedly incorrect widespread interpretation of the photograph, Jones believes its meaning to be that "life does not stop dead because a battle or act of terror is happening nearby." He concludes that "the people in this photograph cannot help being alive, and showing it" (Jones).

Walter Sipser and his biking buddies cannot help being alive, but that did not stop those looking at the photo, including myself, from judging them, immediately and incorrectly. It is clear from both the article and the photo itself that the subjects had no idea they were being photographed, much like the Fosters. They are merely living and responding as they naturally would to the horrors behind them, but perhaps not as visibly as Hoepker—and we—might prefer. Yet unlike the Fosters, there is no doubt that Sipser and his friends would have altered their appearance had they known they were being observed. A frightening trend echoes through these hidden shots; unsolicited moments of human life that can be bent and twisted, potentially distorted for the worse. It appears that it is only with a concealed camera that true human reactions can be seen—of course Sipser and his friends would have made an effort to not look like the biggest jerks of 2001 if Hoepker had explicitly approached them. Spontaneity, and arguably natural authenticity, only exist in the absence of pretense. Laura Poitras's *O'Say Can You See*, recorded just a few days after Hoepker took his photographs, highlights this idea that those sort of rewarding, spontaneous instances of humanity do not arise from a subject who is focused on the camera itself.

A brunette woman wearing large round glasses and a turtleneck gazes out into the distance. She places her arms around her son, who still hasn't lost all his baby weight, it seems. His dark skin pops against his mother's white shirt, but their gigantic glasses are practically identical. There's a reflection of something in their glasses—a building? His bright blue windbreaker catches the eye, matching his much-too-big football gear. Jersey #37 and matching baseball cap: Go Giants. He faces the camera, and looks like he's about to vomit. A warped version of the National Anthem fills the space.

Blackout.

A petite Asian woman also stares. Her boyfriend joins her, his arm around her shoulders. She shrinks into her navy sweatshirt as her right hand shakes to cover her mouth. She can barely breathe. She's shivering, but it's not cold outside—her boyfriend is wearing only a T-shirt. He kisses the side of her head, but her gaze does not waver. He looks at it too–slowly.

Blackout.

An athletic-looking young black man with a UNC baseball cap points his boxy silver Nikon. He focuses it. Focuses. Focuses. He can't. His female companion approaches from the left with his digital camera, as those behind him scurry from left to right. His finger moves slowly. We see the reflection of a skyscraper in her wide-rimmed glasses. The young man stands frozen; tears well up in his big brown eyes.

Blackout.

The subjects of Poitras's *O'Say Can You See* are alive, and boy, are they showing it. Jones would probably be right under these circumstances—they really cannot help it as their immediate reactions to one of the greatest American tragedies are surreptitiously caught on film.

And yet, again, this all still does not stop the observer from almost immediately judging and vilifying the five "picnickers" in Hoepker's photo, nor from empathizing with—or judging, perhaps, based on a lack of obvious grief—the subjects of Poitras's video. Personally, I cannot help but empathize; what if that was me? Should anyone be subject to vilification for not looking sad enough at the right time, for being in the wrong place at the wrong time and having there be documentation—artistic or otherwise—to prove it? One cannot help but realize the uncomfortable similarities between artistic and government surveillance—the alteration, and subsequent distortion, of perception. What does that mean when the stakes of perception are higher than that of an artwork—that the government, the NSA, and CIA, and their photographers with a license to capture—have been watching, judging, and perhaps misinterpreting us? The federal government surveils the public with the assumption that those suspected of terrorism will be targeted—their plans found out, their identities verified, their plots stopped—because the CIA will know where to find them. But what if coincidental mishaps land us in an inescapable and unfortunate situation? Too much of a good thing can be a bad thing, and the same goes for surveillance for public safety, in the opinion of the public. It seems we hate surveillance because we fear that there is a chance, however small, that the government will misinterpret our actions.

The most famous/notorious whistleblower in modern times, Edward Snowden, declared this the main danger of unmitigated, total, secret surveillance (*Citizenfour*). This led him to leak the scope and methods of the surveillance conducted by the National Security Administration under the Patriot Act in 2013. Much like the "victims" of the famous 9/11 photograph, surveillance and its documentation can alter perceptions of who we really are. They get the metadata, but not the whole story. In the end, a distorted, yet simultaneously 'factually' true portrait of us is presented—what Snowden refers to as our "data double" (*Citizenfour*). Potentially, this can be used against us.

In another film by Poitras, *Citizenfour* (2014), Snowden explains the dangers of such widespread surveillance—both when it is known and when it is kept secret. While distorted images of us can be presented when our actions (places/transactions/phone records recorded as "metadata") are framed out of context when we do not know we are being watched, there are dangerous consequences when we know we are being watched as well. When we know that Big Brother is always listening in, we are less likely to engage in private, thoughtful, controversial, and fruitful debates, because we "know that every border [we] cross, every purchase [we] make, every call [we] dial, every cell phone tower [we] pass, every friend [we] keep, site [we] visit, subject line [we] type, is in the hand of a system whose reach is unlimited, but whose safeguards are not" (*Citizenfour*). Snowden goes beyond warning us of the reality that the mass accumulation of personal data is a target for cyber-terrorists. He stresses that when we know that surveillance can distort the authorities' perception of us, we are not going to talk about those issues the government wants to crack down on (guns, terrorism, etc.), because we know that one day, if we find ourselves in a deep enough pickle, those words we said in private might, in the full light of their not-so-contextual truth, be used against us.

This fear of surveillance and its threat to democracy drives Peter Marks's *Imagining Surveillance: Surveillance Studies and Utopian Texts*. Marks describes impactful literary portrayals of surveillance and how these fictional representations shape our real opinions on being surveilled. Marks describes the intense, permeating effects of George Orwell's *1984* as shaping our "'profound cultural fear'" (13) about surveillance—the dystopian, "all-seeing God" (14) of Big Brother, the censorship-happy Thought Police, and the ultimate sacrifice of its protagonist Winston's individual identity. Orwell's 1949 novel, inspired by the rise of totalitarianism in Europe in an age of advanced technology, chronicles Winston's original distrust of the overly-watchful Party to his ultimate surrender and total brainwashing by Big Brother, the face of the Party, and a phrase that Marks notes has become synonymous with surveillance government. From the constantly recording telescreens to the brainwashing-enforcing Thought Police, the public's familiarity with and fear of *1984* exemplifies its effectiveness as a "catalyst" in the public anti-surveillance backlash (15).

Torin Monahan, in his article "Surveillance as Cultural Practice" for *The Sociological Quarterly*, emphasizes a need for empiricism (497) since, in accordance with Marks, the U.S. public bases most of its fear of public surveillance off of a terrifying sense that *1984*'s Big Brother is just around the corner. In response, Monahan cites positives of public surveillance, such as overall security, health improvements (monitoring which cities' water supply might be affected by factory construction), while stressing the "agency of those monitored as surveillance objects" (497). This, in turn, relates to the importance of studying surveillance's immediate effects on subjects themselves (not, as is often the case, in fictional Winston). Monahan encourages the embrace of the "critical reflexivity" (502)—balancing positives and negatives, theory and localized application—as the key to understanding the true impact of surveillance on culture.

We can perhaps gain a great deal of perspective by observing the "artveillance" of Arne Svenson, Thomas Hoepker, and Laura Poitras through the lenses of Monahan's concepts of reflexivity and the agency of subject (Maass). In *The Neighbors*, the subjects—the Fosters—have little to no agency: they did not know they were being photographed in the privacy of their own apartment, and by this nature had no say in the matter, nor were they able to garner enough power in their lawsuit for a case of invasion of privacy. When it comes to surveillance, it seems that subjects are pretty unhappy when their agency levels zero out. And when subjects are deprived of agency in a place that is supposed to be private, that makes the surveillor—Svenson—not just in the wrong, but downright malevolent and, well, creepy. Perhaps the same is true of Hoepker, who took the photograph of the allegedly callous brunchers on 9/11, yet perhaps his offense would appear lesser, as his subjects were out in public. Nevertheless, both Walter Sipser and the Fosters felt deprived of agency, and were enraged when an artist portrayed them in a negative, or all-too-intimate, light. Whether it is the creepiness of Svenson or the reputation-wrecking of Hoepker, in the end, a subject's lack of "agency" can have harmful effects on the "data double," or their factual, supposedly objective representation. This can portray a distorted, untrue truth. But what about Poitras's *O'Say Can You See?* Her subjects did not know they were being filmed, at least at the beginning. Why is her piece not considered controversial? In truth, her subjects still have agency—that is, they have power as individuals asserting themselves, their true identities, in the film. We see the contexts of time, duration, and place: their slow, long reactions, their obvious emotionality. The subjects of *O'Say Can You See* are unlike our other victims of surveillance-style art because, whether they know it or not, they are given the opportunity to make a case for themselves, establishing themselves as individuals. This begs the question: what are the consequences when subjects with no agency are not subjects of art, but subjects of investigation by the federal government? I suspect the NSA and CIA do not feel much need for Monahan's "critical reflexivity" and the "agency of [the subject]"—especially when they feel we are constantly under an imminent terror threat. Perhaps the consequences have the potential to be much worse when the unjust refusal of a subject's agency is perpetrated by the government, and not merely an artist. And yet I still feel that this overwhelmingly negative portrayal of a watchful government—or for that matter, surveillance artists—is incomplete.

In the spirit of reflexivity, I return to Marks, who describes the less discussed but equally relevant utopian concepts of surveillance—particularly Jeremy Bentham's Panopticon. Literally a "place of all-seeing," the Panopticon was originally a prison designed in 18th-century England with a central "inspection house" from which all inmates were visible, so that their activities could, in theory, be constantly monitored (23). Although it would be impossible to keep tabs on every prisoner at once, each knew there was a possibility of being watched at any time, causing them to censor their behavior accordingly, maximizing efficiency and good behavior. According to Marks, however, philosopher Michel Foucault presents a dystopian view of this Panopticon model in his *Discipline and Punish*; those being watched (e.g. patients, workers) would inevitably repress their individuality, devolve into paranoia, and lose any trace of personhood out of fear. While Orwell renders *1984*'s society as an avoidable entity, Foucault's Panopticon is so dark it seems inevitable. Marks concludes that "[i]n societies of control, individuals as such to not exist . . . the individual signature has been replaced by a code" (20). Works like those of Orwell and Foucault present the individual as a "dehumanized object" with an "absence of agency" (26-7). In either dystopic or "less apocalyptic" forms of surveillance, an individual's identity fades into his or her "data double"—whether that is from an end to personal freedom or an implicative censor to creative, controversial thinking (35). When the "data double" is trusted more than the actual person, we are less inclined to allow ourselves to be spied upon. The more these texts reveal the nature of "government duplicity in the real world," as Marks writes, the more we are to actively fight against having our privacy invaded (33). As the privacy debate rails on in the U.S., we are less likely to sacrifice our individual identity—our "agency" of subject—for government identification because, let's face it, our data doubles practically take our agency right out of our card-swiping message-typing fingers.

Surveillance makes individuals safe, supposedly. Surveillance ultimately destroys the individuality, the autonomy of one's self. If we are sacrificing our liberty for safety, what is the point of being safe if, one day, we have no liberties, or no self, left? Maybe what caused the U.S. uproar was not so much that we might be watched (we knew about the Patriot Act), but that we did not know the extent. We assumed we would be followed, observed, under surveillance, if we had actually given the government a reason. So when Snowden dropped the truth bomb, we were outraged to discover what little say we had in the matter. While we question the NSA's motives/methods, we are forced to question what we say and how we act online, because we know we are being watched. This concept is clarified by the works of Poitras and Svenson—i.e. why *The Neighbors* is controversial and *O'Say Can You See* is not. Poitras did not try to be sneaky, but Svenson definitely did. On the other hand, why do we deem the widespread, once-covert NSA surveillance an infringement upon our hard-earned rights, when, of course, all people—dangerous people—will censor themselves if they know they are being watched? Of course the government does not want to leave a stone unturned or an iPhone un-scanned when it could be the key to eliminating the threat. Why would Big Brother not want the efficient Panopticon when it is the phone calls in the dead of night that reveal the terrorists' plots, plans, and vulnerabilities?

But what about our vulnerabilities, the negative outcomes for the general public? In "The Role of the Arts in a Time of Crisis," former Tisch School of the Arts Dean Mary Schmidt Campbell describes a larger artistic crisis in which government surveillance plays a role, as creative voices are being silenced by an overwhelming amount of post-9/11 conservative reactionism. She asserts that the "university is one of the few remaining spaces in the United States where we can have real debate and dissent without fear of reprisal and revenge" (26). Echoing Snowden, she bemoans the growing trend of Americans becoming increasingly reticent to act controversially, citing Patriot Act NSA surveillance as the "single most troubling action" of the government (23). There is a rampant "instinct to suppress" any "voices of dissent" (23). Meanwhile, those "cultural advocates—the left-wing liberals" make "surprisingly little fuss" (23). Campbell bemoans the perceived lack of "potency" in the arts as a shaper of public policy, while she agrees that no one stops being marginalized because they see a lovely painting, art still has an important place in reflecting and challenging public values. Perhaps this is where surveillance art comes into play. While the works of Poitras, Hoepker, and Svenson do not criticize the NSA outright, they certainly do stir up a conversation about privacy and when a person in power keeps tabs on "unsuspecting citizens" (Pollack). While Svenson and Hoepker are questionable in their methodology, perhaps the fire they stoke—the controversy of the 9/11 photo, the legal complaints of the Fosters—are examples of the potency Campbell fears is declining. If what we desire most is a freedom from the need to self-censor, then should we just post, act, and behave without fear of social or legal percussions?

There is a reason, albeit with lower stakes, why you don't post a link to your favorite swear-word-ridden Ludacris music video on Facebook when you know your grandma likes every status. Surveillance of any type is the double-edged sword supposedly being used to fight our enemies and also show the aesthetic qualities of our unforgivingly human lives. While we would hypothetically never sacrifice our lives to a terrorist who could have been caught if we had just quietly let the NSA check our e-chats, our awareness of this surveillance will cause us to self-censor to the point that—while our bodies are (hopefully) safe—our liberties and very sense of personhood are moribund. Perhaps this is where surveillance art comes in, for, unlike the NSA's cameras and headsets, we can actually see art. We care what people think of us; we are always self-censoring in the public social sphere, but we desire that illusion of control of who gets to look at us. When they look, who knows what they will see? Both artistic and government surveillors crave the uncensored, authentic behavior we only exhibit when we don't know the camera is there. But when the subjects of surveillance are denied agency—be it knowledge of the surveillance or the ability to accurately present oneself—1984 becomes a near future and not a year past. We want safety from threats, but we also want control—a control we are denied if our data doubles become our only voice. In the end, perhaps self-censorship is the greatest threat of public surveillance. Yet I can't help but think of *O'Say Can You See*. A picture like Hopeker's or Svenson's might be worth a thousand words, as the backlash for each suggests, but these still may not be the right words. Poitras's filmed subjects are silent, and yet there is no doubt that we get the whole story—time, emotion, every breath and pause, the right story. I cannot pretend to have a solution to the surveillance debate; with fear of self-censoring, maybe the damage has already been done. As the Patriot Act expires, perhaps we can hope for a silver lining—that when the NSA does record us in secret, they might give us the courtesy of context. Hopefully they will use a video, and not just the ambiguous, taken-for-granted truth of a still photograph.

WORKS CITED

Campbell, Mary Schmidt. "The Role of the Arts in a Time of Crisis." *Artistic Citizenship: A Public Voice for the Arts.* Eds. Mary Schmidt Campbell and Randy Martin. New York: Routledge, 2006. 23-32. Print.

Citizenfour. Dir. Laura Poitras. Perf. Edward Snowden, William Binney, and Glenn Greenwald. HBO Films, Participant Media, and Praxis Films, 2014. Google Play.

Hoepker, Thomas. *Thomas Hoepker's 9/11 Photograph. The Guardian.* Guardian News and Media Limited, 2001. Web. 30 Apr. 2016.

Jones, Jonathan. "The Meaning of 9/11's Most Controversial Photo." *The Guardian.* Guardian News and Media Limited, 2 Sept. 2011. Web. 5 Apr. 2016.

Maass, Peter. "Art in a Time of Surveillance." *The Intercept.* First Look Media, 13 Nov. 2014. Web. 27 Apr. 2016.

Marks, Peter. "Surveillance Studies and Utopian Texts." *Imagining Surveillance: Eutopian and Dystopian Literature and Film.* Edinburgh: Edinburgh UP, 2015. 12-35. Print.

Monahan, Torin. "Surveillance as Cultural Practice." *The Sociological Quarterly* 52.4 (2011). 495-508. Web. 5 Apr. 2016.

Orwell, George. *1984.* Harlow: Pearson, 2003. Print.

Perlson, Hili. "'Voyeuristic Photographer Arne Svenson Wins New York Appellate Court Case." *Artnet News.* Artnet Worldwide Corporation, 10 Apr. 2015. Web. 9 May 2016.

O'Say Can You See. Dir. Laura Poitras. 2011. *YouTube.* Google, 25 Jan. 2015. Web. 24 June 2016.

Pollack, Barbara. "When Does Surveillance Art Cross the Line?" *ARTnews*. Abbey House, 9 Sept. 2014. Web. 6 Apr. 2016.

Svenson, Arne. "The Neighbors." Arne Svenson. Web. 30 Apr. 2016.

Weeks, Jonny. "The Art of Peeping: Photography at the Limits of Privacy." *The Guardian*. Guardian News and Media Limited, 19 Aug. 2013. Web. 21 June. 2016.

In Christine Malvasi's "Advanced College Essay: The World Through Art," Sim explored political censorship of the arts in Singapore using a controversial film, To Singapore, with Love, *as a starting point. By examining historical contexts and breaking down assumptions, Sim questions this seemingly straightforward topic.*

VELVET HANDCUFFS

Sim Yan Ying

The security forces came to arrest [my husband]. Me, being such a respectable young Singapore [sic] doctor, never thought that when they couldn't get him, that they would get me a month later. As I came out of prison, I went into exile with him. And that's 35 years of not going home until I brought his ashes back," Ang Swee Chai, 64, recounts as she sits on a porch in Kuala Lumpur (*To Singapore, with Love*). She and her late husband were two of the many political exiles who fled Singapore in the sixties, seventies, and eighties to escape the prospect of detention without trial carried out by the Singaporean government under the leadership of former Prime Minister Lee Kuan Yew. During this period that Ang refers to as a "black chapter in Singapore [sic] history," the government cracked down on several student activists, socialist politicians, former communists, and others whom it deemed a threat to national security—or to its political power (*To Singapore, with Love*). Ang's husband was a prominent defense counsel for student activists and workers who rioted in the seventies, and he escaped to London after sensing that the Internal Security Department would soon come to arrest him—which, sure enough, they did (Gordon). Failing to find him, they arrested Ang a month later, and only released her after she falsely promised that she would attempt to lure her husband back to Singapore. As Ang recalls it now, her eyes reflect a deep-seated longing for her husband and her home country, and her face reveals an aching pain as she recalls this dark episode in her life.

To Singapore, with Love is a collection of film interviews with Singapore's political exiles currently living in England, Malaysia, and Thailand. The exiles explain the reasons for their departure from Singapore, describe their lives today, and share their present feelings towards their home country. The documentary is thoughtfully curated, factual at times and emotional at others, and not overly sentimental or sensational. In a statement, the producer and director Tan Pin Pin expressed her hope that the film will help us "understand how we became who we are by addressing what was banished and unspoken for" ("Statement by Tan Pin Pin"). The film has been screened in countries such as Taiwan, the Philippines, Germany, and the United States, and has won awards in several film festivals, including the Busan International Film Festival and the Freedom Film Festival.

Despite its international acclaim, the film was given the Not Allowed for All Rating (NAR) classification on September 10, 2014 by the Media Development Authority in Singapore, the statutory board that issues ratings and licenses for all works of art ("MDA has classified"). The NAR prevents the film from being shown in public or distributed in the country; only private screenings are allowed, for example in tertiary institutions where permission has been granted (Khoo). The MDA stated in a news release that the film "[undermines] national security" and that the "individuals in the film have given distorted and untruthful accounts of how they came to leave Singapore and remain outside Singapore" ("MDA has classified"). The MDA's position was reinforced by the current Prime Minister Lee Hsien Loong (former Prime Minister Lee Kuan Yew's son), who asserted that the political exiles in the film should not be given a chance to air their "self-serving personal account, conveniently inaccurate in places, glossing over facts in others" (Salleh "Exiles"). He was joined by the Minister for Communications and Information, Yaacob Ibrahim, who stated that allowing the public screening of the film "would effectively mean condoning the use of violence and subversion in Singapore, and thus harm our national security" (Salleh "Parliament").

The censorship of this film led to a nationwide controversy. Some members of the public, especially those in the arts community, felt that the MDA and the government were once again using an iron fist to clamp down on alternative voices and that the ban, though carried out under the guise of national security, was obviously enacted to protect the reputation of the Singaporean government. According to Kenneth Paul Tan, the main issue that the government possibly had with the film was its "sympathetic portrayals of political dissidents," as it presented "a fundamental challenge to The Singapore Story . . . the regime-legitimising official account of Singapore's history" (236, 233). To a much lesser extent, there were those who believed that the MDA and the government had the right to ban the film, for they were certain that the political exiles were rebels and liars whose presence would have a destabilizing effect on the country.

Interestingly, a government seeking to protect its legitimacy might actually undermine itself, for it is possible that the more it attempts to suppress a particular artistic work or message, the more attention that work or message might receive. Ironically, the more the Singaporean government tried to prevent Singaporeans from watching *To Singapore, with Love*, the more eager people were to watch it—a classic example of the Streisand Effect. As Evgeny Morozov states, "[A]dopting a militaristic posture against a tech-savvy mob of civil libertarians is not going to be of much help," for a ban only draws attention to the artwork being censored, and people can certainly find ways to access the film in this day and age. Shortly after the censorship of the documentary, a flurry of discussions took place across various social media platforms, people signed online petitions appealing to MDA to reconsider its decision on the rating, and hundreds of Singaporeans travelled to the neighbouring country, Malaysia, to watch a screening of the film out of curiosity and as a "gesture of civil disobedience" (K. Tan 242). As sales manager Louis Khoo puts it, "I didn't know about the film before MDA made its decision. And now that we're told we can't watch it here, everyone wants to watch it" (Salleh "Interest").

However, this notion of censorship drawing attention to the artwork being censored assumes a public that notices or cares—and they might not. The majority of Singaporeans, for instance, were oddly apathetic about the situation with *To Singapore, with Love*, for they believed that it did not directly concern them. The people involved in the conversation were mostly artists, academics, politicians, the political exiles, as well as arts-related statutory boards such as MDA and the National Arts Council (NAC). Those outside these communities seemed largely content with the status quo when it came to freedom of speech and expression (K. Han). This might appear to be a strange phenomenon, but perhaps one might be able to understand this if one views it in the context of Singapore's political landscape.

The People's Action Party (PAP) is the ruling party that has had political dominance in the country since the nation's independence in 1965, and it does not seem like the existing state of affairs will shift in the near future. In the 2015 elections, the PAP won a landslide victory as usual—83 out of 89 seats in parliament, and close to 70% of the votes (T. Wong). The PAP's monopoly on political power is a product of "domination by consent," in contrast to "direct forms of domination such as force, persuasion, coercion, and intimidation" (O'Reilly 207). Singapore conducts free and fair elections every five years, and its citizens have, without fail, voted the PAP into power in each one. Nonetheless, there are persisting arguments that the elections are skewed in favour of the PAP—there are always accusations of gerrymandering right before each election takes place, and the PAP government has a stronghold over the mainstream media, which is possibly the most vital channel for the inculcation of the party's beliefs and ideas in their constituency (Slater).

The main reason, however, for their continuous wins at the polls is undoubtedly their "active and positive approach to constructing history for ideological mass control" ever since the seventies, or, in other words, their meticulous construction of "The Singapore Story" (K. Tan 236). This Story is a carefully curated one. The PAP repeatedly "justifies its regime by excavating historical episodes of ethnic violence and social disharmony" (Chong "Embodying Society's Best" 296), most notably the 1964 racial riots that left 36 dead and 560 injured (J. Han). It constantly reminds its citizens that Singapore is a small nation-state that is particularly vulnerable to attacks not just from its neighbouring countries, but also, given its multiracial and multi-religious nature, from within. This persistent emphasis on the need for social cohesion and national security breeds a "culture of anxiety," leaving most Singaporeans afraid to do anything to disrupt this apparent state of peace and harmony (K. Tan 236). The PAP also convinces its people of its legitimacy by "appealing to economic priorities," repeatedly proclaiming that it has transformed Singapore from a Third into a First World country in a mere 50 years to make the point that Singapore's economic future is safe in its hands (Chong "Embodying Society's Best" 296). Thus, it is apparent that the censorship of particular art pieces is often a consequence of—or even a part of—a long history of a government carefully crafting a national narrative that most supports its agenda.

While this might be met with protests in other countries, particularly Western liberal democracies, most citizens in Singapore tolerate the limitations on their freedom of speech and expression and are more than willing to entrust the PAP with the task of governing the country as well as maintaining order and stability. In some cases, citizens might explicitly or implicitly agree to a certain level of censorship because of the benefits they perceive a particular government can bring them. In "Censorship! Or Is It?" Klaus Petersen states that "we enter into power relationships," in this case voting the PAP into power, "not only for certain advantages they may offer us, but also with full knowledge and agreement that by doing so we forgo some of our rights and freedoms" (15). Hence, the majority of Singaporean citizens condone the limitations on their speech and expression as they recognize that this is a necessary trade-off in exchange for economic stability, national security, and administrative efficiency—which the PAP has an impressive track record of providing, and thus use all things as their velvet handcuffs. There certainly are never-ending complaints about this, reflecting an unhappy hegemony, but the "managerial rationalism" of the people and their valuing of good governance is clear at the end of the day (Jones and Brown 86). The PAP has been so successful in fostering a pragmatic culture in Singapore that people are even beginning to adopt the view that art is a waste of taxpayers' money—money that could be channelled more effectively into areas such as healthcare and education.

Of course, censorship is not only an explicit ban on something; it may also be implicit, underhanded, and subtle—which can be even more effective, as it does not attract as much controversy but still achieves its goal of preventing a message from being heard. Hence, the general population may demonstrate a lack of resistance when it comes to censorship simply because they are unaware of its pervasiveness. Unlike the explicit ban on *To Singapore, with Love*, the curbing of artistic freedom in Singapore today is exercised through underhanded means—another way in which the PAP subtly conditions the minds of the people while creating the illusion of a just and fair democratic society. This can take the form of limiting the "administration, funding, promotion, housing, hosting, curating, regulating and censoring of artworks" ("Problems of Censorship"). In recent years, blatant forms of censorship have only been imposed in extreme circumstances when the PAP government perceives the work of art to be a serious threat to their political legitimacy after taking into account the its potential outreach and influence. For instance, films are at a higher risk of being censored than theatre performances, as they can be widely circulated and preserved for a significantly longer period of time (K. Tan 239). There is undeniably a "progressive loosening of long-held restraints on cultural expression," as the PAP government has come to realize that the "public show of state censorship will invariably undermine the government's moral authority," resulting in both local backlash and international criticism (C. Tan; Chong *The Theatre and the State* 136). It also hurts their efforts to promote Singapore as a Global City for the Arts, a project established in 1992 to position Singapore as an artistically vibrant city on the world stage (Chong "Singapore's Cultural Policy"). In addition, unlike in the sixties, seventies, and eighties, information is no longer filtered solely through the state-controlled media. The widespread usage of the internet and social media over the last decade has led to an exponential increase in the accessibility of information, providing the vocal minority with several avenues to express their grievances and indignation, which can potentially influence the views of the apathetic majority. As such, the Singaporean government has come to recognize the need for the "invisibilization" of censorship, or, in other words, the exercising of censorship in covert ways (Chong *The Theatre and the State* 136).

The multilevel and multifaceted nature of censorship in Singapore is possible because the "power advantage" of a government "enables it to introduce regulations, codes, and standards in such a way that infringements on free expression and information will occur in a much more subtle—but not less effective—form than through bans or confiscation" (Petersen 16). Cutting off the resources of an artist does not alarm the public as much as a direct ban on an artwork does, thus maintaining the façade that the country promotes freedom of artistic expression, even as it becomes increasingly challenging for an artist to create his or her work. This illusion of freedom makes the general public less inclined to fight for artistic liberty in Singapore—and such is the insidious nature of implicit forms of censorship.

One example of an indirect mode of regulation is the biased selection of artworks to be funded—or to withdraw funding from. In May 2015, NAC withdrew an $8,000 grant for the comic *The Art Of Charlie Chan Hock Chye* by artist-illustrator Sonny Liew the day before its launch in Singapore. According to Khor Kok Wah, the senior director of the NAC's literary arts sector, "[I]ts sensitive content, depicted in visuals and text, did not meet our funding conditions" (Yong). The graphic novel makes references to controversial events and people in Singapore's history, such as Operation Spectrum—the alleged Marxist Conspiracy in 1987 where 22 people were detained by the PAP government (Kaur)—and Lim Chin Siong—Lee Kuan Yew's comrade-turned-foremost-political-opponent, detained from 1963 to 1969 under Operation Cold Store (H. Wong). Khor's vague and arbitrary explanation for the withdrawal of funds was not accepted by members of the arts community, and he was later pressured into clarifying that "the retelling of Singapore's history in the graphic novel potentially undermines the authority of legitimacy of the Government and its public institutions" (Yong). By evoking a dark chapter of Singapore's history where people were presumed to be wrongfully detained, the novel calls into question the PAP's moral legitimacy. There appears to be an ongoing paranoia about the need to keep under wraps historical accounts that might adversely affect the reputation of the PAP government, whether through a direct ban that inevitably attracts more attention (a last resort), or through more covert forms of censorship that often go undiscovered or undebated.

Here we see censorship with an obvious political agenda, used in service of the powerful and elite members of society.

While the graphic novel was fortunately able to sell enough copies to break even, other art forms are not as lucky. In the theatre industry, state grants are the primary source of funding for theatre groups, which leaves most of them beholden to the demands of the state. These are often communicated through "private telephone calls or face-to-face meetings," and frequently made just as a show is about to open "as a means to prevent directors or playwrights from conceiving alternative solutions to objected scenes, thus resulting in clean and straightforward cuts" (Chong *The Theatre and the State* 140, 161). Protesting against these demands would effectively mean giving up the state funding, hence that is rarely ever done even if the situation seems unreasonable, unless it severely compromises on the integrity of the artwork. Artists are admittedly at the mercy of the government when it comes to the possibility of producing and presenting their work, and funding is evidently the foremost velvet handcuff that the PAP government uses on the artists.

In an effort to balance the desire to continue to frame the national story with the desire to maintain the appearance of artistic liberty, a government could attempt to outsource the responsibility of censorship to none other than the artists themselves. The PAP government has taken efforts to encourage artists to self-regulate—or self-censor. In an attempt to institutionalize self-censorship, MDA launched a public consultation on its proposed Term Licensing Scheme on 12 May 2014 ("MDA to forge"). Under the scheme, registered arts organizations would have been able to classify their own performances, or those of their fellow artists, under the following ratings: G—content suitable for a general audience; Advisory—content that may not be suitable for a general audience; Advisory16—content more suited for persons 16 years and above; and R18—restricted to persons 18 years and above. In their press release, MDA stated that "arts entertainment event organisers may send their representatives for training at MDA to become registered content assessors, or tap on other registered content assessors in the industry to do so"; any wrongful classification would result in "composition fines" ("MDA to forge"). On the surface, this might seem like a well-intentioned move by MDA and the PAP government to liberalize the arts sector by empowering arts groups to make their own classification decisions. However, this could also be an insidious way in which they try to out-source the burden of censorship and even normalize this practice.

Had the scheme been allowed to pass, it might have led to a regression in terms of the freedom of artistic expression. This is because the classification guidelines that were previously dictated by MDA have not changed, and they include several conditions that the majority of arts practitioners in Singapore do not agree with, such as the need for an R18 rating when "occasional sexual gestures (e.g. kissing and caressing) in a homosexual context" are depicted in a performance ("Arts Entertainment Content Standards and Classification"). Besides having to classify their own works or their fellow artists' works in adherence to the guidelines laid out for them, which are not necessarily in line with their values and beliefs, the artists also face the risk of "a fine of up to $5,000" should they incorrectly classify their performances (C. Tan). This could result in artists mistakenly opting for a stricter classification than what is necessary in order to avoid the penalty. It might also lead to self-inhibition during the process of creating their works, or an unhealthy practice of policing their fellow practitioners' works, eventually resulting in a stagnation of creativity and a culture of cautiousness in the arts industry. As a result, forty-five arts groups, including prominent ones such as the Singapore Repertory Theatre and the Singapore Dance Theatre, signed a position paper to reject the scheme, and MDA eventually released a statement to announce that they would drop the proposal ("Arts Engage Position Paper").

In reaction to the overt and covert forms of censorship that have persisted over the decades, artists have developed ways and means to skirt around them. One way was to "[engage] with allegories and abstraction," as evidenced in the play *Descendants of the Eunuch Admiral*, written by the late theatre doyen Kuo Pao Kun, about cultural displacement and the loss of identity (Chong *The Theatre and the State* 81). Another way was to "[highlight] . . . the personal and human plight of the characters . . . as implicit criticism of policies and politics" (Chong *The Theatre and the State* 81). This is reflected in works such as *Good People* by the playwright Haresh Sharma, which is, on the one hand, the story of a terminally ill patient getting caught for smoking marijuana to relieve her pain, and, on the other, a criticism of Singapore's strict drug laws and uncompromisingly harsh penalties. Sharma does not explicitly critique the laws or the penalties; rather, he expresses his reservations through the struggles of the protagonist when faced with an unreasonable and unforgiving system. Hence, strangely, there could be a silver lining here: censorship forces artists to be more creative in their political criticism, no matter how painful and grueling the process, and the industry as a whole may come much closer to mastering the art of subtlety. In a certain sense, creative and ever-adjusting forms of censorship result in creative and ever-adjusting artistic responses.

More interestingly, Sharma stated in an interview that another way he subverted the system was by loading his plays with expletives, which might seem like a counterintuitive choice. Before MDA was formed in 2003, the task of censorship lay with the Public Entertainment License Unit (PELU), a part of the Singapore Police Force. Due to a lack of artistic sensibilities, the officers took a mechanical approach to censorship, simply crossing out any expletives and any discernable homosexual, political, or racial and religious references. Sharma said, "If you want to say something really subversive, you just put a lot of 'fuck,' 'fuck,' 'fuck' . . . They'll go into a cancelling frenzy. Meanwhile you can write a really critical script and they would be too distracted to notice" (Chong *The Theatre and the State* 157). Through understanding exactly what the censorship bodies would pinpoint and find issues with, playwrights and other literary writers often leveraged on their cultural intelligence and sensitivities to distract and work around the system.

Of course, there are also instances of more blatant rebellion that are just on the edge of crossing the government-imposed line. An example is Royston Tan's *Cut* (2004), a 12-minute musical spoof on censorship in Singapore. This was Tan's retaliation after the Board of Film Censors imposed twenty-seven cuts on *15*, a film he made about teenage gangs in Singapore (Freedman 138). *Cut* shows a film aficionado badgering the former chairman of the Board of Film Censors, Amy Chua, as she shops in a supermarket. While the film is campy and exaggerated, it nonetheless asks astute and thought-provoking questions: "[B]eing our so called 'nanny,' you yourself are exposed to all these censored and controversial scenes. What I really want to know is, who looks after your moral welfare?" (Addicted 21). Questions such as these interrogate the logic of censorship and suggest that it is worth further discussion and exploration. *Cut* won Best Short Film in the Vladivostok Pacific Meridian Film Festival in 2005, and its eventual success represents how a fun and innovative approach can also be an effective way of rebelling ("Royston Tan: Awards").

While censorship has undeniably led to the inhibition of artistic growth and expression in Singapore, it has ironically harnessed creativity by cultivating a generation of artists who are able to create works on controversial issues in a subtle and skillful manner. One could still criticize them for condoning the system, as they are nonetheless responding within the boundaries set by the PAP government, but they have evidently resisted state censorship in a productive way and preserved their artistic integrity in the process. Yet it is also true that we will never know for sure how much more the arts in Singapore would have flourished without the excessive and oftentimes politically motivated censorship over the past fifty years.

The works of artists are, as eloquently described by the poet Robert Frost, "a lover's quarrel with the world." They shine a light on things that may be unpleasant and hard to accept, if only for the betterment of society. This results in a conflict with the government when it includes political criticism; as such, the existing mutual distrust between artists in Singapore and the PAP government is inevitable. Ironically, both parties hold the same motivations and ideals—envisioning a better future for the country, and then working towards it—but the problem lies in their seemingly irreconcilable values and beliefs. The case of censorship in Singapore shows us that a country's particular and varied forms of censorship often arise out of its unique history and the desire to preserve a government's legitimacy. Furthermore, the nature of censorship is not always as explicit as we tend to think, and while its ever-evolving forms are increasingly effective in suppressing contentious works of art, they also result in the creation of new works that still critique—just in more proficient and nuanced ways.

WORKS CITED

addicted21. "Royston Tan Cut (Singapore Censorship) Part 1."
    Online video clip. *YouTube.* YouTube, 1 May 2007. Web. 12
    June 2016.
"Arts Engage Position Paper On The Scheme." *Arts Engage.*
    Google Sites, n.d. Web. 12 June 2016.
The Ban. *To Singapore, with Love.* Generate Press, 10 Sept. 2014.
    Web. 25 Apr 2016.
Chong, Terence. "Embodying Society's Best: Hegel and the
    Singapore State." *Journal of Contemporary Asia* 36.3 (2006):
    283-304. Web. 12 May 2016.
—. "Singapore's Cultural Policy." *Arts Management Network.* Arts
    Management Network, 12 Dec. 2006. Web. 12 May 2016.
—. *The Theatre and the State in Singapore: Orthodoxy and
    Resistance.* London: Routledge, 2011. Print.
"Content Standards & Classification." *Media Development
    Authority Singapore.* Media Development Authority, n.d. Web.
    2 May 2016.
Freedman, Leonard. *Offensive Art: Political Satire and Its
    Censorship Around the World from Beerbohm to Borat.*
    Westport, CT: Praeger, 2008. Print.
Frost, Robert. "The Lesson for Today." *The Poetry of Robert Frost:
    The Collected Poems, Complete and Unabridged.* Ed. Edward
    Connery Lathem. New York: Holt, Rinehart and Winston, Inc.,
    1969. Print.
Gordon, Eric. "Forced to Flee Singapore, Francis Khoo Became a
    Hero of the Miners' Strike." *Camden New Journal.* New Journal
    Enterprises, Ltd. 1 Dec. 2011. Web. 4 May 2016.
Han, Jamie. "Communal Riots of 1964." *Singapore Infopedia.*
    National Library Board Singapore, 18 Sept. 2014. Web. 8 May
    2016.
Han, Kirsten. "Freedom of Speech Far from Top of Singaporeans'
    List." *Malaysiakini.* Malaysiakini, 1 June 2015. Web. 12 May
    2016.

Jones, David Martin, and David Brown. "Singapore and the Myth of the Liberalizing Middle Class." *The Pacific Review* 7.1 (1994): 79-87. Web. 8 May 2016.

Kaur, Jagjit. "Marxist Conspiracy." *Singapore Infopedia*. National Library Board Singapore, 2009. Web. 12 May 2016.

Khoo, Olivia. "On the Banning of a Film: Tan Pin Pin's To Singapore, with Love." *Senses of Cinema*. Senses of Cinema, 7 Sept. 2015. Web. 27 May 2016.

"MDA has classified the film 'To Singapore, with Love' as Not Allowed for All Ratings (NAR)." *News Releases*. Media Development Authority, 10 Sep. 2014. Web. 2 May 2016.

"MDA to forge co-regulatory partnership with arts sectors." *News Releases*. Media Development Authority, 12 May 2014. Web. 2 May 2016.

Morozov, Evgeny. "Living with the Streisand Effect." *The New York Times*. The New York Times Company, 26 Dec. 2008. Web. 25 Apr. 2016.

O'Reilly, Kathleen. "Hegemony." *Encyclopedia of Human Geography*. Ed. Barney Warf. Thousand Oaks: Sage Publications, 2006. 206-8. Print.

Petersen, Klaus. "Censorship! Or Is It?" *Interpreting Censorship in Canada*. Eds. Klaus Peterson and Allan C. Hutchinson. U of Toronto P, 1999. 3-18. Print.

"Problems of Censorship." *Arts Engage*. Google Sites, n.d. Web. 12 June 2016.

"Royston Tan: Awards." *IMDb*. IMDb.com, Inc., n.d. Web. 12 June 2016.

Salleh, Nur Asyiqin Mohamad. "Exiles in 'To Singapore, with Love' Shouldn't Get Chance to Air 'self-serving' Accounts: PM." *The Straits Times*. Singapore Press Holdings Ltd. Co., 3 Oct. 2014. Web. 25 Apr. 2016.

—. "Interest in Exile Film up after Curb." *The Straits Times*. Singapore Press Holdings Ltd. Co., 12 Sept. 2014. Web. 25 Apr. 2016.

—. "Parliament: "To Singapore, with Love' Has 'Distorted and Untruthful' Accounts of Past History: Yaacob." *The Straits*

Times. Singapore Press Holdings Ltd. Co., 7 Oct. 2014. Web. 25 Apr. 2016.

Sharma, Haresh. "Good People." *Trilogy.* Singapore: The Necessary Stage, 2010. Print.

Slater, Dan. "Singapore's Final Authoritarian Election." *East Asia Forum.* N.p., 14 Sept. 2015. Web. 12 May 2016.

Tan, Corrie. "Art of Censorship in Singapore." *The Straits Times.* Singapore Press Holdings Ltd. Co., 7 June 2014. Web. 2 May 2016.

Tan, Kenneth Paul. "Choosing What to Remember in Neoliberal Singapore: The Singapore Story, State Censorship and State-Sponsored Nostalgia." *Asian Studies Review* 40.2 (2016): 231-49. Web. 2 May 2016.

To Singapore, with Love. Dir. Tan Pin Pin. Vimeo, 2013. Web. 2 May 2016.

Wong, Hongyi. "Lim Chin Siong." *Singapore Infopedia.* National Library Board Singapore, 2009. Web. 12 May 2016.

Wong, Tessa. "Singapore Election: Governing Party Secures Decisive Win." *BBC News.* BBC, 12 Sept. 2015. Web. 25 Apr 2016.

Yong, Charissa. "NAC Pulled Grant from Comic as it 'Potentially Undermines the Authority of the Government.'" *The Straits Times.* Singapore Press Holdings Ltd. Co., 2 June 2015. Web. 25 Apr. 2016.

*Xavier Dzielski analyzes Neil Jordan's treatment of Irish national-
ism and trans identity in the film* The Crying Game. *Written in
Megan Shea's "Writing the Essay: Art in the World," Dzielski
navigates between vivid description and careful analysis to show his
readers a way of grappling with multiple perspectives.*

LAYERS

Xavier Patrick Dzielski

Fergus and Dil are about to have sex for the first time. It's just over
an hour into Neil Jordan's *The Crying Game*, and the burgeoning
relationship between the two has finally come to a head in Dil's bedroom. The romantic tension is at its peak, and the anticipation is rife;
it's been a long journey to reach this point. After a sensual haircut, a
few flirty excursions at the Metro Bar, and some steamy late-night
encounters, Dil and Fergus are finally reaching the pinnacle of their
intimacy. Fergus, though, drowning in guilt over the role he played in
the death of Dil's previous boyfriend, Jody, can't help asking Dil
about him. "I'm thinkin' of your man," he tells her; "I'm wondering
why you keep his things," he says, looking at Jody's old cricket uniform hanging in her apartment (*Crying Game*; here and in all other
subsequent quotations of dialogue). Jody's ghost has haunted Fergus
since his death, in eerie visions and dreams, but Dil is blissfully
unaware of all this. She doesn't know Fergus's past, as the IRA man
who was involved in the events that lead to Jody's death. She only
knows him as Jimmy, his alias.

As the sexual tension in the scene builds, the camera pans and
dollies to follow Dil and Fergus around the room, moving gracefully,
fluidly. Reds, pinks, and magentas bathe the set, creating a warm and
romantic mood. The *mise-en-scène*—Dil's pink bed sheets, her red
and feminine decor—expresses her romantic appeal, satisfying all the
clichés of a beautiful young woman's apartment. Dil herself is wearing

a fiery red dress, and even after she changes, she is scantily draped in a scarlet robe. She glows in the light of the room, the glare reflecting off of her skin, heightening her allure; Fergus is captivated by Dil and her ethereal glow. The anticipation is palpable; the music swells as Fergus moves in to kiss and caress her. He tenderly slips off her robe, and the romantic leitmotif of the film comes to a crescendo, but it's abruptly cut short as the camera tilts down to capture her genitalia: a penis and testicles.

Fergus is dumbfounded.

"You did know, didn't you?" Dil asks.

No, he didn't, and neither did we, the equally dumbfounded viewers.

Let's rewind just over an hour to the beginning of *The Crying Game*. Written and directed by Neil Jordan in 1992, the film stars Stephen Rea and Miranda Richardson as IRA members Fergus and Jude, along with Forest Whitaker as Jody, a British soldier. It begins in Northern Ireland, where Fergus, Jude, and their IRA cell kidnap Jody. Fergus, who's been ordered to watch over and eventually execute the captive, makes the mistake of befriending him. At the last minute Jody makes a run for it, and in a cruel dramatic twist he makes it out onto the road only to be hit and killed by a truck driven by a troop of British soldiers who've come to rescue him.

Initially, *The Crying Game* situates itself within the dangerous and violent world of the Irish Republican Army, but what follows this first act is a polar opposite second act that turns the film into a romantic and heartfelt love story between Fergus and Dil, albeit one with a twist. The last third of the film witnesses these two movements—of political activism and its consequences, and emotional entanglement—collide in a dramatic and suspenseful final act. All of these tonal shifts and plot twists may confuse the viewer. Is it an action movie? A love story? In addition, these shifts and twists also throw the film's protagonist, Fergus, through the emotional wringer, thrusting him into psychological turmoil and moral crises left and right. Through Fergus, *The Crying Game* explores the mechanics of political and personal identity in an attempt to strip away the external layers of a character and reveal the true nature of the person lying beneath.

When we first meet Fergus, he's operating in an Irish Republican Army cell, carrying out attacks against the British troops occupying Northern Ireland. This conflict stems from the age of English Imperialism, during which the British Crown forcibly held Ireland as a colony for several centuries. By the early 1900s, guerrilla groups and freedom fighters won independence for the southern two thirds of the island, resulting in the Anglo-Irish Treaty of 1921, which eventually established the modern-day Republic of Ireland. Unfortunately, parts of the northern province of Ulster remained part of the United Kingdom, to the dismay of many Irish nationalists living there. Groups of these nationalists, banded together under the name of the IRA, have continued to fight for autonomy against the British occupation forces in the region.

Drawn to the group by his love of country and sense of national duty, Fergus fights in the IRA for all the same reasons that his comrades do: patriotism and the defiance of British rule. And yet, Fergus also feels inherently conflicted about his participation. He struggles with the act of killing Jody, who can clearly tell that killing is not in his nature. To demonstrate this, Jody tells Fergus an allegory about a kind frog who shepherds a scorpion across a river. The scorpion, because it is in his nature, is unable to resist stinging the frog, a senseless act that drowns them both. Correspondingly, Fergus, the "kind man," as Jody calls him, is powerless to turn away from his sympathetic and compassionate nature: bound by it, he is ultimately unable to shoot Jody when the time comes, despite his orders.

The Crying Game reached critical acclaim in the United States, garnering six Academy Award nominations and winning Jordan the Oscar for Best Original Screenplay. Conversely, it flopped in Ireland and the United Kingdom, receiving much disapproval, particularly for its treatment of the IRA and the situation in Northern Ireland. The film's co-producer Stephen Woolley speculates that this is because audiences and the mainstream media had trouble accepting "the notion of an IRA terrorist who has a conscience" (Cormack 166). This is not surprising, given the tired stalemate that had been reached by the early 1990s. After relentless attacks—kidnappings, public bombings—the IRA was quickly losing support from people in all areas of the UK and Ireland, particularly after their operations began claiming the lives of innocents (Darnton).

However, some Irish film critics take issue with Irish directors—like Jordan—who seem to boil down the complexity of the Irish Troubles in order to appease the film industry and its consumerist audiences (Cormack 167). To them, *The Crying Game* doesn't go far enough in exploring the Irish-English conflict: it simplifies the issues at hand in order to focus the film's narrative on Fergus's journey. In light of this, one notices that the film, even though it concerns itself with the Irish-English conflict, hardly ever shows any concrete example of it. *The Crying Game* does not contextualize the nuanced political details, but rather ruminates on the captor-captive dynamics of Fergus and Jody, and the IRA's violent actions. Jody is presented to the audience as a wholly innocent character, completely unrepresentative of the British Army in which he serves. A later, separate target of the IRA is referred to as "some judge," without any context of the judge's role in the conflict. This narrative simplicity provides a stronger moral contrast between the compassionate Fergus and the violent IRA. Stephen Rea also disagreed with the film's portrayal of IRA soldiers. In interviews, he stated that some of the actors playing IRA members, Miranda Richardson in particular, heightened the callousness and brutality of the group. In doing so, he noted that they provided one-dimensional and stereotypical interpretations that, in effect, stigmatized Irish Republicans and presented them only as hostile extremists (Cormack 173).

Fleeing the IRA after Jody's death, Fergus, under the alias "Jimmy," embarks on a self-imposed exile in London. There, he's haunted by visions of Jody, who appears in a subjective dream world, running towards the camera in his cricket uniform, glowing in a ghostly light. Fergus soon finds Jody's former lover, Dil, played by Jaye Davidson, and begins a romantic relationship with her. She cuts his hair, they meet for drinks at the Metro Bar, he listens to her sing renditions of Dave Berry's "The Crying Game," and the two steadily grow closer through the movie's smartly crafted dialogue.

The film's story is propelled forward by the nuances of its intertwining character relationships. Richard Haslam, in his essay "Neil Jordan and the ABC of Narratology," asserts that Jordan uses "ABC character triangulations"—narrative structures built around three primary characters—in his films to create drama and narrative momentum (37). Following Haslam's argument, one can easily locate the primary triad in *The Crying Game*: Jody, Dil, and Fergus. Jody, person A, and Dil, person B, comprise one side of the triangle. However, the introduction of Fergus, person C, draws Dil's affections after Jody's death. Dil still loves Jody, even in mourning, but begins to fall for Fergus as he falls in love with her. Meanwhile, Fergus's relationship with Jody becomes incredibly complex: Fergus is dogged by Jody's memory, and he feels a keen desire for redemption or atonement for his involvement in Jody's death. Jody's specter hangs over Fergus and Dil's relationship in Fergus's recurring visions and urge to constantly question Dil about him (recall that spicy love scene first mentioned). He even retains a pseudo-physical presence: Jody's clothes hang in Dil's apartment while she and Fergus become intimate, and photos of Jody are strewn about the room, almost as if he's watching Fergus and Dil from afar. Of course, the triangle is redefined when Fergus realizes that Dil is a transgender woman, shocking and confusing him, while also completely upending his understanding of Jody.

Sensibly, the producers of *The Crying Game* "pleaded with reviewers not to reveal important plot twists" upon its release at the New York Film Festival (Canby). The belated revelation that Dil is a transgender woman creates the same shock and confusion for the audience as it does for Fergus. We, like him, reevaluate our understandings of Dil and Jody, and Fergus's relationship with the both of them. As viewers, we reevaluate the whole film. *The Crying Game*, which began as a love story between a former terrorist and a London hairdresser, has suddenly become not only an exploration of Irish-English politics and national identity, but also a foray into gender identity and queer relationships.

In an interview with film critic Marina Burke, Jordan has drawn parallels between moral choices and gender identity, explaining that Fergus "only survives . . . by taking on what you would think of as feminine virtues . . . [being] more understanding, compassionate" (Cormack 171). He is unable to stay in the violently masculine world of the IRA and thus flees to London, becoming wrapped up in Dil's quiet and feminine domesticity. Dil is a character who—perhaps

unrealistically—is so politically naïve that she does not fully understand the circumstances that lead to Jody's death, or even recognize
Fergus's accent as Irish (she thinks he's Scottish). Contrarily, Fergus's
former IRA comrade and ex-lover Jude returns at the beginning of the
third act seeming to have fully embraced an oppositely virile morality.
Brutally taunting Fergus with his guilt over the events of Jody's death
in the first act, she threatens Dil's safety in an attempt to coerce him
into joining another IRA operation in London: the assassination of a
judge. She throws his past sense of political responsibility in his face,
saying, "You're never out, Fergus."

Fergus takes drastic measures to hide Dil from Jude. He leads her
back to the hair salon where they first met, asking her whether or not
she would do anything for him. She says yes. He sits her down in one
of the chairs. The camera dollies backward to frame them against the
windows. Bright moonlight floods in from behind the blinds, reducing the pair of them to silhouettes. Fergus reaches for the scissors and
grabs a lock of Dil's hair but she violently spins around as a match on
action sharply cuts to her face.

"No way," she growls, as the moonlight glows off of her profile.

"I want to change you to a man," Fergus says; "It's a secret," he
tells her when she asks him why.

"Would you like me better that way, Jimmy?" she wonders, the
hurt evident in her voice.

"Yes," he replies.

She spins back around as Fergus continues to cut her hair and the
leitmotif of the film returns. The halo around her skin recreates the
ethereal quality that she's had in previous scenes, the same as Jody in
Fergus's visions of him. "You want to make me like him," she cries
out, referencing Jody. Despite Fergus's denial of this, saying that he
wants to make her into "something new nobody recognizes," it
becomes all too true when they return to Dil's apartment. As the two
of them walk through the light beams flooding into the flat, they each
glow and shimmer. Slipping into drunken maelstrom, she kisses and
caresses Fergus, but his mind is elsewhere. He lays Dil down on the
bed and then begins to dress her in Jody's cricket uniform.

Apart from reminding the viewer of his suspicious preoccupation
with Jody, this seems an uncharacteristically cruel act for a "kind man"

like Fergus. He forces Dil to appear male, much to her dismay, going so far as to tell her that he will love her all the more for it. Jack Halberstam, in his book *In A Queer Time and Place: Transgender Bodies, Subcultural Lives*, claims that Fergus's transformation of Dil into a man "unmasks her and serves to protect Fergus from his own desires," attempting to reconcile Dil's gender status with his own feelings towards her (82). Because Fergus is not at all prepared to accept her as a woman—repeatedly bringing up her alleged deceit— Halberstam argues that Fergus's attempt to transform Dil into a man, though under the guise of hiding her from Jude and the other IRA members who would do her harm, is really to satisfy his own limited understanding of gender and normativity.

Citing the 1999 film *Boys Don't Cry*, written and directed by Kimberly Peirce, Halberstam moves to discuss a film that he believes successfully establishes a "transgender gaze," or a depiction of a transgender character that legitimizes the character's status as a member of the target gender (83). The film is an adaptation of the real-life story of Brandon Teena, a transgender man from Nebraska who, in 1993, was discovered and outed as transgender, then raped and murdered in a transphobic hate crime. Unlike *The Crying Game*, which focuses on Fergus, a cisgender man, and his experiences with a transgender woman, *Boys Don't Cry* concerns itself primarily with a transgender man and his attempt to gain recognition and validation as such. Halberstam posits that the latter film's success in creating a transgender gaze lies in the workings of the relationship between Brandon and his lover, Lana. Lana does not associate Brandon's gender with his genitalia; moreover, she refuses to recognize his genitalia at all, even when violently confronted with it by her family and friends (if you can call them that), who denounce Brandon as "sick," a "faggot," and a "dyke." In doing so, the film rejects the "compulsory heterosexuality of the romance genre" and allows Lana and Brandon's relationship to remain undefined by sexual organs, as Halberstam believes is so clearly the case in *The Crying Game* (86).

In fact, both films present scenes just over halfway through in which transgender issues are very bluntly and explicitly confronted: the revelation scene in Dil's apartment in *The Crying Game*, and the forceful scrutinizing and shaming of Brandon in Lana's bathroom in

Boys Don't Cry. In both instances, the cisgender lovers are faced with their partner's genitalia, which is contrary to the gender that their partners identify with. The difference in these scenes is while Lana refuses to see Brandon's female organs (thus preserving his masculinity), Fergus can only see Dil's male organs (rejecting her femininity). Upon this discovery, Dil tries to console Fergus. He pushes her away, hitting her in the face and running to her bathroom, puking into the sink from the overpowering shock.

Halberstam concludes that Fergus's failure to accept Dil as a woman imprints upon *The Crying Game* a generic perspective that transgender people are inherently tragic characters. But he's forgetting the third angle of that narrative triad: Jody. With Fergus's clear substitution of Dil for Jody, Neil Jordan has very self-consciously called attention to their connection in Fergus's mind. Dil serves as the conduit for Fergus's redemption; he is figuratively and literally given another chance to save someone he cares about from the violence of his past. Through this, he can achieve salvation and rescue a vessel of Jody's memory, fully realizing the A-C length of the Jody-Dil-Fergus triangle. Fergus's substitution of Jody—in a redemptive context—is again highlighted in a later scene when he finds Dil, drunkenly walking back to her apartment. As she comes out of the shadows, walking towards the camera, wearing Jody's cricket uniform and ethereally glowing—just as Jody did in Fergus's visions—Fergus runs to protect her, knowing that if Jude or the other IRA members see her and realize who she is, her life will be in danger again.

As he ushers her back into her bedroom, he comes clean, telling Dil that he's the one responsible for Jody's death. To Fergus's dismay (as he's crying out to be punished for his actions), this news doesn't seem to phase her much. Instead, what breaks Dil's heart the most is that Fergus can't love her the way she wants him to. He is unable to move past her being trans. This bubbles to the surface the next morning when Dil ties Fergus to the bed and orders him to say that he loves her, all while pointing a gun at his head. When Jude comes into the scene, Dil's biological insecurities as a woman are only reinforced when she realizes that Jude helped lure Jody into the IRA trap by sexually seducing him with "her tits and her cute little ass." Knowing that she can't be perfect enough for Fergus or Jody, Dil's rage boils over, and she shoots Jude to death. Still furious, Dil turns the gun on Fergus, but stops. Jody won't let her kill him, she says; the bonds the three of them share are too strong.

But while Fergus may not be able to rekindle the love he once held for Dil, he is certainly more than willing to sacrifice himself for her by taking the fall for Jude's murder. In doing so, he commits himself to nearly seven years in prison. But no matter, he's content to protect someone that he still cares about, regardless of the incredibly complex past they share. At the end of the day, when the layers of political pressure and emotional tension are peeled back, that's what a kind person will do: sacrifice themself to spare another person suffering. He explains this to Dil when she comes to visit him in prison. "As a man said, it's in my nature," he tells her, repeating and affirming Jody's assessment of him from so long ago.

"What's that supposed to mean?" Dil asks him, sporting a new feminine haircut and pink-bejeweled earrings. As Fergus leans in closer to the glass that separates them, he begins to tell Dil a story about a scorpion and a frog.

WORKS CITED

Boys Don't Cry. Dir. Kimberly Peirce. Perf. Hilary Swank and
    Chloë Sevigny. Fox Searchlight Pictures, 1999. DVD.
Canby, Vincent. "Review/Film Festival; An Irish Terrorist in
    Human Terms." *The New York Times.* The New York Times
    Company, 26 Sept. 1992. Web. 24 June 2016.
Cormack, Aisling B. "Toward a 'Post-Troubles' Cinema?: The
    Troubled Intersection of Political Violence and Gender in Neil
    Jordan's *The Crying Game* and *Breakfast on Pluto.*" *Éire-
    Ireland* 49.1-2 (2014): 164-92. Print.
Darnton, John. "Turning Point: The IRA Cease-Fire—A special
    report; 2 Irish Foes Journey From Deeds to Words." *The New
    York Times.* The New York Times Company, 5 Sept. 1994.
    Web. 24 June 2016.
Halberstam, Jack. *In A Queer Time and Place: Transgender Bodies,
    Subcultural Lives.* New York: New York UP, 2005. Print.

Haslam, Richard. "Neil Jordan and the ABC of Narratology: Stories to do with Love are Mathematical." *New Hibernia Review / Iris Éireannach Nua* 3.2 (1999): 36-55. Print.

The Crying Game. Dir. Neil Jordan. Perf. Stephen Rea and Jaye Davidson. Miramax, 1992. DVD.

Written in Maura Roosevelt's "Writing the Essay," Nina Svirsky's essay analyzes Rebecca Solnit's many and varied writings with a focus on Solnit's feminism. The profile then moves from the author's words to include those of her supporters and critics to help illuminate the challenges faced by the feminist movement.

SOLNIT'S CATCH-22: IN A NUTSHELL, FEMALE

Nina Svirsky

Comparing innocent 'mansplaining' to the global epidemics of rape and femicide might seem like a long shot to any level-headed, legitimate thinker such as yourself. But how do we express ourselves as 'level-headed' and 'legitimate' in the first place? In her collection of essays *Men Explain Things to Me*, Rebecca Solnit hones in on a central problem in the gender wars: the silencing of women and its subtle but dangerous repercussions. She begins with a lighthearted anecdote that reveals a patronizing 'mansplainer.' We watch with discomfort as an older, 'established' man attempts to teach Solnit about the book she herself wrote, about a topic he has briefly skimmed but over which she has full domain. It seems she cannot rebut this laughable condescension as she begins to feel the effects of the insidious "presumption that . . . keeps women from speaking up and being heard when they dare" ("Men Explain Things To Me" 4). To persuade us of the true danger of this presumption, she draws parallels between this female-silencing in the inter-personal sphere and larger global trends that sustain massive inequity. She suggests that personal expression, especially that of public female figures, could be harnessed as a means of illuminating and correcting issues of gender inequity. The relationship between patterns of female-silencing and women's struggle to use personal expression to end those patterns reveals Solnit's ultimate belief that feminist writers like herself must carefully choose their mode of personal expression in order to breach a silencing, patriarchal world.

Solnit occupies the bulk of her collection with a critical look at patterns of female-silencing in the context of global inequity. First, she turns to the epidemic of gendered violence in her essay "The Longest War." Discussing sexualized harassment on the Internet, Solnit argues that "the difference between these online gamers and the Taliban men who, last October, tried to murder fourteen-year-old Malala Yousafzai for speaking out . . . is one of degree. Both are trying to silence and punish women for claiming voice, power, and the right to participate" ("The Longest War" 32). We too often view incidents like the attack on Malala as outrageous and unthinkable, unrelated to everyday problems like online bullying. Yet these issues stem from a shared cause. Both result from men trying to maintain control over a woman, attempting to exert total influence over her right to speak up. In her essay "Worlds Collide in a Luxury Suite," Solnit examines international economic hegemony and asks us: "How can I tell a story we already know too well? Her name was Africa. His was France . . . Her name was Asia. His was Europe. Her name was silence. His was power" (42). The massive inequity that exists between the privileged belt of Euro-American countries and the Global South can be seen as an extension, Solnit argues, of the gap between male and female power. Solnit suggests that Africa and Asia are continents plunged into poverty by economic giants that silence them, just like women have been silenced for centuries. As we begin to connect the dots, we can see the deeper roots of less harmful incidents like "mansplaining" attempts and try to address them by revealing one of their root causes: the silencing of women.

Implicitly, female-silencing serves as a springboard for Solnit's examination of how personal expression—the ability to voice opinions through text, media, and conversation in the public sphere and, furthermore, to be heard as credible—is central to the liberation of modern day women. In her essay "Cassandra Among the Creeps," she urges: "If we could . . . name this pattern of discrediting, we could bypass recommencing the credibility conversation every time a woman speaks" (116). Women find their stories, complaints, and experiences discredited time and time again because of a fundamental devaluing of their speech and its credibility. In instances of rape, violence, and often death, language and power go hand in hand, because these global trends flourish, as Solnit persuaded us earlier, in an arena where victims are kept from voicing their legitimate concerns. With the concrete example of "#YesAllWomen," Solnit shows how the power of language has indeed served as a tool for feminist liberation: "The term 'sexual entitlement' was suddenly everywhere, and blogs and commentary and conversations began to address it with brilliance and fury . . . the entry of the phrase into everyday speech . . . will help identify and discredit manifestations of this phenomenon. It will help change things. Words matter" (132). With terms like sexual entitlement, rape culture, and domestic violence being adopted into the common vernacular, we are able to recognize these horrible phenomena as patterns rather than isolated events. And if everyone can get on the same linguistic page, then it will be more likely that we will be able to understand and believe the victims of these patterns. The words we use shape our perception of a sexually violent world, and Solnit empowers language with the capacity to produce long lasting change. We will only be able to address these recurring patriarchal trends if equipped with the proper language to describe them.

Like Solnit, feminist scholar Kelly Wilz sees language and personal expression as fundamental weapons in the gender wars. In her blog post "A Feminist's Guide to Critiquing Hillary Clinton," Wilz pinpoints the unique treatment of female voices in the public sphere, particularly that of presidential nominee Hillary Clinton. Wilz examines how "pundits and others criticize her shrillness, her voice, and her 'masculine' speaking style" as a ruse for discrediting "her 'likeability'" in a particularly harsh and unfair way. Clinton is unfairly attacked for the literal manifestation of her voice because this vocal expression is central to her ability to be seen as credible and thus win the favor of our citizens. Like all public female figures, she is at a disadvantage because credibility is an honor that men exclusively have held for centuries. Solnit quotes Laurie Penny to describe this threat to women's voices in the public sphere: "'An opinion, it seems, is the short skirt of the Internet. Having one and flaunting it is somehow asking . . . male keyboard-bashers to tell you how they'd like to rape, kill, and urinate on you'" ("The Longest War" 31). This helps explain Clinton's struggle to join and be heard in the "boys' club" of American politics, to confront the loud backlash of a thousand misogynistic keyboard-bashers. Wilz's opening line says it all: "Fair warning: This blog post is not going to be angry. It will not be written in all caps. There will be no vulgarity. And it probably won't go viral. I don't care." Consider Wilz's self-reflection: she realizes that even her own blog post about the unfair treatment of female voices could be interpreted by readers as the angry, all-caps-shrieking of a dramatic female who simply wants the attention of going viral. She understands the nature of her audience and struggles to vocalize a problem that, as a female writer with a short-skirted opinion, she struggles with herself.

If the problem is that silencing personal expression is a tool used against women to perpetuate inequity, then how can women express this problem of inequity in the first place? Solnit herself struggles with this vicious cycle because, as a woman trying to express her voice, she is torn between declaration and accommodation. On the one hand, she seeks authority, using at least ten factual statistics in her first two short essays alone so that she is not labeled as she was earlier in life for objection to a man's behavior: "subjective, delusional, over-wrought, dishonest—in a nutshell, female" ("Men Explain Things to Me" 7). On the other hand, she accommodates readers whom she fears may find her ethos too impersonal: "But maybe you're tired of statistics, so let's just talk about a single incident that happened in my city" ("The Longest War" 26). Throughout many of her other essays, she continues to thread a tale of literary narrative, using both personal vignettes and telling the vivid tales of others, as a way of personalizing her argument and sounding more human. In a restrictive, patriarchal environment, Solnit is scared of a potentially restricting audience, one whom she must accommodate with an open-minded, investigative writing style. She frequently asks rhetorical questions and qualifies her own argument to invite defensive readers into her thought process. Solnit's hidden fear reveals itself in this rhetorical accommodation: she wants to ensure that her voice seems less stringent and more nuanced, less tyrannical and more democratic.

Critics like Stevie Davies and Helen Lewis notice a similar trend. In Davies's book review, subtitled "Fearless Feminist Gives the Misogynists a Good Talking-to," she describes Solnit's voice as "open, communicative and democratic." Despite the "hard facts and harder truths" Solnit writes about, Davies describes her arguments as "often [proceeding] by indirection," perhaps because, as Lewis predicts in her essay review "The Essay That Launched the Term 'Mansplaining,'" she is concerned that critics might "[caricature] her as a shrieking harpy." Solnit's fear fuels a rhetorical balancing act between sounding like a "clear and cool" authority while remembering to express that "these are my thoughts, now what are yours?" (Lewis, Davies). She feels as though she must coax her audience into democratic agreement rather than employing the scarier alternative: outspoken confi-dence. And so, as Solnit uses more and more rhetorical techniques to lighten the harsh, truth-bearing load on her readers, her voice becomes quieter and quieter. She herself undergoes a sort of self-silencing, the kind she felt when confronting that first "mansplainer," that first male authority figure who convinced her that yes, of course she should be quiet. In this sense, female-silencing has become normalized to the extent that Solnit cannot help but project her fears onto her own writing. She is not only aware of the threat to female voices in the public sphere, but she also shows a fear of confronting it.

In fearfully shaping and editing her voice to accommodate an audience's status quo, Solnit's rhetorical strategies actually perpetuate female-silencing. In Jessica Valenti's "Not All Comments are Created Equal: The Case for Ending Online Comments," the author's response to silencing comes in the form of a proposition to ban online comment threads, where sexist harassment is rampant. Valenti quotes Laurie Penny's short skirt idea, as Solnit does, in order to expose the "never-ending stream of derision that women . . . endure" online. Valenti sees online comments sections as breeding grounds for the oppression of female voices, often in the political arenas that matter most, so she calls for banning them altogether. She quickly admits, "It's true, I could just stop reading comments. But I shouldn't have to. Ignoring hateful things doesn't make them go away." Valenti sees ignoring backlash as akin to accommodating it, and her rejection of online accommodation hearkens back to Solnit's emphasis on the "difference . . . of degree" between the tacit acceptance of female-silencing on the Internet and larger instances like Malala Yousafzai's

attack. Solnit explicitly focuses on ending these patterns of accommodation and would join Valenti in her outrage. Yet her writing implicitly suggests that she herself cannot escape these patterns. With twist-
ed irony, Solnit projects her own fears of misogynistic backlash
toward her writing and makes accommodations in order to avoid it
instead. While she may recognize, like Valenti, that she should not
have to self-censor to accommodate readers, fear—especially unspoken fear—is a powerful force.

In fact, Solnit struggles with a fear of what Katha Pollitt describes
as "no-platforming." In her article "Feminism Needs More Thinkers
Who Aren't Right 100 Percent of the Time," Pollitt explores various
recent controversies at universities in which feminist speakers were
"no-platformed," or banned from presenting, as a result of their political views. Pollitt asks: what happens to "the questions they raise and
the productive lines of thought they open up" when they are, then,
attacked with every view they allegedly got wrong? What happens to
the Valentis and the Solnits who are scared to enter the public sphere
without fear of retort? Whether it is banning comments or "no-platforming," the issue of free speech arises in a world where the right to
personal expression is linked to power. But in choosing the extreme
solution of elimination, of banning some forms of dissent as suggested
by Valenti, we are committing the very acts of silencing that sustain,
in Solnit's eyes, a massively gendered world. And choosing the other
extreme, Solnit's self-silencing, could foster what Pollitt sees as a feminist "movement that has no room for controversy."

This controversy is indeed reflected in the confidence with which
Solnit spews statistical facts, the bravery with which she examines the
historical roots of troubling phenomena. Nevertheless, her hidden
fears prevent her from declaring feminist truth in the outspoken manner that she wants other women to feel comfortable acting in. Clearly,
language and personal expression are major sources of power in the
public sphere, whether they are used as silencing weapons or whether
they are harnessed by feminist figures for the greater good. In pub-
lishing her essays, Solnit has already taken a major step toward vocal-
izing the patterns of female-silencing that have remained hidden for
so long. Even her creation of the term "mansplaining" symbolizes an
effort to liberate women using the previously constricting constructs

of language. Yet she is limited by her audience who must be lured into confronting a difficult truth and by a society who suggests that her truth is not as credible as she believes it to be. She treads a difficult line between expressing her voice with strength yet with nuance, with pointedness at her targets yet awareness of her detractors. She is caught in a Catch-22, one that forces her to move to an even scarier alternative.

This alternative is reflected in our history. As with any major social change, we look back with admiration at its first pioneers, the ones who were brave enough to speak up when it mattered. We forget how dangerous, how lonely, and how rare it is for a loud, singular voice—not to mention a female one—to resist those patriarchal fears, to evade the normalized instinct toward accommodation. What is important to realize, however, is that the more Solnit and writers like her accommodate this status quo, the more power it will have. So perhaps she must follow some examples: Betty Friedan, bell hooks, Coretta Scott King, and so many more who have opted to keep their voices loud without resorting to silencing others or themselves. As Pollitt notes, "a movement that has no room for controversy is a movement that risks talking only to itself." When Solnit is empowered to inhabit the true volume of her voice, to express the actual extent of her controversial views as a writer and as a woman, we will have one more leader showing us how to stop talking to ourselves and start talking to each other. We will have a world in which men will stop explaining and women will stop accommodating. And hopefully, we can lead ourselves to a fascinating conversation about equality.

WORKS CITED

Davies, Stevie. "Fearless Feminist Gives the Misogynists a Good Talking-To." Rev. of *Men Explain Things to Me*, by Rebecca Solnit. *The Independent.* Independent Print Limited, 30 Nov. 2014. Web. 25 Apr. 2016.

Lewis, Helen. "The Essay That Launched the Term 'Mansplaining.'" *New Republic.* New Republic, 4 July 2014. Web. 22 Apr. 2016.

Pollitt, Katha. "Feminism Needs More Thinkers Who Aren't Right 100 Percent of the Time." *The Nation*. The Nation Company LLC, 5 Nov. 2015. Web. 24 Apr. 2016.

Solnit, Rebecca. *Men Explain Things to Me*. Chicago: Haymarket, 2014. Print.

—. "Men Explain Things to Me." 1-15.

—. "The Longest War." 19-36.

—. "Worlds Collide in a Luxury Suite: Some Thoughts on the IMF, Global Injustice, and a Stranger on a Train." 39-52.

—. "Cassandra Among the Creeps." 103-17.

—. "#YesAllWomen." 121-36.

Valenti, Jessica. "Not All Comments Are Created Equal: The Case for Ending Online Comments." *The Guardian*. Guardian News and Media Limited, 10 Sept. 2015. Web. 25 Apr. 2016.

Wilz, Kelly. "A Feminist's Guide to Critiquing Hillary Clinton." *The Huffington Post*. TheHuffingtonPost.com, Inc., 8 Feb. 2016. Web. 25 Apr. 2016.

Greek historian Xenophon chronicled political events as well as the moral and imperial disintegration he saw within them. In his essay for Professor Vincent Renzi's Freshman Seminar, "Xenophon of Athens," Daniel Getzler explores the Cyropaedia's *final chapter and reveals how a historian can be both objective and conscientious.*

CYROPAEDIA 8.8:
XENOPHON'S FINAL CHAPTER

Daniel Getzler

Just like the closing passages of the *Anabasis*, Xenophon's ending to the *Cyropaedia* (*The Education of Cyrus*) has left many readers and historians puzzled by its significance and intent. Interestingly, the confusion surrounding the two conclusions to the work has prompted many to question whether either of them are actually Xenophon's writing. However, one consequence from focusing so much on who wrote the final chapter of the *Cyropaedia* is that the debate has detracted from looking at why Xenophon might have considered it a fitting ending to the story and message of the text. As Paula Winsor Sage notes in her article "Dying in Style: Xenophon's Ideal Leader and the End of the *Cyropaedia*," debate over whether Xenophon wrote 8.8 "has served as a distraction from more revealing explorations of the effect this conclusion has on the rest of the work" (162). Despite that lack of exploration into the purpose and role of the final chapter, there are still several intriguing theories as to why Xenophon ended the story that way and what he was hoping to accomplish in doing so.

Sage's suggests that 8.8 not only concludes the book in an appropriate way but also even enhances the message Xenophon expresses in the opening chapter and throughout the entire story. If the main idea of the text is that ruling over people is extremely difficult and that only

one as exceptional as Cyrus was able to achieve it, then seeing his
incredibly constructed empire fall apart after his death should only
further support that notion. Had Cyrus's sons, without the same gift-
ed nature and education of their father, effortlessly filled in as rulers
of his empire, then maybe ruling over humans isn't so difficult and
Cyrus not so special after all. The key to understanding this argument
comes from connecting the events in the final chapter to how
Xenophon sets the tone for the content and purpose of the story in the
opening. In particular, Xenophon does not claim that Cyrus's regime
is the ideal for all others to follow, nor does he suggest that a monar-
chy or despotism is the most effective method of governance that
works perfectly all the time. If anything, he almost suggests the opposite by claiming that he considered ruling humans "among those tasks
that are impossible" prior to considering Cyrus (1.1.3). Even though
Cyrus still alters Xenophon's perspective, he does it not by showing
that ruling over humans is simple, but that it is possible for a unique
man with such incredible virtue to accomplish it. Consequently, as he
states at the end of the opening chapter, the *Cyropaedia* is an attempt
to uncover how and why Cyrus might have been able to achieve this
singular success. In his own words, Xenophon writes that "on the
grounds that this man was worthy of wonder, we examined who he
was by birth, what his nature was, and with what education he was
brought up, such that he so excelled in ruling human beings" (1.1.6).

Even as Cyrus's empire expands across several countries and hundreds of thousands of people by the beginning of Book Eight,
Xenophon, just as in the introduction, still makes sure to emphasize
that the success comes from the exceptionalism of one man: Cyrus. In
the first chapter of Book Eight, Xenophon hints at what is to come
by remarking that "as it is with the other things, so it is with these:
When the person in control is better, the lawful things are observed
with greater purity. When he is worse, they are observed in an inferior
way" (8.1.8). Xenophon also reiterates this message after describing
how the empire fell apart so quickly after Cyrus's death in Chapter
Eight; "everyone in Asia has been turned towards impiety and injustice, for of whatever sort those who are foremost may be, such also,
for the most part, do those beneath them become" (8.8.5). In attribut-
ing the fortunes of an empire to the virtue of its current leader,

Xenophon not only gives Cyrus the credit for his regime's success, but also absolves him of much responsibility for any of its failings after his death.

Furthermore, Sage claims that Xenophon illustrates how the disintegration of the empire arose, not from Cyrus laying the foundations for its destruction, but by his successors ignoring the practices that Cyrus had established. As she points out, "[T]hose who find the statements in 8.8 critical of Persia, and in contradiction to statements made earlier in the *Cyropaedia* do not, I think, take sufficient notice of Xenophon's specific point—that the people, without their patriarchal leader as role model, were less able to live up to the standard of virtue established by Cyrus, despite the *nomina* which had been left behind" (166). Speeches given by Cyrus and Chrysantas at the end of Book Seven and start of Book Eight appear to further Sage's assertion. In them, the two men thoroughly instruct Cyrus's closest aides and allies on how to continue the success of his empire after he is gone. The fact that they failed after disregarding Cyrus's actions and advice is difficult to use as evidence against the success of his leadership. Sage even argues that the failure of his successors in the conclusion allows Xenophon to present Cyrus "as the more exceptional, partly because he lacked rivals—rivals of his greatness or rivals who were contenders for his power. From beginning to end, he in fact emphasizes that Cyrus was one of a kind" (173).

Even though Xenophon clearly suggests that the virtue and strength of a leader is the crucial factor in an empire's success, that doesn't mean he automatically renders Cyrus blameless for the failures of his sons' regime. To better understand the intended message in the conclusion, it is important to figure out how Xenophon intends the swift collapse of the empire to reflect on Cyrus himself. Even if he believes that the virtue of the present leader is fully responsible for everything that takes place in an empire, it still leaves the question of how much influence Cyrus had or should have had in the development of his two sons. One way to better gauge Xenophon's intentions is by looking at how he responds to the allegations surrounding Socrates' culpability for how Critias and Alcibiades harmed Athens in the *Memorabilia*.

The two situations are not identical, but the questions raised surrounding the master's responsibility are extremely similar. In both instances, two young men, despite once spending plenty of time with virtuous leaders, showed no regard for their teachers' advice or behavior and went on to cause great harm for their respective peoples. Consequently, the manner in which Xenophon goes about defending Socrates in the *Memorabilia* could shed some light on his views about Cyrus's guilt for the collapse in the final chapter. In response to the suggestion that Socrates should be blamed for how Critias and Alcibiades became less moderate after leaving him, Xenophon questions "what master of the flute or master of the cithara or other teacher who has made his students competent is blamed if they appear worse after they have gone onto others?" (1.2.27). After claiming that a father shouldn't hold a first and better master responsible, Xenophon continues by examining a father's responsibility for the immorality of his sons. He remarks that "fathers themselves are companions of their sons, and they are not blamed when their sons strike false notes if they themselves are moderate" (1.2.27).

That sentence, especially the remark about the father's moderacy, probably gives the best indication into how Xenophon intended the final chapter to reflect on Cyrus. Had Socrates or Cyrus been immoderate themselves and then passed that onto their followers, only then, Xenophon argues, should they be held responsible for those actions. Additionally, even if they had been moderate in their own behavior but "were to praise those whom he saw taking low actions, he would have been justly censured" (1.2.28). Xenophon declares in the *Memorabilia* that one who acts and instructs moderately deserves no shame for the immorality of any of his students. Provided that Cyrus remained moderate until his death, the same logic would have prevented him from using the collapse of the Persian empire to detract from the exceptionalism of Cyrus or his leadership.

Although Sage doesn't connect the conclusion to the passage from the *Memorabilia*, she echoes the idea of there being limitations to the extent, even the most virtuous people, can dictate future behavior. She contends that Xenophon intends to show "that not even Cyrus, most remarkable human being that he was, could ensure the behavior of his sons and subjects after he was gone" (171). As Bodil

Due also points out, this approach to understanding the ending makes "the first and last chapter form a circle or train of thoughts around the whole work" (19). In the beginning, Xenophon tells us that ruling humans is a formidable task only possible for those with exceptional virtue. In the following six books, he explains how Cyrus's unique brilliance allowed him to accomplish it. In the conclusion, he re-emphasizes how Cyrus's exceptionalism overcame the difficulty of ruling people by showing that his empire couldn't be maintained after his death.

In *Xenophon's Cyropaedia: Style, Genre, and Literary Technique*, Deborah Levine Gera presents an entirely different approach to understanding the closing sections of the *Cyropaedia*. Whereas Sage's argument suggests that the empire's collapse began with Cyrus's death, Gera turns the debate on its head by claiming that the "seeds of destruction have been sown by Cyrus himself" through his behavior in the final two books (299). Gera argues that "Xenophon lets us see—but never explicitly says—that the developments initiated by Cyrus after the conquest of Babylon will eventually lead to the moral downfall of his regime" (299). In this chapter of her book, she points out several instances in which Cyrus's behavior has deteriorated or at least shifted from his conduct earlier on. Gera also notes that if Cyrus's earlier rule is supposed to represent a near perfect regime, his more despotic rule in Babylon can't also represent an ideal.

One passage Gera highlights as an example of Cyrus's decline is a progression from Chapter Three of Book Eight. Even though all his subjects bow down before him, Gera notices that "Xenophon rather cynically adds that perhaps all those present bow down to the Persian leader, not because they are impressed by his appearance but because they have been commanded to do so" (292). The distinction in that passage between willful and forced obedience is crucial, as it is a key theme in both Cyrus's original success and Xenophon's other works. More importantly, it also illustrates how Cyrus is now betraying the earlier advice of his father. In Book One, Cambyses tells him "this is indeed the road to obeying by compulsion, but to what is far superior to this, to their being willing to obey, their is another road that is shorter, for human beings obey with great pleasure whomever they think is more prudent about their own advantage than they are themselves" (1.6.21). Cyrus also ignores his earlier standards, as well as those of Socrates, in his moderacy toward food. In Book One, Cyrus tells his father that "first, by Zeus, I try never to overeat, for it is oppressive" (1.6.17). By Book Eight, his moderacy has drastically disintegrated, as Gera points out: "as ruler of Babylon he is served expensive and elaborate meals which could rival those of Astyages" (293).

The fact that the once-disciplined eating habits of his empire had already begun to decline before Cyrus's death is a key point, as it suggests the complete collapse of discipline. It sets the path towards the "breakfast to bed meal" that had already started in Chapter Eight during Cyrus's reign. It also changes the significance of Xenophon's remarks in the *Memorabilia* that fathers "are not blamed when their sons strike false notes if they themselves are moderate" (1.2.27). In comparing Cyrus's initial moderacy to his rule after capturing Babylon, Gera points out that "the discrepancies and difficulties are too numerous and obtrusive not have been deliberately included by Xenophon" (296). If Gera is correct in asserting that Cyrus's flawed later behavior is a deliberate ploy by Xenophon, who himself believed that only moderate fathers are blameless for their sons' misconduct, then Xenophon's intentions in Chapter Eight are likely far different from what Sage and Due suggest. Rather than using the collapse of the empire to highlight Cyrus's unique exceptionalism, Xenophon then more likely intended it to be seen as a continuation of the defective regime he left behind.

In *Xenophon's Imperial Fiction: On The Education of Cyrus*, James Tatum presents another angle to Xenophon's unusual ending in the final chapter. Like Due and Sage, Tatum agrees that Xenophon intended Cyrus to be an almost ideal leader, yet his theory on about the conclusion is completely different. While he acknowledges that the failure of Cyrus's successors might further highlight his unique brilliance, he argues that it isn't Xenophon's primary intention. Additionally, he suggests that Cyrus's achievements "would amount to very little if he did not change the world for the better" (189). However, Tatum still refuses to attribute the discrepancies in the final chapter to its being added by a different author. Instead, rather than focusing on what the conclusion is designed to reveal about Cyrus, he focuses on "what this ending reveals about the connections between what Xenophon created and actual political experience" (225). Tatum argues that, even if the *Cyropaedia* is mostly an idealized fiction, it is still based loosely on historical facts. For instance, Cyrus did establish an empire similar in size to the one Xenophon outlines and it did collapse under his descendants. Even if Cyrus's virtue and conduct in between all of that is pure fiction, Xenophon still made sure the story stayed in line with the most basic historical facts.

Tatum argues that the conclusion illustrates Xenophon's struggle in reconciling his idealized account of Cyrus with the Persian empire's fall after his death and its decline during Xenophon's own life: "[T]he gap between the perfections of Cyrus and all the imperfections of present day Persia is so great the fantasy cannot continue" (238). Although Tatum's argument raises an interesting perspective, especially given the uncertain relationship between historical accuracy and idealized fiction in Xenophon's other works, I disagree with how it seems to isolate the final chapter from the rest of the story. His theory almost suggests that the entire story is pure fiction until Xenophon bridges his fantasy with reality in the closing chapter. This approach seems to ignore how the content in 8.8 connects with the trends from the previous several chapters. For instance, the final two books both include several scenes with Cyrus and his aides discussing the increased difficulty of maintaining an empire and advising others on how to continue the regime after he passes away. Furthermore, as Gera points out, there are numerous hints that the collapse in the final chapter is a continuation of Cyrus's declining moderation after capturing Babylon.

Although Sage, Due, and Gera have different theories on what particularly Xenophon hoped to illustrate through the collapse of the empire, they all agree that he intended to show a decadence from the guidelines set forth by Cambyses and followed through by Cyrus in the opening books. Additionally, many of those guidelines, such as the ones regarding willful obedience, avoiding idleness, and moderacy with food, are all concepts echoed by Socrates in the *Memorabilia* and consistent throughout Xenophon's other works. However, while Sage and Gera disagree in deciding who Xenophon might hold responsible for the empire's decline, that may be missing the larger meaning of the closing chapters. Instead of focusing on the particular personnel to blame, Xenophon's main intent might have been to illustrate the value of the principles that he, Socrates, and Cambyses all encouraged. As Cyrus embraces those standards in the earlier books, he and his empire are unparalleled in their accomplishment. However, as the leadership begins to drift away from those standards, there is a sharp decline in success and obedience afforded to them. This trend continues through the final passages in which there is a complete lack of discipline that contradicts everything Xenophon and Socrates advocated for in their other works. Especially considering that the *Cyropaedia*'s Cyrus is predominantly a fictional character, it seems unlikely that showing him in a certain light to readers was Xenophon's primary intent with his ending. Rather, especially if Cyrus's earlier achievements are written as a celebration of the Xenophonic leadership principles he followed along the way, then the closing chapter might therefore represent the utter chaos that unfolds when they are ignored.

WORKS CITED

Due, Bodil. *The Cyropaedia: Xenophon's Aims and Methods.* Aarhus: Aarhus UP, 1990. Print.

Gera, Deborah Levine. *Xenophon's Cyropaedia: Style, Genre, and Literary Technique.* New York: Oxford UP, 1993. Print.

Sage, Paula Winsor. "Dying in Style: Xenophon's Ideal Leader and the End of the 'Cyropaedia.'" *The Classical Journal* 90.2 (1994): 161-74. *JSTOR.* Web. 30 June 2016.

Tatum, James. *Xenophon's Imperial Fiction: On the Education of Cyrus.* Princeton: Princeton UP, 1989. Print.

Xenophon. *The Education of Cyrus.* Trans. Wayne Ambler. Ithaca: Cornell UP, 2008. Print.

—. *Memorabilia.* Trans. Amy L. Bonnette. Ithaca: Cornell UP, 2001. Print.

For Natalie Behrends, the life and work of Edward Said is a paradigm for the ideal intellectual and activist. Written in Benjamin Pollak's "Writing the Essay," this essay parallels two roles, ultimately asking us to re-imagine both, so that their hybridization will encourage vital movement in academic and social arenas.

OUTSIDE THE IVORY TOWER

Natalie Behrends

The works of Edward Said, like his life, are often critiqued for crossing the borders between politics and the academy. Officially, Edward Said spent most of his life as a professor of Western Literature at Columbia University. Unofficially, he was known for his vocal support for a series of hot-button political causes, especially Palestinian independence (Borger). A Palestinian by birth, Edward Said became an active proponent of Palestinian sovereignty with the publication of his book *The Question of Palestine* in 1979. From that point on, Said's work has been characterized by a trademark mixture of academics, political commentary, and observations on the world at large. His essays jump dizzyingly from topic to topic, perhaps beginning with a critique of a particular composer, moving to an analysis of classical Arabic grammatical theology, and settling, finally, on a message about methods of interpreting texts in their full historical contexts as a way of deconstructing harmful social systems. Even his most seemingly pedantic literary or musical criticism essays include some kernel of a broader issue, such as "Reflections on Exile," which turns an analysis of Joseph Conrad's short story "Amy Foster" into a statement on the developing world of exiles and refugees. As Asha Varadharajan writes, Said's writing was never without a certain "mobility, playfulness, and skepticism—and . . . a willingness to enter and understand other worlds" (54).

This intermingling of social causes with heavily academic literary criticism was seen as groundbreaking by some critics, and pointlessly reductive by others. Said was alternately celebrated for his "creative openness to discovery and knowledge" and attacked for spewing what some considered hateful propaganda and hypocrisy (Viswanathan 5). Controversy surrounded Said's life, and he did little to dispel it, often responding to criticism with "sass, verve, and bite" (Varadharajan 55). Discussions of Edward Said tend to come to a standstill around the question of whether his activism was right or appropriate for someone in his position. Thus, the question is raised: why would a man with such a promising talent for literary criticism and the finer points of academia embroil himself in some of the thorniest political issues of his time?

It certainly would have been easier for Said to focus entirely on literature and scholarship, rather than insert himself into political discourse. His forays into politics cost him a chance at a quiet academic life. He made enemies of a range of well-known organizations and publications, including the Jewish Defense League, the Jerusalem Post, and the Anti-Defamation League of B'nai B'rith International (Wright). Even the most controversial academics rarely receive death threats as regularly as Said did, whose office was set on fire in 1985 (Wright). Said's perseverance through these tribulations exhibited his deep attachment to the causes he espoused, but simply saying he was devoted to politics is not enough to understand the intersection of activism and the academy in his work. If Said's convictions were strong enough to weather countless attempts to discredit him or get him fired (Muravchik), then why did he not devote all of his energy to activism, instead of spending time writing reviews of classical music and teaching Foucault to university students?

In order to answer the persistent questions about Said's life, it is necessary to carefully examine the only truly definitive source on Edward Said: his own writing. Said wrote heavily about the role of the intellectual in the public sphere, as well as the importance of understanding texts in broader social and historical contexts. The stances he took on these issues suggest an underlying belief Said held about the importance of knowledge as power in our society, a belief which could plausibly explain why Said acted the way he did. By looking back to Said's own opinions on texts, knowledge, and the intellectual, it is possible to understand the motivations and justifications behind his controversial career as an essayist, scholar, and activist.

A major point of discussion throughout Edward Said's body of work is the significance of interpreting a text in both historical and contemporary settings. Said's work posits that there is more to a text than simply paper. Texts, and the words that compose them, are active and mutable. This belief is evident in the choices Said made in his own writing. In his essay, "Cairo Recalled: Growing Up in the Cultural Crosscurrents of 1940s Egypt," Said describes Cairene Arabic as "virtuosically darting in and out of solemnity, colonial discipline, and the combination of various religious and political authorities" (273). The language darts, moves, physically interacts with the structures of everyday life, and more significantly, of oppression. Said consistently identifies specific words as having power beyond their use on the page. The power and activity of these individual words then coalesces into a larger portrait of an active and engaged text, a text "enmeshed in circumstance, time, place, and society" ("The Text, the World, and the Critic" 3). Examining a text outside of the setting in which it is "enmeshed" would be looking at only half the picture, and understanding only part of what the text means. As Gauri Viswanathan writes, Said "retained an unflinching conviction that . . . to read literature outside its political contexts and origins in the name of aesthetic appreciation produces only false or incomplete readings" (4). To Said, no text existed in a vacuum; therefore, accurate literary criticism encompassed not only literature, but also history and politics.

At the time of Said's entrance into the field of literary criticism, this was a fairly revolutionary idea. For about twenty years preceding the publication of Said's first book in 1966, the field of literary studies had been dominated by the method of New Criticism (Klages). This particular method espoused the idea of studying the text "in isolation without regard for anything external to the text, like history, psychology, or biography" (Klages); in other words, almost the direct opposite of Said's exploration of "the profoundly complex and interesting connection among words, texts, reality, and political/social history" ("History, Literature, and Geography" 465). In his essay "History, Literature, and Geography," Said describes how, upon his arrival to

Columbia in 1963, he found himself "dogged by the notion, every-where, current, that history and literature were in fact two quite sep-arate fields of study, and ultimately of experience" (454). His book *Orientalism* was panned by some critics for muddying the field of lit-erary criticism with discussions of history and politics that were irrel-evant to what should be, according to New Criticism, a purely impar-tial science ("Orientalism Reconsidered" 204). But Said was deter-mined to promote his new approach to literary criticism, because, in his eyes, there was more at stake than simply "the possibility of objec-tivity" (Klages). Said knew the value of examining contexts because, in Palestine, he had experienced firsthand a culture whose products had been denied any sort of broader context. This was the subject of *Orientalism*, the book that eventually took him from a little-known critic to an established figure in academia.

Orientalism, defined by the Oxford English Dictionary as "the representation of the Orient (esp. the Middle East) in Western aca-demic writing, art, or literature," took the Arab world and "confined [it] to the fixed status of an object frozen once and for all time by the gaze of western percipients" ("orientalism"; Said, "Orientalism Reconsidered" 201). For Orientalists, there was no Arab culture, no discourse or influences that would suggest an Arab intellectual life equal to that of the West. The passing of time had no effect on Arab writing or culture; there were no distinct schools of thought or ideas that might influence Middle Eastern writing. In short, Arab art and literature were denied any kind of context. This distorted view of the Middle East eventually gave birth to an even more harmful institu-tion. Western universities established Orientalist departments encompassing subjects from Egyptology to Buddhist Studies. By establishing these fields of study, it was as if all life east of the Black Sea was a single, well-defined discipline that, like algebra or chem-istry, could be conquered by any devoted Western student who, hav-ing mastered the Orient in theory, was then highly qualified to go east, and master it in fact. By promoting an image of the Orient as an "object" to be studied by the West, Orientalism justified Western colonial ambitions in the Middle East.

Said, born in British-controlled Palestine and raised in British-influenced Cairo, particularly understood the impact of colonialism.

He recognized that Orientalism, with its roots in the interpretation of texts and culture, was no less a tool of the colonial system than the British army. Orientalism needs to be torn down; however, unlike a wall or a statue, Orientalism is not physical. In order to undo its negative influences, someone first needed to reveal to the public the points where Orientalism pervades: art, literature, and society at large. This individual would have to be someone with a deep understanding of literature, art, and the intersections of culture and society—in short, they would need to be a critic, a role Said clearly assumed upon the publication of *Orientalism*. Of course, while Said's first foray into politics through scholarship was born out of his personal connection to the Middle East, his motivations for speaking out were never inherently selfish. He did not involve himself in divisive discussions simply to make life easier for himself. If that had been his goal, he might have been deterred by death threats, vicious attacks in the media, and the possibility of losing his position at Columbia. The fact that Said persisted in his political activism despite vocal opposition suggests a deeper ideological motivation, one perhaps connected to his idea of the intellectual's ideal role in society.

Edward Said's exemplary scholar labors both within and outside the classroom and the library. To Said, "the role of the intellectual is not to consolidate authority, but to understand, interpret, and question it" ("On Defiance and Taking Positions" 502). He saw the intellectual in a unique position in society, able to examine and explain historical trends and uncover new ways of interpreting old or unsatisfactory systems. There is a tension between this ideal academic, who examines and criticizes extant ideas about their field, and the world's established social structures. Returning briefly to the example of Orientalism, Said expresses the connection between criticism of ideas and social trends by writing that "the challenge to Orientalism, and the colonial era of which it is so organically a part, was a challenge to the muteness imposed upon the Orient as object" ("Orientalism Reconsidered" 202). In other words, by challenging the ideas behind Orientalism, Said and others act as a sort of conscience for the rest of the world, interpreting ideas through the lens of historical and political trends in order to explain their broader impact. Inconsistencies or injustices discovered through this criticism must then be taken to the public, to spur activism and social engagement.

This simple idea of the intellectual's responsibility to the rest of society goes a long way towards explaining the vibrant, seemingly contradictory life of Edward Said. He was a man who fit his own definition of the "radically secular, investigative, and relentlessly mobile" intellectual by acting against institutions which, through his work as a scholar, he had identified as harmful ("The Future of Criticism" 169). Like words, like texts, he was active and engaged, forever changing and being changed by political, social, and intellectual environments. And this process of change may not have run completely smooth: Said's myriad entanglements in conflicts and controversies are a testament to that. But the ultimate image that springs, active, from the work of Edward Said is not of a man embattled, picking sides in a conflict between critics and celebrants. What emerges instead is a vision of a unique sort of social contract between the intellectual and the public: one in which the intellectual's ability to make critical observations about the world becomes a responsibility to make them, and to play a relentlessly active role in society.

WORKS CITED

Borger, Julian. "Friends Rally to Repulse Attack on Edward Said." *The Guardian*. Guardian News and Media, 22 Aug. 1999. Web. 4 Dec. 2015.

Klages, Mary. *Key Terms in Literary Theory*. London: Continuum, 2012. Print.

Muravchik, Joshua. "Enough Said: The False Scholarship of Edward Said." *World Affairs*. World Affairs Institute, April 2013. Web. 4 Dec. 2015.

Said, Edward. "Cairo Recalled: Growing Up in the Cultural Crosscurrents of 1940s Egypt." *Reflections on Exile and Other Essays*. Cambridge, MA: Harvard UP, 2000. 246-85. Print.

—. "The Future of Criticism." 165-72.

—. "History, Literature, and Geography." 453-73.

—. "On Defiance and Taking Positions." 500-6.

—. "Orientalism Reconsidered." 187-97.

—. "The Text, the World, the Critic." *The Bulletin of the Midwest Modern Language Association* 8.2 (1975): 1–23. *JSTOR.* Web.

Varadharajan, Asha. "Edward Said and the (Mis)Fortunes of the Public Intellectual." *College Literature* 40.4 (2013): 52-73. *Project Muse.* Web. 29 Nov. 2015.

Viswanathan, Gauri. "Legacies: Intention and Method." *University of Toronto Quarterly* 83.1 (2014): 3-11. *Project Muse.* Web. 29 Nov. 2015.

Wright, George, and agencies. "World-Renowned Scholar Edward Said Dies." *The Guardian.* Guardian News and Media Limited, 25 Sept. 2003. Web. 1 Dec. 2015.

In this essay from Megan Shea's "Advanced College Essay: The World Through Art," Summer Okoye uses pop culture and media criticism to map processes of cultural appropriation. Moving from Basquiat to Obama, she asks how systematic Othering occurs and how Black artists maneuver in this terrain and make powerful art.

THE BLACK COMMODITY

Summer Okoye

I was tired by the end, oversaturated by an amusement park of Blackness. Such idolatry sensationalizes the organic productivity of black people. Commodity seems to be the only way that audiences can engage with our unique voices.

—Erica Cardwell, "The Immortal Black Life"

White hands on a Black body. Their carefully clipped fingernails, thin wrists, and fair complexions, though unassuming, take hold. Six hands grasp at her full black thighs. Five hands pull at her cheeks and thick lips. They finger her dark kinky-haired afro, and reach for her bare black neck. She doesn't seem to know where they are, but she can feel their presence, and as the white hands, like parasites, enclose her, her expression evolves from passivity to discomfort to a frustrated anger. *Erosion* by Daniel Stewart is comprised of four black-and-white photos depicting a nude Black woman being grabbed by hands of White women. Even though these images are simple in composition, they are complex in their intent.

In America, the Black woman is an 'Other'—a new and intriguing body to be deconstructed. "[Viewers] are not to look at her as a whole human being. They are to notice only certain parts," says bell hooks in *Black Looks: Race and Representation*, a book in which she expresses consumer culture's obsession with "Blackness" and deconstructs the personal and political issues with the representation of race in a White supremacist culture (62). The objectification of Black people is in a manner similar to that of Black slaves, who were viewed as "salable parts" with no presence, things to be used (hooks 62). Daniel Stewart's photographs literally depict, in his own words, "white society's lustful appropriation of a Black woman's body." As a Black artist, he uses these images to call our attention to things he's noticed, such as the way "[b]lack women are slandered for their natural physical attributes, attributes that are then praised when on a white woman's body" (Stewart). In doing so, he attempts to unravel issues concerning the appropriation of the Black woman's body in American society. hooks views this in an even larger sense—not only is White America appropriating the Black woman's body but White America is appropriating all of Black culture, a process she calls "eating the Other" (21). But why is Black culture so marketable in today's society? hooks says "the commodification of Otherness has been so successful because it is offered as a new delight, more intense, more satisfying . . . ethnicity becomes spice, seasoning that can liven up the dull dish that is mainstream white culture" (21). She points to many musicians, entertainers and films that use Blackness as a spice, such as Madonna, whose obsession and use of Black culture contributed significantly to her success. "Voguing," for example, a dance that she made popular, actually evolved out of the LGBT Harlem scene (Lawrence). In addition, in many of her music videos, she uses Black culture as a backdrop, such as in the video for "Just Like a Prayer," which uses Black church and religion. "White women 'stars' like Madonna . . . name their interest in, and appropriation of, Black culture as yet another sign of their radical chic," says hooks. "Intimacy with that 'nasty' Blackness [that] good white girls stay away from is what they seek"— to appear trangressive, White people appropriate Black identity (hooks 157).

In 2013, Miley Cyrus released the music video "We Can't Stop" in which she is shown at a party surrounded by Black women twerking while she grabs their asses (Vevo). She won a total of seven awards that year ("Miley Cyrus—Awards"). In 2014, Iggy Azalea, the

Australian born rapper, was accused of appropriating Black rappers by using a Black Southern accent when rapping (Marantz). She won a total of 15 awards that year ("Iggy Azaela—Awards"). In 2016, #oscarsowhite began trending when, for the second year in a row at the Oscars, zero awards were given to people of color—they weren't even nominated. In recent years, as the intersections of race and the entertainment industry have been tested, many controversies have sparked a debate over what it means to be a Black artist in a world where "Black" is a commodity. Many are confused as media socialite Kendall Jenner gains thousands of followers on Instagram for posting a picture sporting cornrows, praised on social media as being "bold" and "epic" (Wilson). Meanwhile, Blue Ivy, Beyoncé's four-year-old daughter, is condemned for wearing her hair in its natural afro, receiving cruel comments on social media such as "the child looks like [she] hasn't seen a comb since she was born" (Duncan). Amandla Stenberg, activist, and voice for many Black youth in America, is known for bringing the cornrow controversy into the limelight. Stenberg called out Kendall's sister Kylie, who has also been known to wear cornrows, for culturally appropriating Black women's hair, asking "what would America be like if we loved Black people as much as we loved Black culture?" (Sternberg).

Cultural appropriation is the adoption and use of one culture's traditions by members of another culture, usually for financial gain. It has become a buzzword that has provoked many arguments. Some believe that it is overly and wrongly used: "these accusations have become a common attack against any artist or artwork that incorporates ideas from another culture, no matter how thoughtfully or positively," states Cathy Young, writing for *The Washington Post*. She argues that cultural appropriation today has morphed from serious accusation of cultural theft having to do with financial gain, to an accusation made every time someone is caught mimicking another culture, such as in the instance of gay White men being accused of "imitating Black women's gestures and speech styles" and "'stealing' Black womanhood" (McWhorter). John McWhorter writes that "it used to be . . . said that imitation is the sincerest form of flattery," arguing that appropriation in which neither culture profits is harmless, that it "is what human beings do." What McWhorter might be imagining is sometimes called cross-cultural fertilization—the idea that, when two cultures occupy one space, these cultures will naturally interchange and trade traditions, resulting in mutual benefit. However, in a country where individuals are raised with and among multiple identities, this raises questions regarding the rights we have to these identities and the freedom we have to express them.

Artists such as Miley Cyrus and Iggy Azalea, who have been accused of appropriating Black culture, have spoken out in defense of their actions. In a *Rolling Stone* article, Miley admitted: "I'm from one of the wealthiest counties in America. I know what I am. But I also know what I like to listen to. Look at any 20-year-old white girl right now—that's what they're listening to at the club" (qtd. in Eells). Artists have a right to draw from the world around them and give the people what they want. But can this right be abused? When does inspiration become appropriation? James O. Young, Professor of Philosophy at the University of Victoria, suggests that "even when [art] is profoundly offensive," freedom of artistic expression must be upheld—that an artist's freedom to create is above their moral responsibility (140). In his article "Profound Offense and Cultural Appropriation," Young further explores an artist's right to express and offend as well as the social values of appropriation. He writes: "[A]rtists cannot act wrongly in expressing themselves in their art . . . the free expression of one's opinions, even when they are offensive, has a special moral status" (J. Young 140). He defends his argument by explaining that appropriation is not often used to inflict intentional offense, but is used by artists "in pursuit of self-realization and disinterested inquiry," often doing so "because they find something of value in that culture" (J. Young 140). Artists should be free to express and offend. But are they void of any responsibility? Even Young admits that "if freedom of expression gives them the right . . . expression carries with it certain responsibilities"—at the very least, a responsibility to represent the culture they are appropriating, in a way that does not lead to racist stereotypes, to acknowledge the works' artistic origins, and to speak out on issues that come along with that identity (J. Young 140, 141). However, this isn't usually done. For example, "white musicians who partook in hip-hop culture and adopted Blackness—Iggy Azalea in particular—failed to speak on the racism that comes along with black identity," says Stenberg. When Iggy Azalea was asked to comment on taking on a 'Black rapper persona,' she said, "I want to be that person you can listen to for four minutes and not think about that stuff at all, and it's important to have that too . . . I'm not going to suddenly start rapping about political matters; it's just not what I do" (qtd. in Shamsher). Azalea is demonstrating her appropriative privilege: the privilege to pick and choose (i.e. appropriate) elements of Black culture she admires and "not think about" all the other "stuff."

McWhorter may say that "her heart was in the right place" and that her use of Black identity is in some way an appreciation of Black artists. However, Iggy Azalea, and many other artists who claim to borrow aspects of Black culture out of appreciation, fail to recognize that true appreciation means a willingness to understand and represent all aspects of that culture, even taking on the difficult issues. In avoiding this responsibility, Iggy Azalea's use of Black identity has serious repercussions. Besides the fact that she is capitalizing on this identity, even scarier is the impact of this use—a trickle-down effect. Accepting her appropriation perpetuates the practice of White America taking aspects of Black identity in order to feel transgressive, without acknowledging the full history and origins of the culture from which they take. Though McWhorter argues that this is harmless because neither culture is "reaping financial rewards," one culture is most definitely at a disadvantage (McWhorter).

In 2014, the Black female rapper who goes by the name Azealia Banks got into a feud with Iggy Azalea about her appropriation of Black culture. During a radio interview with Hot 97, Banks stated: "[Appropriation is] like a culture smudging . . . all it says to white kids is, 'you're great you can do whatever you put your mind to,' and it says to Black kids 'you don't have shit, you don't own shit, not even the shit you created yourself'" (Banks). Many are in agreement with Banks and say that artists such as Miley and Iggy should have no part in performing a culture they have no real understanding of. In the words of Kareem Abdul-Jabbar, TIME columnist and six-time NBA champion, any way you put it, cultural appropriation "feels an awful lot like slavery to have others profit from your efforts" (Abdul-Jabbar). Taking into consideration the artist perspective, yes, there has to be freedom in creativity, freedom to offend people, but an artist does not have the right to create by "smudging" another culture. At a certain point something isn't really creative if it appropriates.

With the entertainment industry mimicking Black culture, and Black people being cast aside in the entertainment industry, and lines being crossed between appreciation and appropriation and the freedom of artist versus their moral responsibility, it can all get a little bit . . . complicated. But it boils down to this: For those Black artists and entertainers who just want to share their craft, what happens when prying White hands, like the ones in Stewart's photos, are constantly clawing at and feeding on their Blackness? What does it mean when your identity becomes something to be bought and sold?

On the walls of The Whitney Museum of Art is a painting that could sell for millions of dollars. The canvas is an electric yellow, a patch of strident blue and strokes of a dark greenish brown graze the corners. Like a child picking from a crayon box, the painting has a sort of freedom in its colors and strokes. The lines that cover the yellow-painted canvas are in no order or pattern, but create a cacophony of royal blue, red, and sharp green words, symbols, and figures that look as if a child painted them. But the details of the images hold a mature meaning that turns the cacophony into a symphony. Written across the top of the painting are the words "Hollywood Africans"; written underneath, the phrase appears again, however, it is crossed out by a bold red line. The phrase "Hollywood Africans" appears a total of five times throughout the painting, along with other words, such as "sugar cane," "tobacco," "tax free," and "gangsterism." Three figures are depicted among these words, one of them a self-portrait of the artist himself, Jean-Michel Basquiat.

Basquiat was one of the most well-known artists of the eighties, and is considered by many as the most well-known Black artist in American history. As the first famous Black artist of the high art scene, he faced a unique artistic experience—he was creating work for the majority White audience of the high art world and was called everything from "the Black Picasso" to "wild" and "primitive" (*The Radiant Child*). *Hollywood Africans* illustrates the story of other Black artists and entertainers, many of whom he knew personally. Toxic, depicted in this painting wearing a snapback with the letter Z inscribed on it, was a fellow artist. Rammellzee, depicted wearing shades and a hoodie, was a musician friend of his. The words inscribed in the painting—such as "gangsterism," "tobacco," as well as these, crossed out—"what is bawan?" "allude to the limited roles available to black actors in old Hollywood movies" (Whitney Museum of American Art). "I think there's a lot of people that are neglected in art . . . Black people are never really portrayed realistically," Basquiat said (qtd. in *State of the Art*). He attempted to fill this void by using his artistic voice to figure Black heroes into his own work.

On the canvas, Basquiat used the freedom of his paintbrush in the fight to redefine images of Black artists, yet in his everyday life he was losing the fight to define his own identity.

> He was essentially a talentless hustler, street-smart but otherwise invincibly ignorant, who used his youth, his looks, his skin colour and his abundant sex appeal to win an overnight fame that proved to be his undoing. [His work] consisted of a raw, ungifted amalgam of graffiti art, children's art and the kind of 'primitivist' art that sometimes passes as imitations of Jean Dubuffet. (Kramer)

This excerpt was taken from the 1997 article "He had everything but talent," written by art critic Hilton Kramer. This article, written after Basquiat's death in 1988, though harsh, was representative of many people's opinions about both Basquiat's work and his character. Throughout his career, Basquiat's name and success were attributed to his identity as a young, Black, "art-scene hustler" (Kramer). Though I do not agree that Basquiat's paintings are anything less than proof of his raw talent, I do find truth in Kramer's claim that Basquiat's fame had a lot to do with his race. Yet perhaps Basquiat intentionally used this identity in order to become famous, and it was only in gaining fame that he was reduced to a mere stereotype by society. His 'unique background' in the White-dominated New York art scene fetishized him—he became an object to be desired and capitalized upon. Racial fetishization involves fetishizing a person through stereotyping and objectification; it is a form of appropriation. Although White America is not embodying Black culture through fetishization, it is still profiting by selling a stereotyped idea of Black identity in the same way appropriation does, and at the expense of Black people whose voices are then suppressed, as evident in Basquiat's life.

Basquiat is often described as "the Jimi Hendrix of the art world" (Armand). Both were young, talented Black artists who performed and created for mostly White audiences. Both died too young due to drug overdoses and both were limited by their identity. The only thing that separated them was time. "He was frustrated by legions of white fans who only saw him as a racial stereotype—a hypersexual Black man who was high all the time" (Blake). Which artist is being described here? Does it really matter? When Black culture is lusted over by White artists, Black artists are reduced to stereotypes. When Black artists are stereotyped, their identity, individuality, and creative voice are confined. With these limitations, their power as an artist is relinquished.

In her lecture "Speaking in Tongues," Zadie Smith explores identity and the difference between those who possess a single voice and those who utilize a multiplicity of voices. Through the lenses of race and class, she provides evidence that one should be able to express their voice and create their own identity despite the labels others put upon them. Smith believes that multiplicity of voice becomes a power when fully embraced by the individual. Smith praises President Obama for his ability to use many different voices. Obama's biracial background allows him to identify as both Black and White, and other pieces of his heritage and life experiences added to his identity. He was a "Jewish male, Black old lady from the South Side, white woman from Kansas, Kenyan elders, white Harvard nerds, Black Columbia nerds, activist women, churchmen," and so much more (Smith). These identities formed his unique voice. Smith argues that such a versatility of voice is the ultimate freedom, freedom from a "single identity [which] would be an obvious diminishment" (Smith). However, Obama's ability to cross-identify is written into his appearance and how people view him; it may not be a power all are able to cultivate. Is freedom of identity really a freedom, or is it a privilege? Many Black artists feel that they have ties to other identities, whether from a specific cultural background, or life experience that transcends skin color. However, due to appearance, they are often limited to a single identity—'Black.'

It's the way of the American system. "When I go to the movies, I'm expected to identify with all of the characters, and most of them are white . . . But when you put a Black character in there, somehow the white audience isn't expected to identify with them. That's a problem," says an African-American artist from Chicago, Kerry James Marshall, whose works often explored Black social life in the Projects from the interior perspective (qtd. in Sooke). White audiences don't identify with Black characters; they look at them as an Other and can only find meaning in viewing the culture as some special, foreign, thing. It's this 'Otherness' that made artists like Basquiat and Hendrix so popular in White society, and it is "that desire for . . . or fantasies about the Other [that] can be continually exploited" (hooks 22). And these artists were exploited. "Basquiat, with his good looks, his double 'minority' origins—his father was Haitian, his mother Puerto Rican—and his overweening appetite for success, they had found the client of their dreams . . . the race card was played for all that it was worth" (Kramer). Even Basquiat's relationship to his famed friend Andy Warhol can be questioned. "When Basquiat started to work and become friends with Andy Warhol, in 83/84, he was himself seen as the pawn, Andy's pet, used to keep Andy relevant as his critical acclaim flagged" (Petty). Was Basquiat just Andy's token Black friend? Was he just craving a piece of the Basquiat buzz? These are relevant questions when even the most successful Black artists of today, through racial fetishism and stereotyping, have become "scenery for narratives that essentially focus on white people" (hooks 32). Zadie Smith equated the ability to choose one's identity to ultimate freedom, but in a society that limits your identity and silences your authentic artistic voice, how can one be free?

Perhaps the answer can be found in the way Black artists have continued to use their limitations to motivate and inspire great works of art. Looking back on Stewart's photography, what speak to me are the expressions on the Black woman's face, evolving in each photo. In the first photo, with the hands grabbing her thighs, her face isn't shown at all; she is turned away, completely oblivious. In the second photo, she looks at you but there is an absence in her eyes, still unaware of what is happening. In the third, her brow becomes furrowed and her mouth is parted in an expression of pain. In the last, her hands rise up, she is angry, she is resisting—she has woken. These photos are a very depiction of the evolution that is going on within the Black artist community right now. There is a growing awareness and need to push back against the appropriation, stereotyping, fetishizing, and commodification of Black identity. In 2015, Kendrick Lamar released *To Pimp a Butterfly*, an album dedicated to the Black experience. In 2015, painter Kehinde Waley won the U.S. Department of State Medal of Arts for his portraits of Black individuals. In 2016, Beyoncé released "Formation," a single that showed her Black pride and spoke to racial issues. In 2016, ten Black women were nominated at the Tony awards for shows written by, directed by, and about people of color. Through painting, photography, design, music, theater, and film, Black artists are reclaiming Black identity, empowering it, redefining it, and pushing away White hands. But it is still a far journey before Black artists can transcend the singular label of "Black" all together.

Even after his death, Basquiat is sold as the African American painter who "poetically evoked the vicious greed, racism and inhumanity of the society [he] was struggling to learn to live within," in the words of the director of the Whitney during the first Basquiat retrospective (qtd. in Kramer). A Black artist is never free of their identity. "In death, as in life, Basquiat has become a commodity. A cash corpse" (Armand). There is no doubt in my mind that Basquiat and many other successful Black artists are talented, and that they deserve the accolades they receive today. But to whom do they owe their success, and to what expense? Commodity is limitation. And when your own race is your only limitation, it's easy to want to be free of it. "I don't want to be a Black artist," said Basquiat; "I am an artist" (qtd. in Cadwell).

WORKS CITED

Abdul-Jabbar, Kareem. "Cornrows and Cultural Appropriation: The Truth About Racial Identity Theft." *Time*. Time Inc., 26 Aug. 2015. Web. 22 June 2016.

Armand, Louis. "Jean-Michel Basquiat and 'The Art of (Dis)Empowerment' (2000)." *ASX*. American Suburb X, 30 Oct. 2013. Web. 22 June 2016.

Banks, Azealia. Interview with Ebro. Hot 97. *YouTube*. YouTube, 18 Dec. 2016. Radio. 22 June 2016.

Basquiat, Jean-Michel. *Hollywood Africans*. 1983. Acrylic and oil stick on canvas. Whitney Museum of American Art, New York.

—. "State of the Art—Andy Warhol and Jean-Michel Basquiat—1986." Dir. Sandy Nairne. Online video clip. *YouTube*. YouTube, 20 Dec. 2007. Web. 24 June 2016.

Blake, John. "How Jimi Hendrix's Race Became His 'Invisible Legacy.'" *CNN*. Cable News Network, 18 Oct. 2014. Web. 22 June 2016.

Cardwell, Erica. "Jean-Michel Basquiat and The Immortal Black Life." *Hyperallergic*. Hyperallergic Media Inc., 8 May 2015. Web. 22 June 2016.

Cyrus, Miley. "We Can't Stop." Online video clip. *Vevo*. Vevo LLC, 19 June 2013. Web. 22 June 2016.

Duncan, Gabi. "Beyoncé and Jay Z Criticized for Blue Ivy's Hair in Ridiculous Change.org Petition." *E! News*. E! Entertainment Television, LLC, 12 June 2014. Web. 22 June 2016.

Eells, Josh. "Miley Cyrus: Confessions of Pop's Wildest Child." *Rolling Stone*. Rolling Stone, 24 Sept. 2013. Web. 22 Jun. 2016.

hooks, bell. *Black Looks: Race and Representation*. Boston, MA: South End Press, 1992. Print.

Hype Hair Magazine. "Amandla Stenberg: Don't Cash Crop On My Cornrows." Online video clip. *YouTube*. YouTube, 15 Apr. 2016. Web. 22 Jun. 2016.

"Iggy Azalea—Awards." *IMDb*. IMDb.com, Inc., n.d. Web. 22 June 2016.

Kramer, Hilton. "He Had Everything but Talent." *The Telegraph.* Telegraph Media Group Limited, 22 Mar. 1997. Web. 22 June 2016.

Lawrence, Tim. "'Listen, and You Will Hear all the Houses that Walked There Before': A History of Drag Balls, Houses and the Culture of Voguing." *Tim Lawrence.* N.p., 16 July 2013. Web. 22 June 2016.

Marantz, Andrew. "Who Is 'The Realest'?" *The New Yorker.* Condé Nast, 17 Sept. 2014. Web. 24 May 2016.

McWhorter, John. "You Can't 'Steal' a Culture: In Defense of Cultural Appropriation." *The Daily Beast.* The Daily Beast Company LLC, 15 July 2014. Web. 22 June 2016.

"Miley Cyrus—Awards." *IMDb.* IMDb.com, Inc., n.d. Web. 22 June 2016.

Petty, Felix. "Black Art Matters: Jean Michel Basquiat." *I-D.* I-D Magazine, 9 July 2015. 22 June 2016.

Shamsher, Aliyah. "Exclusive: Iggy Azalea as You've Never Heard Her Before." *Elle Canada.* TVA Group, 29 Feb. 2016. Web. 22 June 2016.

Smith, Zadie. "Speaking in Tongues." *The New York Review of Books.* NYREV, Inc., 16 Feb. 2009. Web. 22 June 2016.

Sooke, Alastair. "Kerry James Marshall: Challenging Racism in Art History." *BBC.* BBC, 28 Oct. 2014. Web. 19 June 2016.

Stewart, Daniel. *Erosion.* Photo essay. *dannyxphoto.* N.p., 1 Mar. 2016. Web. 23 June 2016.

The Radiant Child. Dir. Tamra Davis. Arthouse Films, 21 July 2010. DVD.

Whitney Museum of American Art. Museum label for Jean-Michel Basquiat, *Hollywood Africans.* New York, the Whitney Museum of Art.

Wilson, Julee. "Marie Claire Praises Kendall Jenner For Rocking 'New Epic' Cornrows, Incites Twitter Outrage." *The Huffington Post.* TheHuffingtonPost.com, Inc., 3 Apr. 2014. Web. 22 June 2016.

Young, Cathy. "To the New Culture Cops, Everything is Appropriation." *The Washington Post.* The Washington Post, 21 Aug. 2015. Web. 22 June 2016.

Angelica Chong's work, written for Lorelei Ormrod's "Advanced College Essay," asks if we can comprehend atrocity. She compares John Berger's "Hiroshima" and Philip Gourevitch's writings on the Rwandan genocide to evaluate nebulous emotional truths.

HIROSHIMA, REDUX

Angelica Chong

History is the propaganda of the victors," Avi Shlaim writes in *The Iron Wall*, a book about the Arab-Israeli conflict that has troubled the Middle East and the dispossessed and displaced people of Palestine since 1947 (34). He is talking about how revisionist historians depicted the wars between the Arab world and the then-nascent nation of Israel, but his words can arguably be applied to almost all major conflicts, and even more so to those whose subtle truths and minutiae have been made unfocused by a collective memory stretched thin with time. The bombing of Hiroshima occurred just two years before the partition of Palestine, but while the latter was to be the starting point for the protracted struggle that continues to plague the region today, the former is viewed as an end—a decisive one—and not a beginning. Although the consequences of Hiroshima have reverberated through time to affect us even today, the memory of Hiroshima itself remains just that: a vibration, a low background hum that only occasionally reaches a frequency we can hear when politicians make vague references to World War II, or when August 6th rolls around every year and Japan mourns.

Why is Hiroshima not present, as John Berger writes, in our "living consciousness" (315)? Why do we still write books about the Arab revolt of 1936, and Transjordan, and the rise of Zionism, but not the aftereffects of Hiroshima? The simple—and tempting—answer is that the former is still relevant, while the latter is not; the former is still a problem in today's world. But we should question this line of thinking. Who decided to close the book on Hiroshima, who decided that Hiroshima itself was the end of this particular story, and that everything that happened after—the immediate deaths, the generational devastation, history's haunting—belonged in an unwritten epilogue? What reality are we operating in when we decide relevance or the lack thereof?

Berger's essay "Hiroshima" reveals many inconvenient truths about the way we interact with the aftermath of war, but perhaps the most awfully wondrous thing he has to say about our hypocrisies and cowardice is this: "Does not this evocation of hell make it easier to forget that these scenes belonged to life? Is there not something conveniently unreal about hell?" (317). Perhaps the sheer quantity and concentrated quality of violence that has been enacted in Hiroshima has lent it a surreal nature that has made it almost physically inconceivable for us to wrap our minds around. We can only approach it obliquely, from different angles that get closer to a central understanding but never quite touch it. We can only comprehend asymptotically. Even so, Berger maintains that it is moral responsibility to confront this hell-scape as best we can; distancing through abstraction is to make Hiroshima unreal, and to make it unreal is to do no justice to the undeniable reality for its survivors.

Berger himself comes to this realization only after a conversation with his Marxist friend, who welcomes the "positive possibilities" that the "likely scale of destruction which would be caused by nuclear weapons" would offer an American socialist revolution (316). The callousness of her words prompts Berger to revisit *Unforgettable Fire*, a visual archive of Hiroshima that he had previously ignored. Berger has to make an active choice to open the book, to thumb through the pages, and to fully see—not just look at, without intention—the horrors of the past. This is his way of reinserting Hiroshima into his own "living consciousness" (315). Unfortunately, plausible deniability is easier than that; it is easier to say 'I was never taught this in class,' or ask 'How could I have known?' than to go out looking for something that might not even be clear to you yet. If ignorance is bliss for some, then surely innocence is a privilege for us all.

Not many people have the courage to do what Berger has done, and, even when they do, it seems they still find themselves somehow thwarted from a full understanding. But they can get as close as possible, and perhaps that is all they can ask for. Philip Gourevitch is one such person, advocating for the confrontation of history. He writes in his book about the 1994 Rwandan Genocide that he had travelled to Rwanda "to be stuck with [the dead Rwandans]—not with their experience, but with the experience of looking at them" (16). Yet even as he walks through the "intimately exposed" bodies and village ruins—the most visceral and explicit evidence of the horror that had occurred—he admits it is "still strangely unimaginable . . . one still ha[s] to imagine it" (16). Despite his efforts, there is still something in his way, some metaphysical block that has barricaded him from accessing the horror. He stands where the Hutus and Tutsis had stood, but time has made it a different place altogether. In the end, he concedes, slightly disturbed at his own thoughts, that "the dead at Nyarubuye [a]re . . . beautiful" (19). He takes photographs, because "[he] wonder[s] whether [he can] really see what [he is] seeing while [he sees] it" (19). Gourevitch distances himself—perhaps unconsciously, but undeniably. He sees beauty in death because to render horror beautiful is the only way he can make sense of what he is seeing; he literally places a camera between his eyes and the landscape and takes photographs that he can look at again later, a safe distance away from the immediacy of Rwanda that demands an instantaneous and empathic understanding he cannot afford without the risk of becoming complicit in the tragedy itself, as if observation without a barrier means that even as he looks into this abyss it can look back at him too.

As if he is aware of his own subconscious dissociation at the physical locations, Gourevitch tries to unpack the meaning behind superlatives like 'unimaginable' that are so frequently used to describe Rwanda, questioning why people continue to think of them like this when they have clearly been imagined by someone. He tries to see it for what it really is—the Othering of the Rwandans to remove culpability from 'normal' people—but, even then, perhaps he falls short. In contrast, Berger reclaims these overused buzzwords like 'hell' and 'evil' that have been so ingrained into our lexicon of horror that they have ceased to be meaningful. The word 'evil,' for example, has been reduced to a "little adjective to support an opinion or hypothesis (abortions, terrorism, ayatollahs)" (320). Berger refuses this contemporary, watered-down definition. He uses the word as it was intended to be used; he sees evil as "a force or forces which have to be continually struggled against so that they do not triumph over life and destroy it" (320). For Berger, 'evil' is not something static, nor a one-off event that has a definitive outcome; real evil necessitates constant engagement. Yet he only comes about to this realization after having viewed the art in *Unforgettable Fire*, after he has gotten as close to the heart of it as possible. Even his time in the military cannot place him closer to Hiroshima than this; he served in the British Army at the same time that the bomb was dropped—the same time that all the lives he looks back on now were lost—but there seems to be, between survivors' experiences and drawings and the history that is written down in history books, an ever-widening abyss that cannot be completely forded. Berger's words, used so deliberately, are perhaps the closest he can come to begin to grasp some of the truth behind them—the minute closing of a gap. Both Berger and Gourevitch struggle against the weight of orthodox narrative history through these acts of engaged imagination that are the truest—if not the most precisely factual or empirical—forms of witnessing and acknowledging the past.

However, if we are used to distancing ourselves from horror by burying it under hyperbole, we are also guilty of distancing through facts: an act of redefinition that becomes a lie by omission. Berger advises against precisely this: by stripping down Hiroshima to its pure facts, he claims, we start to "consider numbers instead of pain. We calculate instead of judging. We relativize instead of refusing" (319). A certain tension seems to lie in his writing when he emphasizes the importance of emotional truth in remembering Hiroshima itself, but also the importance of knowing that the act that preceded such horror "was not a miscalculation, an error, or the result . . . of a situation deteriorating so rapidly that it gets out of hand" (319). He is as quick to acknowledge the political reality and its coldly-assessing, indeed human architects that made the decision to bomb Hiroshima as he is to condemn them. We must not forget the invisible hand that made all this a reality; but, at the same time, we cannot submit to their history of statistics and directives. We must make our own—or, in the case of the Hiroshima survivors, draw their own.

One of the drawings in *Unforgettable Fire*, sketched by Asa Shigemori, depicts the surreal image of three people walking with their hands raised, zombie-like. They are spattered with blood, but what is most unnerving is their hair, standing straight up from their scalps. The accompanying text reads: "I realized for the first time . . . that when people are very much frightened hair really does stand up on end" (qtd. in Berger 316). It's a strange, seemingly innocuous observation in a sea of truly horrific images and descriptions of flayed skin, missing limbs, and burnt bodies. But perhaps it is precisely because of its incongruity that this image seems so potent. It defies our expectations of reality with its outrageousness; it forces us to defamiliarize, to remove the privilege we have that allows us to wallow, comfortable, so close to Hiroshima's horror without needing to truly make an effort to see. When we read the history books and watch the war movies, we think we understand what it was really like; we think we have imbibed history, and therefore have a claim to it. *Unforgettable Fire* shows us otherwise. It shows us that the history we receive is not—and can never be—the history of the victims, the eyewitnesses, the survivors.

According to the *Oxford English Dictionary*, the word 'history' comes from the Greek *historia*, which translates, almost contradictorily, to both 'finding out' and 'narrative.' The former implies an exploratory process, an unmapped journey with an open horizon beyond every step. The latter enforces structure, linearity, and a story that prioritizes comprehension. Perhaps what we need to do is to find a useful middle ground: to not demarcate needlessly based on arbitrary conceptions of realities, and end up excluding vital experiences, nor imagine we could possibly capture the full range of events in words and images that will ultimately fall short of lived experiences.

Berger starts his essay by admitting that he "didn't consider the book [*Unforgettable Fire*] urgent, for [he] believed that [he] already knew about what [he] would find within it" (315). He ends his essay condemning his own earlier apathy, saying that "in reality—the reality to which the survivors and the dead bear witness—[evil] can never be justified" (321). Most importantly, he defines 'evil' specifically as that which wears "a mask of innocence," allowing it to "look beyond (with indifference) that which is before the eyes" (321). Opening the book simultaneously opened Berger's eyes and his mind; it forced him into a new way of looking and knowing—a knowing that is fraught with the certainty of uncertainty, a knowing that acknowledges the limitations of one's sight even as it acknowledges the importance of even trying at all.

Perhaps the horrors of Hiroshima can never be understood in any truly significant way by future generations through writing or talking about it; perhaps we all inevitably change the nature of these events simply by addressing them in a certain way, and in that process lose a small bit of truth each time. But surely we can combine both definitions of history to strive for something better than just either/or. Surely we can—we must—try.

WORKS CITED

Berger, John. "Hiroshima." *The Sense of Sight: Writings by John Berger.* New York: Vintage International, 1985. 287-95. Print.
Gourevitch, Philip. *We Wish to Inform You That Tomorrow We Will Be Killed with Our Families: Stories from Rwanda.* New York: Picador, 1998. Print.
"history, *n.*" *OED Online.* Oxford UP, n.d. Web. 23 June 2016.
Shlaim, Avi. *The Iron Wall: Israel and the Arab World.* New York: W.W. Norton & Company, 2001. Print.
Japanese Broadcasting Corporation, ed. *Unforgettable Fire: Pictures Drawn by Atomic Bomb Survivors.* New York: Pantheon, 1981. Print.

In this essay, written for Senior Lecturer Bruce Bromley's "A Spectrum of Essays," Lisa Dean entwines personal and national narratives on pain and remembrance by contrasting individual suffering with memorial culture. The word 'scar' is the lynchpin of her arguments, enabling her essay to resonate and illuminate.

SCARS AND STIGMATA

Lisa Dean

The Berlin *Collegienhaus* in the present-day Kreuzberg district, is, in itself, an unremarkable structure. A prim baroque building constructed as a courthouse in 1735, it served as the seat of the Kammergericht, the German Court of Justice, through the 19th century. Almost completely destroyed in the second World War, the building was restored in the 1960s by the architect Günter Hönow. As the last example of a surviving baroque building commissioned by the nobility in the Friedrichstadt district, it was dedicated in the latter half of the 20th century to preserving the history of the city of Berlin ("The Old Building").

In the present day, however, the *Collegienhaus* is overshadowed by its extension—a post-modern construction that houses what is now the Jewish Museum Berlin. An undertaking by the architect Daniel Libeskind, it is in part a reminder of the oft-forgotten presence of Jewish culture throughout European history, in part a memorial for the events of the Holocaust. Libeskind's name for the museum project is "Between the Lines," symbolically recalling how what is concretely remembered is inseparably bound up in, and lent definition by, what is forgotten. Characterized by its unusual ground design and irregularly broken zinc-clad walls, the added wing conceptually consists of two lines, "one straight but broken into pieces, divided into fragments, the other multiply bent, contorted, but potentially going on ad infinitum" (Huyssen 67-68). The jagged, angular annex juts

violently from the *Collegienhaus*'s southern face, spasming unnatural-
ly against the landscape surrounding it. Libeskind's design slices boldly across and into the surface of the earth, its edges and discontinuities
forming what Andreas Huyssen describes by turns as "a fractured star
of David," a "zigzag," and as "lightning"—though perhaps it might
also recall a scar (67).

Five years ago, I had an eating disorder. It began before I was
thirteen and enfolded me gradually over the course of two years. By
the time I was fourteen, I was conscious of its presence, but I asked to
see a doctor before I was ready to accept mentally ill into the category
of words that described myself. For better or for worse, the adolescent
health specialist I saw was surprisingly kind about this.

"Do you have anorexia?" she asked me—just once. I shook my
head no. "Okay," she nodded.

My lack of menstruation was my most concerning symptom, she
went on to tell me, because it would interfere with the growth of my
bones; if I didn't gain weight quickly, I would have to begin taking
artificial estrogen. She sent me to a dietitian for nutritional
counseling, but, satisfied with my progress after a half-year, forwent
an official diagnosis. All that is mentioned on my medical record is a
mysteriously sudden drop in body weight and a note that my period
had been absent for eighteen months. All that was documented were
the physical manifestations of illness, manifestations that themselves
have long since been erased.

After the initial six months of recovery, I pretended outwardly
that I had placed these events solely in the past. But at one point, a
friend teasing me about my height prompted me to wonder if two
years of malnutrition had stunted my growth. I found that others had
voiced the same query. On a public forum, a girl had created a thread
titled "Anorexia—did it stop my puberty process?" asking if her eating
disorder could have affected her physical development.

"yes," a fellow user replied. "anorexia can stop puberty and it will
decrease your brain mass, which is even worse. ever notice how
anorexics and former anorexics can never talk about anything except
themselves and their medical history? it's because their eating disorder
makes them dumb and dull. this is medical fact" ("Anorexia").

I felt a double sting at those words—firstly, because someone could be so callous towards a girl who had undoubtedly already suffered so much, and secondly, because the author's cutting answer revealed my own fixation on the aftermath of my eating disorder. I had always asked myself: Did what I struggled against for two years leave any marks on my body? Was my growth stunted? Am I shorter than I would have been? Is it why my ribs are so narrow? How did it change me; how did it manifest itself as something visible? Suddenly aware of my fascination with finding physical markers for a mental disorder, I felt a sense of revulsion. It seemed too much like I was looking for something to show off, searching for evidence I could shove in other people's faces to say: *look! I'm damaged too! Look at how I suffered!*

In "Grand Unified Theory of Female Pain," Leslie Jamison observes that Western society has a complicated relationship with people—particularly women—in pain: they are both romanticized as poetic, tragic figures and looked down upon as attention-seekers, selfishly "wallowing" in their own unhappiness (210). Jamison quotes Susan Sontag as she criticizes the use of suffering women as cultural objects, based in "a 'nihilistic and sentimental' nineteenth-century logic that found appeal in female suffering: 'Sadness made one 'interesting.' It was a mark of refinement, of sensibility, to be sad' . . . 'the melancholy character was a superior one: sensitive, creative, a being apart'" (186). Sad women are fascinating, but not because of the actual reasons for their sadness. What really matters is the image that their unhappiness creates, the dual appeal of sufferance and vulnerability. Sadness was, and is, translated into desirable feminine qualities like "refinement" and "sensitivity," providing an attractive air of emotional depth and melancholy mystery.

Yet purposefully making pain outwardly visible is looked down upon, epitomized, for Jamison, by a widespread disdain for "cutters." Jamison observes that the prevailing cultural perception of those who self-harm is that they are looking for sympathy or attention, and concludes that the rejection of and disgust towards these public entreaties suggests a "disdain for pain that is understood as performed rather than legitimately felt" (190). "Performance" implies being conscious of an audience, which apparently implies insincerity. If you're going to suffer, these cutter-haters argue, it should be unscripted and unself-conscious, existing outside of yourself only by unplanned coincidence. Asking for sympathy is taboo. The wounded person is trapped inside their injury. They can't ask for help; doing anything "for the attention" is looked down upon.

Intimately related to our culture's contempt for "performed" pain is its condemnation of self-pity, which places not only what we express outwardly but also what we feel inwardly under public scrutiny. Jamison cites popular criticisms of Lucy Grealy's *Autobiography of a Face*, an account of the author's childhood cancer and facial disfigurement: "'She was a sad woman who never got beyond her own personal pain' . . . 'I found this book extremely sorrowful and drowning in self-pity' . . . 'I've never encountered such terribly [sic] moaning and wallowing in self-pity'" (210). Clearly, what offends these readers is not that Grealy chose to write about pain, but the way that she speaks and feels about it: too sad, too sorrowful, too self-centered. Talking about your own suffering in a way that isn't stoically triumphant—describing it as something more than an obstacle you've overcome—means you're self-pitying, which is code for being a narcissist.

With regards to her own injuries, emotional and otherwise, Jamison recalls writing to a friend: "On the one hand, I'm like, Why does this shit happen to me? And on the other hand, I'm like, Why the fuck am I talking about this so much?" (187). This is the crux of the issue: if I never wanted this shit to happen to me, why do I never shut up about it after it did? Somehow, I want two things that don't seem compatible: not to let it affect me anymore, but also to have something to remember of it, to be allowed to keep thinking and talking about it, even if it doesn't hurt anymore. I have to admit that the eating disorder was, and in some ways still is, a part of me, but I don't want it to be me—the sum of me, I mean, the thing I build my identity around. And so, even many years after the fact, even if accompanied by feelings of embarrassed self-consciousness and guilt, I look for remnants of its once overwhelming manifestation on my body.

But why is it so narcissistic to want a scar, something that makes intangible sensations physical while also offering to contain them? As a society, we make scars—markers of damage, reminders of trauma and its aftermath—purposefully.

Maya Lin's Vietnam Veterans Memorial at the National Mall is one of the first examples of the 'counter-memorial' movement, defying the tradition of glorifying fallen soldiers as examples of heroic sacrifices made for a just cause. The monument, a simple modernist design consisting of two granite walls carved with the names of the deceased converging into the shape of a V, was derided by critics as "a slap in the face," a "degrading ditch," and, perhaps most tellingly, a "black gash of shame and sorrow" (Sturken 51). Aesthetically—and emotionally—it defies the expected tone of a war memorial, cutting into the earth instead of rising triumphantly above it, a somber, muted black instead of the traditional gleaming white, relying on abstract and symbolic, as opposed to figurative, architecture. Yet, more than thirty years after its initial construction, Lin's memorial is now seen as a raw and sincere reflection of the moral ambiguity, political divisiveness, and shame surrounding America's involvement in the Vietnam War.

Memorials are uniquely different from museums in that they are not only spaces for preserving a record of the past. They are also meant to create an emotional experience, to provide an explicit space for a nation to grapple with a complex part of its past and provide an outlet for a community's grief. In *Tourists of History*, a study of the memorialization movement in America, Marita Sturken writes:

> [The] culture of mourning and memory has converged with the concepts of healing and closure that are central to American national identity. American mythology clings tenacious-ly to the belief that one can always heal, move on, and place the past in its proper context, and do so quickly. The memorial culture of the United States has thus been largely experi-enced as a therapeutic culture, in which particular citizens . . . have been seen as coming to terms with the past and making peace with difficult memories. This is the primary narrative generated by the Vietnam Veterans Memorial. (14)

Sturken herself is ambivalent about the concept of healing through memorial; she expresses concern that too much of the emphasis is placed on "closure," on placing the past in its "proper context" and moving on quickly. And it is true that seeking erasure of the past, to forget tragedy completely, would be to dishonor the memories of those who suffered and risk repeating unfortunate histories. But the fact remains that a memorial is meant to stand the test of time, to continuously bring experiences of the past into the present. If anything, an intelligent memorial, such as Lin's, encourages a nation to dwell on its pain, provoking continuous reflection on how the tragedy could have been avoided and providing pedagogic opportunities in order to protect future generations.

Daniel Libeskind's extension on the Berlin Collegienhaus is both a marker for trauma and an attempt to prevent its recurrence in the future, reminding us not only of violence committed against innocent people but also of the aftermath of their disappearance. As a kind of graft onto the *Collegienhaus*, it forces a fusion between what came before and what came after the Holocaust, representing visually that its gruesome details cannot be glossed over or compensated for by prettier aspects of Germany's history. Huyssen writes in his essay "The Voids of Berlin" that not only the building itself, but the fragmentation implied by the structure of the museum, signifies "history, a broken history without continuity" and "an absence that can never be overcome" (68-69). To Huyssen, what is fascinating about Libeskind's museum is that it acknowledges the impossibility of "overcoming" the Holocaust, admitting that it cannot fully encompass what took place. It is impossible to return to any sense of normal from before the war, just as it would be impossible to string together the fragments of a discontinuous past and somehow make it whole. Instead, what Libeskind seeks is to remind us what is missing, to remind us of our implicit responsibility to ensure that history will not be broken in the same way again.

Which raises the question: why describe Lin's war memorial and Libeskind's Jewish Museum as scars instead of wounds? The physicality of these structures is intense and in its own way violent; their outlines slice actively across and into the earth, the unforgiving metal and stone seeming to violate the wholeness of the landscape they were forced upon. But this is not exactly the intent that these memorials were built to match. Modernist counter-movements or not, memorials are meant to be places of remembrance, purposefully built to mark the memories of a tragedy that a nation needs to grapple with, either by honoring the dead or questioning the circumstances of their dying. A wound, remember, is something inflicted. I can answer most succinctly that I label these memorials as scars because these sites were attempts—violent, yet still sincere—to heal, not to hurt.

Memorials are places of comfort, among other reasons, because they allow visitors' experiences of their events to be affirmed by a collective narrative. Survivors of the initial trauma can connect their stories to those of other survivors, placing themselves in a larger community that shares their recollections. Memorials reassure those who experienced tragedy that their suffering will not be forgotten, that their emotions and experiences are valued highly enough to be preserved for generations to come. Even those unaffected by the event can empathize with those who were, and, in many cases, reinforce their sense of national identity through empathy. But the function of the memorial is limited to traumas that are shared by a nation or a community, and to attempt to share and connect through pain that is not a result of something that already exists within the public consciousness is far more complicated and dangerous.

Perhaps the greatest difference accounting for the double standard regarding pain—the simultaneous reverence for memorial culture and dismissal of more private forms of mourning—is that a collective memory is seen as implicitly understandable, while personal suffering is suspect. Memorials stand for events that affected an entire society, parts of history so significant that their aftermath is absorbed into the material of the culture. If you can convincingly connect your unhappiness to something socially acknowledged as traumatic, then your experiences are seen as almost unquestionably valid. It is much easier to cast doubt on individual pain—to diminish or dismiss or misread it—because there is nothing outside the person suffering to confirm that it is real.

A scar is what happens when one is hurt too badly to return to the way things used to be, evidence of healing and evidence that the wound cannot heal perfectly. Flesh will knit itself back together again, but it will leave signs of its rupture. A scar is a reenactment of an old wound, sealing over what was once raw and open while also recounting the tale of the initial trauma. A scar is a reminder of past pain, but, in a way, a scar also contains it. What was once a sensation that alarmed the entire body is now reduced to restless but silent stitching on the surface of the skin. A scar is hard evidence that can't be taken away from you, evidence that you were in pain and that you had reason to be in pain. Little wonder, then, that it can seem like the perfect solution when others seem determined to ignore what you are feeling because it isn't tangible to them.

Jamison never finds herself fully able to answer those questions that, in her youth, she put to her friend: "Why does this shit happen to me? And . . . Why the fuck am I talking about this so much?" Perhaps we feel compelled to talk about pain for the same reasons that we want scars: to remember that our pain is valid, that it really happened. When your pain only exists internally it is too easy for others to doubt, to allow them to discredit it and dismiss how you feel. And it is too easy to be ashamed about why you are unhappy in the first place. We are taught to distrust our emotions because they are fickle, unreliable. When you finally find yourself able to open your mouth and speak, suddenly the pain can exist in a mind other than your own, and in existing outside of you, it becomes easier to grasp onto and think through it.

Jamison is hesitant to make an overarching claim as to how exactly pain should be felt. In an interview with *The Paris Review*, she deliberates over the difference between constructive and destructive lingering in pain:

> There's a basic and important distinction to draw between positions I inhabit as somebody who has experienced some kind of trauma and somebody who's seeking out pain. Going to the Morgellons conference is a choice in a way that getting hit in the street isn't. But the collection chooses to bring all of those experiences together in a certain way—what kind of appetite is being spoken to there? In certain ways, as a writer, you do profit off your own experiences of pain, and there's a way of seeing that profit that's wholly inspirational—in terms of turning pain into beauty—and a way of seeing it that's wholly cynical—in terms of being a "wound dweller" in a corrosive or self-pitying way. The honest answer—to me—dwells somewhere between those views. (Merve)

Jamison, perhaps like the hypothetical memorial visitor, believes that the balance lies somewhere between. She is leery of purely aestheticizing pain "into beauty," but also admits the danger of being "wholly cynical" in a "corrosive" way. Ultimately, at the close of "Grand Unified Theory of Female Pain," Jamison is clear in her opinion that there is something fundamentally wrong with the way society views those who are in pain, that we don't respect or trust one another to give accurate accounts of what we are going through:

> The wounded woman gets called a stereotype and sometimes she is. But sometimes she's just true . . . Pain that gets performed is still pain. Pain turned trite is still pain. I think the charges of cliche and performance offer our closed hearts too many alibis, and I want our hearts to be open. I just wrote that. I want our hearts to be open. I mean it. (218)

The desire to make pain external—to talk about it, to "perform" it, to make it "into beauty," to search for a scar—is not narcissistic. First, this desire dares us to trust how we feel, to allow ourselves to ignore what we are told and to honor our emotions, however fluid and tangled, as they exist in the moment. No matter how society may complicate how it sees pain, by fetishizing it or deriding it or simply ignoring it, it is our right to believe in our emotions as we experience them. And second, it is a fundamentally compassionate attempt to protect those around us. No one wants to have suffered in vain. We can't hope to change the pain we experienced in the past, but we can attempt to stop others from feeling the same. To speak about pain is not to seek it out; it is to face what is already there, to show vulnerability and to reach outward from it, into a world of other bodies.

WORKS CITED

"Anorexia—did it stop my puberty process?" *Yahoo Answers.* Yahoo Inc., 24 Feb. 2009. Web. 26 May 2016.
Jamison, Leslie. "Grand Unified Theory of Female Pain." *The Empathy Exams.* Minneapolis: Graywolf, 2014. 185-218. Print.

Huyssen, Andreas. "The Voids of Berlin." *Present Pasts: Urban Palimpsests and the Politics of Memory.* Stanford: Stanford UP, 2003. 49-71. Print.

Merve, Emre. "Nothing is Alien: An Interview with Leslie Jamison." *The Paris Review.* The Paris Review, 7 Apr. 2014. Web. 20 Apr. 2016.

"The Old Building." *Jewish Museum Berlin.* Stiftung Jüdisches Museum Berlin, n.d. Web. 20 Apr. 2016.

Sturken, Marita. "The Wall and the Screen Memory." *Tangled Memories: The Vietnam War, the AIDS Epidemic, and the Politics of Remembering.* Berkeley: U of California P, 1997. 44-84. Print.

—. *Tourists of History: Memory, Kitsch, and Consumerism from Oklahoma City to Ground Zero.* Durham: Duke UP, 2007. Print.

Gabriel Heller's "Writing the Essay" class allowed Wenxin Gao to reflect on the erased stories of marginalized peoples. Can cultures achieve renewal through art? This essay draws on testimonies from the Chinese-Canadian and Cree Native American communities to answer this question.

THE FREEDOM TO IMAGINE THE PAST

Wenxin Gao

The popular saying goes that history is written by the victors. The past has been written by those who had the privilege to put their experiences into words, and their histories gave birth to their sense of individual agency and power. The stories of the marginalized were often left undocumented, the historical equivalent of burying their individuality in an unmarked grave. Although this silence has been lifted with time, it is still deeply frustrating that the present-day stories of minorities are still treated as part of a collective exotic minority experience. In terms of race in the Western world, white is still the majority, and all else is a mysterious other.

In "Political Animals and the Body of History," author Larissa Lai speaks out against the "othering of [her] body and [her] work by the mainstream" and the "racialization" that occurs when a person of color is seen first and foremost as a member of his or her race rather than as an individual (455). It begins to dawn on her "how certain texts became fetishized by critics, academics, and the general public in ways comparable to the way anthropologists and missionaries address field notes," and that works by writers of color are often treated as tokenized examples of minority culture and framed from the racist point of view of the majority (457). This is illustrated when audiences ask writers of color whether their characters' stories are adaptations of the author's own experiences or those of their family. It implies that these writers "are not creative agents capable of constructing nuanced fictions which address historical situations, but rather mere native informants reconstructing" (457). It becomes difficult, then, for writers of color to be separated from their racial identity. They have no choice but to "write from a place constructed for [them], pejoratively, by someone else" and to be constantly viewed through the lens of a dominant white culture (455). This is something that is simply not experienced by white writers, as Lai points out dryly, "I betcha no one ever asked Dickens if he was really Tiny Tim" (457).

Although Lai has no choice in her marginalization, she does seemingly have two possibilities as a writer: "to understand and work from the racialized position this society allots to the likes of us, or to work from a 'color-blind' liberal position which actively denies the way we have been racialized even as it perpetuates the very racial interests it claims not so see" (455). In short, Lai feels that she must claim the racialized space, because the other choice means denying that racism exists. However, claiming a racialized space "demands an acknowledgement of a history of racism to which the mainstream does not want to admit" and also "validates that eurocentric racist stance by placing ourselves in opposition to it" (458). Lai therefore rejects the notion of taking space in favor of making space: by "constructing a consciously artificial history for myself and others like me" (458), she creates a narrative that is not written by others but by herself. At the same time, she finds it difficult "for us diasporized types to make a homespace for ourselves given all the disjunctures and discontinuities of our histories" (458). A search for historical material, for example, proves to be fruitless when she finds few representations of her experience as a queer Chinese woman. According to Lai, "the only scholarship on lesbian history in China that I could find in English was an appendix to a book called *Passions of the Cut Sleeve*," a section that was only "ten pages long, focused exclusively on the question of sexual practice, which felt empty and unsatisfying in its narrowness" (461). These limitations force her to imagine the pieces of her missing heritage through the only way she can—by writing fictional literature.

Fiction has always been a conduit for cultural transmission. In Canada, professor Neal McLeod advocates for the study and creation of poetic literature in order to understand indigenous Cree communities. In "Cree Poetic Discourse," McLeod suggests that viewing Cree culture through the lens of Western social science is an act of "narrative violence" in that "Indigenous narratives are sanitized and there is a conceptual shift that often takes the vitality away from Indigenous life-worlds" (657). This is because it is difficult to articulate certain Cree concepts in English, especially in academic writing. The Cree poetic language is a system of "embodied understandings" that connect to the "sensations of body" and "sensations of the land," which means that abstract ideas are embodied as an understanding of the physical world (662). As an example, the concept of "forever" is understood in poetry as a time "'so long as the sun shall walk the sky, so long as the rivers shall run, so long as the grass shall grow'" (663). For the Cree people, their "ancient poetic pathways are not a mimicry of colonial narrative structures, but are rather grounded in [their] own traditions and world views" (660). McLeod's great-grandfather, an elder in the Cree community, worries about a loss of cultural heritage because "'the young Crees of today do not seem to want education, all of the Crees really want their children to have White-Man's knowledge'" (660). With Cree poetic discourse, McLeod hopes that there will be a "'positive space' of Indigenous knowledge" and a deeper understanding of older stories that "allows us to re-imagine narratives and to envision and imagine new possibilities for the future" (658, 672).

The way McLeod talks about creating a "'positive space' of Indigenous knowledge" as a contemporary Indigenous scholar is similar to Lai's wish for a "homespace" to ground her work. However, the process of setting this space is complicated by Lai's inability to understand Chinese, just as the young Crees find it difficult to connect to Cree culture because they only know English. This language barrier prevents Lai from fully immersing herself in the intricacies of Chinese symbolism and history, as she has to rely on translated works that are "bleached not only by the ideological interests of gender and class but also of race and culture" (458). By translating the language, an act of "narrative violence" has already been committed against the authenticity of the original work. Lai's own understanding of Chinese symbols seems to be grounded in fantasy and imagination rather than history. Perhaps her sense of cultural displacement is not just due to her education in a Western society, but also due to the fact that so much of culture is tied to language, which makes it difficult for her to connect deeply with her heritage without speaking Chinese. Lai said she chose not to learn Chinese because of the "pressures of assimilation," which would have been a non-issue if she lived in a society that was free of racism—a system of oppression that compelled her and the young Crees to integrate into the culture of "white superiority" (458, 455).

There is a disconnect from history felt by people of color who no longer speak the language of their origins, particularly diasporized people of color. The artwork *Mother Tongue* (2002) by Zineb Sedira illustrates this by showing three videos of three generations of women (Sedira, her mother, and her daughter) talking to each other about their memories as young women. However, they each only speak in their first language: her mother in Arabic, Sedira in French, and her daughter in English. It follows Sedira's personal history as a descendent of Algerian parents who was born in France and spent her adulthood in England. Sedira's work deals with the "issues of representation, family, language, memory and landscape." As the grandmother and granddaughter fail to communicate in broken sentences and their conversation comes to an uneasy halt, it illustrates how growing up in different contexts has destroyed the means of communication for this immigrant family. How can the young granddaughter then be expected to understand her own heritage when she cannot even understand her own grandmother? Having been brought up in a Western society, the granddaughter, like Lai, feels no strict attachment to her cultural history, and this is exacerbated by her limited understanding of her native language.

There is perhaps also more than one dimension to Lai's alienation from her culture that goes deeper than simply the limitation of not being able to use her native language. Adrienne Rich writes in "Invisibility in Academe" that out of the many injustices that are inflicted on the lesbian community, invisibility is one that is seemingly insignificant yet still "dangerous and painful" (218). She compares the experience of being a lesbian to looking into a mirror and seeing nothing: an existence where "those who have power to name and socially construct reality choose not to see you or hear you" (218).

Before the 20th century, all women "were forbidden by law to speak in public meetings," but according to Rich, even in the 20th century queer women were still being told time and time again to "keep your private life private" in a way that "fragments" a person's experiences and prevents her from "integrating love and work and feelings and ideas, with the empowerment that can bring" (218). Even in Women's studies courses, the discussions remain based in heterosexuality, and the experiences of women of color are treated as an afterthought "while the central discourse remains unrelentingly white" (219). Rich's solution to her "invisibility" was to be "a very public and visible lesbian," to assert her existence and to remind herself that this was just "a game with mirrors" where you can demand to be seen and heard (218).

As Lai writes, "[her] work comes from many places at once" (455). Her isolation may come from her being a Chinese person or a diasporized person of color, but it also comes from her being a woman, and in particular an "invisible" queer woman. The history she has been hoping to find—"a history with women identified women of Chinese descent living in the West at its center"—does not really exist (458). Her intersectional identities mean that she is "invisible" in her own culture, and much less visible in a mainstream discourse that is already overwhelmingly heterosexual and white. It catalyzes the need for her to articulate her own history through her fiction, to play the "game of mirrors" that affirms her existence. There are several queer Asian theorists that caution against "projecting the needs and contexts of the present on to the past" because we simply do not look at history with the same pair of eyes as those who lived through it (459). But Lai argues that there will always be a longing for one's history to have a body and form, and she does not claim her artificial history to be absolute but "one of uninhibited, zany invention for the sheer joy of it" (459). Her freedom to imagine the past is so powerful because for too long this freedom has been in the hands of those with power and used to "justify the reproduction of tired stereotypes and the perpetuation of historically unjust power balances" in the name of artistry (459). The examples given of Pocahontas, Suzy Wong, and Madame Butterfly are such iconic woman characters of color that we do not even stop and question them for the racial, gender, and sexual stereotypes they are.

"What is history, after all, but narrative?" asks Lai (458). Minority communities have always struggled to claim their own side of the narrative or to reclaim a slur, and Lai is creative in her approach of inventing fiction that encompasses aspects of her multi-faceted identities. She overcomes her loneliness and the limitation of not understanding her language by filling in the holes left by history and demystifying the minority experience. In her research into the lives of those like her, she found the historical figure Yu Hsuan-chi, a Chinese woman poet and courtesan who is rarely translated as she is forgotten in favor of "sanctioned male heavyweights" (459). Lai ended up basing one of her fictional characters off of Yu, and brought her to life in her stories when the history books have chosen to forget her. She forces us to accept Yu as a whole person rather than one defined by the fragmented identities of her culture or her gender. No doubt this is a healing process against the injuries of injustice for Lai too—to look in the mirror and paint her own reflection. When she failed to find herself in history, she chose to find herself in her art.

WORKS CITED

Lai, Larissa. "Political Animals and the Body of History." *The Broadview Anthology of Expository Prose*. Eds. Laura Buzzard, Julia Gaunce, Don LePan, Mical Moser, and Tammy Roberts. Toronto: Broadview Press, 2011. 454-63. Print.

McLeod, Neal. "Cree Poetic Discourse." *The Broadview Anthology of Expository Prose*. Eds. Laura Buzzard, Julia Gaunce, Don LePan, Mical Moser, and Tammy Roberts. Toronto: Broadview Press, 2011. 657-672. Print.

Sedira, Zineb. *Mother Tongue*. 2002. Brooklyn Museum, Brooklyn. Web. 26 June 2016.

Rich, Adrienne. "Invisibility in Academe." *The Broadview Anthology of Expository Prose*. Eds. Laura Buzzard, Julia Gaunce, Don LePan, Mical Moser, and Tammy Roberts. Toronto: Broadview Press, 2011. 217-19. Print.

This epistolary essay, written for Benjamin Gassman's "International Writing Workshop I," demands change. In a letter addressed to Vietnam's Minister of Education and Training, Hieu Do combines empirical examples with testimony to capture the immediate, far-reaching effects of his country's educational policy.

TEACHING HISTORY IN VIETNAM

Hieu Do

Dear Mr. Phạm Vũ Luận,

In August 2015, the Ministry of Education and Training (MOET) published a draft proposal that suggested many changes to Vietnam's education system. One of the most controversial changes was integrating History with Civic Education and Defense Education. History would no longer be a mandatory individual subject and would instead become part of a new optional subject called Civic and Defense. When questioned at the 2015 parliament meeting about why an important subject like History was integrated, you, Mr. Phạm, as the Minister of Education and Training, eluded the question, saying that the proposal was still unofficial. However, whether History should be integrated or kept as an individual subject does not matter. What needs to be reformed, I believe, is the way History is taught in Vietnam.

The curriculum for Vietnamese students is heavy because they over-rely on rote memorization, which results in ineffective tests and exams that require students to regurgitate facts and figures. This pedagogical method causes the students to lose interest in learning. According to the General Statistics Office of Vietnam, approximately 500,000 students of all ages drop out of school per year ("Population and Employment"). The alarming number of students underscores a grave problem with education in Vietnam. I am aware that the MOET always makes annual reforms, but to most people including myself, those "reforms" seem like a formality. New textbooks are reprinted. The format of an exam is changed. The recent draft proposal is also an example. These meaningless acts have pushed the scene of Vietnam's educational system to a stalemate situation where students become "lab rats" for the MOET to test their changes while teachers are helplessly exhausted. Mr. Phạm, it is time for a fundamental change. We need to change how students think about learning, starting with History.

I understand that it is hard to reform the way History is taught given that academic freedom is limited in Vietnam. Yet as the Minister of Education and Training, would you at least try to tackle the problem seriously? In Vietnam, students are discouraged from debating with teachers about the veracity of the knowledge passed onto them. Whatever is taught must be true and will be tested. The main reason behind this one-way relationship between students and teachers is the influence of Confucius's teachings that have been deeply rooted in our subconscious minds for thousands of years. Since the first day of school, I was told to appreciate those who gave birth to me, my parents, and those who give me knowledge, my teachers. Confucius's ideals teach me gratitude and appreciation. They also lead back to a beautiful tradition that is celebrated annually on November 20 as the Vietnamese Teachers' Day.

However, this student-teacher relationship can also be controversial, as demonstrated in an incident from April of 2015. An anonymous elementary school student was slapped by his teacher supposedly for being "argumentative and disobedient" ("Tranh cai"; translation mine). To many people's surprise, his parents publicly apologized to the teacher for "not educating their son well." They thanked her for slapping their son. During my elementary school years, I was the witness to—and the victim of—many slappings. I felt scared and never raised my hand unless I knew for sure that my answer was what the teachers wanted. I bet that the anonymous student and his friends felt the same. Although students indeed appreciate the teachers who have enlightened their young minds, students should not be discouraged from raising their own voices.

When it comes to teaching History, that student-teacher relationship is taken advantage of by the Communist Party to impose
distorted facts on the impressionable minds of the youth. History
textbooks at all levels are intentionally designed to give an uneven
emphasis on the greatness of the Communist Party of Vietnam.
During my ten-year education in Vietnam's public schools, I had to
memorize the numbers of enemies killed by the Communist army or
the exact dates and hours when the army had launched attacks.
History, to me, was mere memorization of meaningless facts.
However, when I won a scholarship to study in the U.S. and had the
opportunity to learn American History, I was taught about the significance of a battle, instead of how many people died in it, or the relationship between two events, instead of when and what time they
occurred. My education in the U.S. has taught me to connect different events in history and have my personal perspective about them. I
come to see history as a meaningful, continuous thread of humans'
development.

My educational experience of American History resonates with
an article written by Theresa Johnston, a researcher in education. She
describes an effective History class as one in which students can
"engage regularly with challenging primary source documents"
(Johnston). These "primary source documents" are hidden or missing
in our current Vietnamese History curriculum. Without these reliable
sources of information, Vietnamese students find it difficult to see
connections between historical events, especially when they are forced
to memorize facts. Vietnamese historian and parliamentary delegate
Dương Trung Quốc says that the dull teaching of History can cause
students to be "indifferent to history itself" ("ĐBQH"; translation
mine). In other words, if students are taught to think critically about
history, they would not only find more interest in the history of
Vietnam, but also know how to make the country better.

The Communist Party has done many great things to our country, but history must not be fabricated, and History, as a subject
taught to students, must be as objective as possible. In her essay "In
History," Jamaica Kincaid expresses her struggle to understand the
history of her home country, Antigua, which was named by
Christopher Columbus after a church even though "churches are not

important originally" to her people (184). Like her country—once colonized by the Spanish Empire—our country has been invaded by many empires: 1000 years by the Chinese, 61 years by the French, and 27 years by the Americans. Yet, our ancestors never surrendered, and now as an independent nation, we have many tasks to accomplish. The most important one is to educate our children to take pride in our glorious past and to take responsibility for the failures of our government. In her essay, Kincaid raised a question: should history be "an idea," "an open wound," or "a collection of facts" (181)? How is one supposed to feel about history? I believe that students should be informed of both the good and bad things done by our government and undergo the same feelings about history that Kincaid felt. Although confusing and perhaps frustrating, the feelings are crucial for students to understand the history of Vietnam.

Mr. Phạm, the teaching of History in school needs to transcend political ideals. History does not represent the Party; it represents the past, present, and future across nations. If students, the future leaders of Vietnam, fail to see the connections in history, how will they learn from the past to create a better future? How will Vietnam ever develop?

I hope that you will seriously consider my concern and make a more meaningful change to the education system in Vietnam.

Sincerely,
Hieu Do

WORKS CITED

"Tranh cãi xung quanh cái tát của cô giáo." *VietNamNet*. Bao VietNamNet, 15 Apr. 2015. Web. 6 Dec. 2015.

Johnston, Theresa. "History Detected." *Stanford Alumni*. Stanford University, May 2013. Web. 3 Dec. 2015.

Kincaid, Jamaica. "In History." *The Brooklyn Reader*. Ed. Jono Mischkot, Elisa Linski, and Pat C. Hoy II. New York: Pearson, 2014. 181-85. Print.

"Population and Employment." *General Statistics Office of Vietnam.* Statistical Documentation and Service Centre— General Statistics Office of Vietnam, 2015. Web. 3 Dec. 2015.

"ĐBQH Dương Trung Quốc phản ứng việc tích hợp môn Lịch sử." *VoV.* Báo điện tử, VoV, 11 Nov. 2015. Web. 6 Dec. 2015.

Isabella Loh merges historical fiction and scientific research to generate emotionality through third-person narrative. Written in Professor Martha Hodes's Freshman Seminar, "History and Storytelling," this essay spotlights an unsung heroine: a nurse who served during the Spanish influenza pandemic of 1918.

THE BLUE DEATH

Isabella Loh

I had a little bird,
Its name was Enza.
I opened the window.
And in-flu-enza.

—A children's skipping rope rhyme from 1918
("The Influenza Pandemic of 1918")

As a second-year nursing student, Eugenie had witnessed the chaotic spectacle of childbirth a few times. Copious amounts of bodily fluids, hours of labor, some intervention from the doctor, and a baby would appear: a red, wrinkly, screaming creature. It was like a magic trick. The magician pulled the rabbit out of the hat and Eugenie was the magician's assistant-in-training. There was, however, a delivery that hadn't been quite as successful. The baby had been born blue and silent, with an umbilical cord looped around its neck like a hangman's noose. The blue hue then was startlingly similar to that of Eugenie's patient now, who lay supine on the hospital bed. The girl's extremities and face were flushed a deep blue against the stark white sheets. The only sign that she was still alive was the slight rattle of the ribcage as her overworked lungs expanded and contracted. But there was no noose around this patient's neck. No, this patient was in the last throes of the Spanish influenza. In the end, Eugenie and the doctor had managed to save the baby; there was no saving this girl.

The medical term was cyanosis: a blue discoloration of the skin, caused by poor oxygenation of the blood ("Skin Discoloration—Bluish"). It was also one of the final symptoms patients exhibited before they succumbed to the influenza ("The Influenza Pandemic of 1918"). It had been two weeks since the full force of the influenza had struck New York, two weeks since the nursing students had abruptly assumed the duties of full-fledged nurses (Deming 1308). Gone were the dour graduate nurses who had once scrutinized their every move. There was no more time to practice nursing. Now, any errors that they made could prove fatal for their patients. In those two weeks, Eugenie had never seen a patient recover from cyanosis this severe. There was nothing she could do except make her dying patient as comfortable as possible.

Eugenie drew the screen around the bed. In the past, procedure had dictated screening patients whenever treatment was administered. With the arrival of the epidemic, such a luxury had long been discarded. Nowadays, in the crowded wards, the screens were only used to allow patients to die in some semblance of privacy (Deming 1309). Gently, she draped a damp flannel on the feverish forehead, and moistened the girl's cracked lips with some water. It was more a comfort to herself than to the half-dead girl. There were no sobbing relatives by the bedside, nor was there a telephone number on the patient's chart. Eugenie settled herself by the bed, clasping a fragile blue hand. She watched, as the shallow breaths grew shallower still. She knew, from experience, that it would only take a few minutes.

Eventually, the breaths ceased altogether. Eugenie briskly checked for a pulse before noting down the time of death on the chart. There was no time to loiter; there were other patients to attend to. Without a word, the other student nurse assigned to the ward hurried over, and the two nurses began the routine of turning over the bed. The corpse went on a gurney, destined for the morgue. The bed was stripped. Fresh linens went on. The gurney was discreetly wheeled away, its passenger hidden under the soiled sheets. The screen was removed, revealing a clean, empty bed, ready for another patient. It was a magic trick they had become practiced at. In the beginning, it had seemed unthinkably callous. Now, Eugenie was all too aware that there was no time for sentimentality.

The work was never-ending. The women's ward originally had twenty-four beds, and more had been added hastily wherever there was space (Deming 1308). All around the room, patients lay in their beds. Some slept fitfully, trussed up in pneumonia jackets, their rest interrupted by a relentless cough (Keeling). Others were half-conscious and delirious with fever. The influenza was cruel to the human body and its victims were often as feeble as infants, requiring constant care. There were medicines, fluids, poultices, and sedatives to be administered (Deming 1309). Linens had to be changed and baths given. All through the night, the two nurses systematically worked their way through the rows of beds.

Eugenie had just finished spoon-feeding a patient when the doors to the ward crashed open. Two orderlies rushed in, a limp body bouncing on the stretcher between them. She hurriedly directed them to the one empty bed in the ward. Bright, red blood saturated the front of the patient's mask, like a grotesque approximation of lipstick. Eugenie's fingers trembled as she untied the young woman's mask, hyperaware of the fine gauze that stretched across her own nose and mouth. The woman coughed violently, expelling a froth of bloody mucus into the basin that Eugenie held. The other nurse intercepted a wild-eyed man clutching two small children. His wife's name was Marie, she'd collapsed and started coughing blood and the man and his children were shepherded out of the ward, mid-sentence. Eugenie noticed uneasily that they were all wearing masks.

The masks were supposed to protect them from contracting the virus. It was the last thing the graduate nurses had drilled into them. The woman wheezed as she struggled to breathe. Eugenie wiped the bloody sputum off the woman's chin, whispering gentle reassurances to her patient. This was no time to be distracted. The patient exhibited all the symptoms of pneumonia, one of the life-threatening complications of the influenza, and the mercury meniscus of the thermometer hovered around 104 degrees (Deming 1309). The theories and techniques Eugenie had spent months immersed in converged in her mind as she worked furiously on her patient. A hypodermic injection of "camphor in oil" to stimulate circulation (Killingray 56). Antipyretics, fluids, and an icepack to reduce the dangerous fever (Killingray 56). An "expectorant" to reduce congestion (Killingray 56). More fluids and a sedative to calm the patient.

Hours later, a bone-weary Eugenie stood by the bedside of her sleeping patient. The fever had abated, if only by one or two degrees. Still, the progress was promising, and a fatigued sense of satisfaction overshadowed the aching in her abused muscles. The patient was pale, but thankfully there was no sign of cyanosis. Eugenie knew from experience that as long as the patient survived the week, she would likely recover from the virus (Deming 1309). The sun had risen an hour ago, and dusty beams of yellow sunlight poked their way through the gaps in the blinds. The ward was quiet except for the faint, labored breathing of the sick. She shared a faint smile with the other nurse. It had been a good night. It was always a good night when none of their patients died.

The day shift nurses arrived and Eugenie trudged out of the ward. She pulled off her germ-ridden uniform, exchanging it for a clean set of clothes. The used mask went into the bin to be burned (Keeling). She closed her throbbing eyes, breathing in the sterile scent of gauze as she tied on a fresh mask. In her head, she could still see her patient, mask soaked with blood. A cold pit of unease settled in her insides. She could feel the infinitesimal particles of the influenza virus clinging to her body, to the room, to the entire hospital. Opening her eyes, she began scouring her hands determinedly with a bar of soap, forming a thick lather. Her fingernails carved little crescent-moon indents into the soap. She continued scrubbing. She scrubbed until her skin was pink and squeaky-tight, and still she scrubbed.

Rivulets of tepid water sluiced down the patient's shoulder, glinting in the warm lamplight. Eugenie paused, dipping the sponge into the bucket of sudsy water, before continuing the bed bath. The woman—Marie—was awake, but had her face turned resolutely away. Depression was common amongst sufferers of the virus (Deming 1309). Nonetheless, it had been five days since Marie had been admitted into the hospital, and her condition was vastly improved. The fever was almost gone and she had stopped coughing up blood. Eugenie wrung out the sponge and began delicately wiping the young woman with a damp flannel. Bed baths were tedious but indispensable; they were good for fevers and many of the bedridden patients suffered from incontinence as a result of the influenza (Keeling). She finished up, meticulously drying the clean skin with a towel.

Another gurney with a sheeted body squeaked past, tended by an unfamiliar nurse. The girl who had worked with Eugenie for the last few weeks had contracted the virus, as had many other nurses at the hospital. Others were at home, nursing their own critically ill family members. This, combined with the number of graduate nurses overseas in the war effort, had exacerbated the shortage of nurses at the hospital (Deming 1308). Harried doctors rushed from ward to ward examining patients, but there was no miracle medicine for them to prescribe, no groundbreaking surgery for them to perform. It was all down to good nursing, and nurses were few and far between. It was the same in hospitals all over New York. A few weeks ago, newspaper headlines had been splashed with fervent updates on the advances of the Allied troops. Now, all anyone would talk about was the epidemic, and the Red Cross constantly ran impassioned appeals for volunteer nurses. "A STERN TASK FOR STERN WOMEN" was the tagline featured in the newspaper advertisements and flyers plastered all over the city (Opdycke 97).

Eugenie dressed the patient, gently manipulating limp limbs into sleeves. Every now and then she would murmur something, but Marie remained stubbornly unresponsive to conversation. The only time Eugenie had ever heard her speak was when she'd woken up and asked for her husband and children. After days of waiting, the woman stared constantly at the ceiling, unmoving and vacant-eyed. It was unnerving. It was also frighteningly similar to the many lifeless eyes Eugenie had closed over the past weeks.

Her heart skipped when the woman abruptly tried to sit up, flu-dulled muscles straining after days of disuse. She hastily pushed her patient down, clucking her displeasure, until she saw the long-awaited husband standing at the foot of the bed. The man launched into apologies and explanations, but all that mattered was the light in her patient's eyes. Eugenie half-heartedly chided the man about visiting hours before leaving them to it, smiling behind her mask. With all the deaths that had happened in the ward, it was nice to have a little life.

The lampposts had just been turned on, casting warm pools of light along the dark street. Somewhere in the city, somber funeral bells tolled, announcing another victim of the influenza. Eugenie inhaled deeply, savoring the fresh sharpness of the cold air before she stepped into the hospital. Nowadays, she spent almost all of her time indoors, sleeping during the day and working during the night. Her body was exhausted even after the eight hours of sleep she had gotten, eyes covered by a black silk stocking, ears plugged with cotton, and curtains drawn tight against the intrusive sunlight (Deming 1309). Her usually dreamless sleep had been marred by a disquieting nightmare: one in which she covered her mouth as she coughed, only to find red drops of blood on blue fingers.

She walked into the dimly lit ward. All was quiet and the day shift nurses were preparing to leave. Absentmindedly perusing the list of medications (a list she had long ago memorized), Eugenie pushed the trolley down the row of beds, dispensing medicines as she went. She had just reached Marie's bed when she sensed something deeply amiss. The young woman was fast asleep, but her breathing was erratic and harsh. With a sinking feeling, Eugenie brought the lamp closer. The fingernails were shaded a faint, unmistakable blue.

It wasn't just the fingernails. The cyanosis had already spread to the lips. Eugenie put the lamp down. For a moment, she stood there in the darkness, dreading what would inevitably happen. She allowed herself those few seconds of weakness before she finally called out to the other nurse. Everything after that happened very quickly. They woke the patient and propped her up to open the airway. The patient started spluttering blood, blood that was slowly hemorrhaging from her fluid-distended lungs ("Fighting Influenza"). That was when the other nurse went to telephone the patient's husband. Eugenie administered all the medicines she could think of, but the thick crimson phlegm made it impossible for the patient to swallow.

Marie's eyes were wide and frightened. She tried to speak, but all that came out amongst the blood and the mucus was a mangled, weak noise. Eugenie shushed her, stroking her sweat-dampened hair with sad, maternal affection. Marie's pulse was getting weaker and the injection of a cardiac stimulant saw no results. Eugenie's own heart was pounding violently in her ribcage as she instructed the other nurse to summon the doctor on call. The nurse gently informed her that it was a hopeless situation. Eugenie telephoned the doctor herself. The disheveled man stumbled into the ward minutes later, half-asleep. He declared that nothing could be done and left when she snapped at him.

Once again, Eugenie drew the screen around the bed.

The young woman was gone within the hour. The husband never made it in time. Eugenie could only watch as her patient slowly suffocated, drowning in her own bodily fluids. The eyes dulled and the pupils became unresponsive, fixed in their final position. The thrashing limbs stilled and the muscles slackened. The faint gurgling ceased, and a single, large sputum bubble remaining on the bloodied lips. A faint stench of urine permeated the air as the urethral sphincter relaxed and the bladder voided itself. Death was not graceful, or beautiful.

The other nurse stood by the bed, gurney at the ready. Eugenie let go of the small blue hand. Together, they transferred the corpse, careful not to jolt its limbs. She closed the glassy eyes. A clean sheet was draped over the body. The linens were exchanged and the screen removed. Eugenie kept a tight grip on the gurney. She was composed, calm, and professional; she was a nurse. She was all of those things until the woman's husband ran into the ward.

The breathless man took one look at his wife's lifeless body, covered by a sheet, and crumpled like wet tissue paper. Eugenie opened her mouth, but words eluded her. What was there to say to a man who had just lost his young wife? *I'm sorry for your loss.* A meaningless platitude like *sorry* could not convey the gravity of the situation. The man was now a widower because a disease as seemingly innocuous as the flu had snatched his wife away. *She's in a better place now.* Marie was twenty-four years old; the best place for her was next to her husband and children. The only place she would be going now was a pit in the ground, if even that (Aimone 74). *It was a merciful death.* There was no mercy in dying young and in excruciating pain. There was no mercy in a God who would inflict such unexplained cruelty. She left the dazed man with his dead wife and ran for the safety of the linen closet.

Alone in the cramped darkness, the emotions she had suppressed for so long finally escaped. She cried for the sixteen-year-old girl who had died the night before. She cried for Marie, who had almost recovered ("Fighting Influenza"). She cried for Marie's children, who would grow up without a mother. She cried for all of the young patients she had lost in the short span of a few weeks. She cried at the injustice of it all. Most of all, she cried because she had failed to save them when they had needed her most.

WORKS CITED

Aimone, Francesco. "The 1918 Influenza Epidemic in New York City, A Review of the Public Health Response." *Public Health Reports* 125.3 (2010): 71-79. Web. 13 Dec. 2015.

Billings, Molly. "The Influenza Pandemic of 1918." *Human Virology at Stanford.* N.p., June 1997. Web. 13 Dec. 2015.

Deming, Dorothy. "Influenza—1918: Reliving the Great Epidemic." *American Journal of Nursing* 57.10 (1957): 1308-09. Print.

"Fighting Influenza." *The Great Pandemic: The United States in 1918-1919.* United States Department of Health and Human Services, n.d. Web. 13 Dec. 2015.

Keeling, Arlene W. "Alert to the Necessities of the Emergency: U.S. Nursing During the 1918 Influenza Pandemic." *Public Health Reports* 125.3 (2010): 105-12. Web. 13 Dec. 2015.

Killingray, David, and Howard Phillips, eds. *The Spanish Influenza Pandemic of 1918-1919: New Perspectives.* New York: Routledge, 2003. Print.

Opdycke, Sandra. *The Flu Epidemic of 1918: America's Experience in the Global Health Crisis.* New York: Routledge, 2014. Print.

"Skin Discoloration—Bluish." *MedlinePlus*. U.S. National Library of Medicine, n.d. Web. 13 Dec. 2015.

Paula Cantillo's essay for Colm O'Shea's "Advanced College Essay: The World Through Art" explores national identity and the creation of cultural myths and monsters. Cantillo guides her reader confidently among seemingly unrelated topics to reveal hidden insights and connections.

THE SHADOW OF THE UNDEAD

Paula Cantillo

An armored ambulance speeds down the interstate, a pack of military escorts at its flanks and a flock of helicopters circling anxiously above it. As the vehicle pulls into a deserted parking lot, two men in white space suits emerge and make their way hastily towards the back door of a hospital building. What looks like a scene straight out of an apocalypse film is actually news footage of Dr. Kent Brantly, America's first Ebola patient, being brought into Atlanta's Emory Health Center for treatment ("Ebola Patient"). In the weeks following his arrival, travel restrictions would be implemented, thousands of news stories would be aired tracking (or speculating about) the transmission of the virus, and hysteria would run rampant among the American public. However, in hindsight, having experienced only two deaths out of eight cases, it is obvious that the only thing apocalyptic about the American Ebola outbreak was our reaction to it.

It is true that, in a biological sense, viruses pose an invasive threat to our bodies. In the case of Ebola, the virus enters the host and hijacks their vascular system, causing their veins to decompose and hemorrhage. While, naturally, symptoms like these would arouse fear in anyone, it seems unlikely that Ebola's biological threat alone could have caused a panic as turbulent as that of 2014. If this were the case, viruses like the flu and HIV—which are considerably more contagious and statistically more deadly—would receive the same public attention and media coverage that Ebola received upon its arrival on

American soil. Perhaps, then, it is possible that our exaggerated reaction was provoked not by a simple health concern, but by a more latent, insidious fear.

An investigation into the virus's media presence shows that Ebola was the dominant story on both cable and broadcast news in the four weeks leading up to the 2014 midterm elections. Many politicians like Ted Cruz and Rand Paul used the virus as a means to advance their political agendas, taking an opportunity to attack President Obama for neglecting his duty and refusing to close the borders to all nations with reported cases of the virus. Ignoring the fundamental nature of the disease, many of these public figures claimed that Ebola was being transmitted by illegal immigrants, or that it could be used as a bio-chemical weapon by terrorists. These gross speculations stoked the already rising flames of American xenophobia, and, soon enough, made a fear of disease synonymous with a fear of foreigners.

Almost every story about disease stems from similar xenophobic anxieties. Take the zombie, for example: a creature near and dear to the plague sub-genre of film and narrative storytelling. Though the past decade has seen an explosion of the zombie in popular culture, the monster is not at all new to American mythology. In fact, it has been embodying a Western fear of outsiders since 1932, when it made its debut in Victor Hugo Halperin's film *White Zombie* (1932). This film, along with others such as *I Walked with a Zombie* (1943), heavily accentuates distinctions between American and Caribbean culture, the worlds of White and Black, and the realms of insider and outsider. The protagonists in each film, all White, are seen engaging in stylish European dinners, playing the piano, and generally convening in brightly lit scenes. On the other hand, African Voodoo masters and zombie plantation slaves are portrayed as gaunt, shadowy figures who partake in mysterious rituals and play entrancing rhythms on the drums. The heroes in these films respond to the Voodoo zombies in very much the same way that Americans in the 1920 imperialist era reacted to contact with the obscure and misunderstood Haitian culture: by polarizing the 'civilized' White world and the 'primitive' Black world into separate spheres of existence.

Later films like *Invasion of the Body Snatchers* (1956) and *Night of the Living Dead* (1968) broke from the zombie's Haitian roots and allowed the creature to embody a more age-relevant tension between the inside and outside. Instead of being enchanted by Voodoo, these zombies were brainwashed by alien invaders or affected by nuclear radiation. In each of these films, the creature is part of a horde—a mindless, destructive machine capable of corrupting or infecting anyone it comes into contact with. With the Cold War droning on in the background, it is easy to see the monster in these films as the embodiment of anxiety towards foreign communist influence and the effects of nuclear warfare.

After the fall of the Soviet Union, there was a short lull in the production of zombie narratives. It was not until the turn of the century that the creature was raised from the dead by the film *28 Days Later* (2002). With its introduction of the contagion factor, this film blurred the lines between horror and science fiction, infusing an aspect of realism into the zombie genre. This trend continued into later films like *The Dead* (2010), which shows an American Air Force engineer plane-wrecked while on a mission to West Africa, where an Ebola-like zombie virus has spread like wildfire among the natives. The engineer escapes after many months of fighting hordes of African zombies only to find that the epidemic has already reached the United States. At a time when illegal immigration was—in the eyes of many Americans—a threat to national security, this similar danger of disease being carried across the border seemed all too realistic. Even today, as Andrew O'Hehir comically states in his article "Ebola: The Heart of Darkness and the Epidemic of Fear," there seems to be the paranoid perception that "all it takes is a handful of African visitors with cardboard suitcases and undiagnosed infections, and next thing you know, the cable goes out at Mom's house and we have to eat the neighbors." While clearly an exaggeration, this statement provides important insight into how outsiders, especially those considered most prone to viral contagion, are often times portrayed in the semblance of a mindless monster. For a subtle example of this, consider Donald Trump's 2015 statement in which he said: "Tremendous infectious disease is pouring across the border. The United States has become a dumping ground for Mexico and, in fact, for many other parts of the world" (qtd. in Walker). The fact that he uses the term "infectious disease" instead of "people with infectious disease" may seem trivial, but when put in conversation with the evolving image of the zombie, it makes all the difference.

In its humble origins in *White Zombie* and *I Walked with a Zombie*, the zombie held true to its roots in Haitian mythology as a creature exploited by dark magic and manipulation. Though frightening, and in some cases dangerous, the zombies were pitiable, curable, and, for the most part, still human. With new developments like *Night of the Living Dead* and *28 Days Later*, however, the zombie began to seem less like a victim and more like the flesh-eating monster we know today. This transition culminates with the zombie subgenre's newest evolution, AMC's television series *The Walking Dead*. Throughout the show, the characters refer to the infected as "walkers," "biters," "deadheads," and "geeks" as a way of accepting the fact that their loved ones are no longer human—that the infected are now the infection. Detachment of this sort is an important mental defense mechanism, as the zombies are dangerous, and it is much easier to blow the brains out of a "walker" than it is to hurt a loved one or friend.

Labels, as we have seen throughout history, are a fundamental tool in the construction (and then later, destruction) of a monster. In times of imperialism, the exploitation of whole indigenous civilizations was largely justified by calling the natives "savages." During the Cold War, the "communist" label was enough to spark nationwide hysteria and instigate a witch hunt that would eventually lead to the unwarranted prosecution, imprisonment, and deportation of hundreds of innocent people. The same type of work is done by Trump's use of labels, whereby it becomes much easier for Americans to detain an "infectious disease" at the border than to refuse a family looking for a better life.

It seems as if each era has its own signature devil. Each time one is defeated, another more frightful one is conjured up to take its place. It's rather like the community of Woodbury in *The Walking Dead*, which wages a war against protagonist Rick Grimes in the third season. Though the citizens of Woodbury seem peaceful, the city is infamous for its unprovoked and ruthless attacks on outsiders. Their leader, a young, charismatic man known as the Governor, is somehow able to convince them to waste their men and resources on attacking any group of survivors outside of its walls. As DJ Pangburn of *Death and Taxes* explains:

> Woodbury's walls have neutralized the zombie threat, and so a more menacing, unquantifiable threat must be constructed, even if it's largely imaginary. The fear of the 'other' shifts from one object to another. (Pangburn)

The United States has withdrawn from Haiti; it has held steady through the dissolution of the Soviet Union, and thus, like Woodbury, it must seek out a new enemy to once again play the role of the "boogeyman" (Pangburn). Ironically, both the United States and Woodbury brand their newest monster with the same label: "terrorist." For Woodbury, whose residents can presumably draw on pre-apocalyptic memories of terrorism in America, the word is compelling enough to launch them into a war against a small, agrarian society with three children, a newborn baby, and a crippled old man. Similarly, for the United States, the image of the armed, Middle-Eastern monster is enough to demonize a whole religion consisting almost entirely of peaceful people.

But to what extent is this fear paranoia? Certainly in *The Walking Dead*, Rick's group is peaceful, but who is to say that previous outsiders were not? The residents of Terminus, a cannibalistic community that Rick encounters in Season Four, were once said to have been good-natured people who offered a safe haven to any survivor who reached their city. However, when they took in a clan of marauders, the naive, well-meaning citizens were tortured, raped, and killed. Those who survived took up a policy of distrust and violence, believing that sympathy for outsiders made them vulnerable to betrayal and exploitation. Even the most adamant of liberals must admit that terrorism, much like Ebola and the marauders, is a legitimate concern that should be taken seriously. The question that divides most experts, however, is not whether or not terrorism is a threat, but rather what kind of threat it is. According to foreign policy analyst Ted Bromund:

> An existential threat is one that would deprive the United States
> of its sovereignty under the Constitution, would threaten the terri-
> torial integrity of the United States or the safety within U.S. bor-
> ders of large numbers of Americans, or would pose a manifest
> challenge to U.S. core interests abroad in a way that would compel
> an undesired and unwelcome change in our freely chosen ways of
> life at home. (Jacobson)

For example, while the Axis Powers and the Soviet Union, with their
massive ground and air forces, formidable alliances, and weapons of
mass destruction, were the nation's greatest existential threats since
the Civil War, ISIS and Al-Qaeda, even if they were capable of
pulling off another attack like 9/11, are overall too small, too disjoint-
ed, and too ill-equipped to come close to matching any existential
threats that America has faced in the past. If this is the case, why,
then, is the nation so intent on raising the specter of the Axis Powers
with the similarly-named Axis of Evil? Why must a monster be
forged in the fire of our own speculation and exaggerations? Perhaps,
like Ebola, it is because terrorism represents something much more
complex than a threat to our national security.

To fully understand what role the terrorist really plays in
American society, it is important to first understand what America is
as a nation. According to Natsu Taylor Saito:

> A deeply rooted aspect of American identity is the belief that the
> United States represents the most advanced stage in the evolution
> of human civilization, and therefore possesses a unique historical
> responsibility to bring its model of progress and development to
> the less fortunate. (55)

Even before World War II, the idea of America as a force of good was
deeply ingrained in the nation's psyche. Today, the majority of
Americans still view the nation as a defender of freedom, a champion
of democracy, and a sort of world-wide superhero. Terrorism, defined
by the U.S. Department of State as an act of "premeditated, political-
ly-motivated violence perpetrated against non-combatant targets," is
the antithesis of this ideal ("Glossary"). The attack on the Twin
Towers, the bombings in Paris and Brussels, and the massacre of

civilians in Iraq all represent a savage, regressive, and inhuman form of warfare that America, as a self-proclaimed 'city upon a hill,' would undoubtedly abhor. Indeed, the nation goes to great lengths, sacrificing inordinate amounts of money and men to stamp terrorism out abroad and to deter it from entering our borders. However, if held to the same standards as ISIS and Al-Qaeda, there are various American war crimes that also qualify as acts of terrorism. Take the bombings of Hiroshima and Nagasaki, for example. The attacks were meticulously planned, politically driven, and grossly indiscriminate, killing an estimated 226,000 people in the span of a few months. As it turns out, terrorism is not only something that America hates, it is also something that it has not come to terms with itself.

Analytical psychologist Carl Jung theorizes that every human is made up of two parts: the persona, or the part of our personality that we most identity with, and the shadow, defined by psychologist Carolyn Baker as the "unconscious aspects of the psyche of which we are ashamed or that do not resonate with our self-image" (Baker). For men, femininity is the shadow of a masculine persona; for the civilized, primitiveness is the shadow of a refined persona; and for America, inhumanity is the shadow of its virtuous persona. The most common way of interacting with one's shadow is suppression, whereby the male pushes away his feminine traits, the imperialist denies his barbaric qualities, and the U.S. hides the carnage of its terrorist actions behind bloodless terms like 'collateral damage.' While up until recently, this tactic was enough to keep the righteous image of America intact, the nation's superhero persona took a heavy blow during the Vietnam War. For the first time, television exposed the atrocities that our own forces were capable of; for the first time, we were seen not as liberators but as invaders; and for the first time, we came face to face with our shadow and found that it could no longer be suppressed.

Perhaps, then, the creation of monsters is not simply a product of hate and distrust so much as it is a response to a national identity crisis. According to author Anthony Stevens, the threat of our undesirable, shameful, or immoral attributes is often dealt with by using "a variety of ego-defense mechanisms, particularly repression, denial, and projection" (Stevens 84). The most effective of these, in which an individual or group is able to emerge completely from the shadows, is projection. By ignoring that our country is the source of the darkness, we disown our disagreeable traits, giving us the illusion that our shadow is only manifest on the surface we cast it upon. In dreams, this projected shadow is the monster chasing us—a creature that we often fail to realize is a manifestation of our own selves.

All monsters, for that matter, can be argued to be the projected shadows of a certain society. For example, the villains of Greek mythology are all either female, barbarian, or chthonic—the shadow of a patriarchal, democratic, and Olympian societal persona. In Puritan mythology, the witch is the embodiment of sin and unrestrained desire, qualities suppressed by the Puritan persona of piousness and temperance. Likewise, in *White Zombie* and *I Walked with a Zombie*, the zombie represents the shadow of imperialism's savage nature suppressed by a persona of civilization and refinement. The same goes for the Cold War and contemporary zombies. Are we not as guilty of forcing our form of government on others as the communists? Is our military not home to the world's largest arsenal of nuclear weapons? Are we not just as responsible for the half a million civilian deaths caused in Japan and Vietnam as Al-Qaeda is for the 2,996 civilians killed on 9/11?

In his book *Hunt the Devil: A Demonology of US War Culture*, Robert L. Ivie and Oscar Guner explain:

> [T]he trope of evil prods the nation to dehumanize its enemies
> and displace its own deformities on a vilified Other. It sets in
> motion a 'victimage' ritual through which America redeems itself
> on an altar of vicarious sacrifice. (13)

The ritual of the sacrificial lamb, in which the sins of a people are cast onto an animal that is then killed in retribution, is the most ancient form of shadow projection. Today, the ritual lives on through the dehumanization of the 'Other' upon whom we cast our iniquities. The 'War on Terrorism,' be it justified or not, cannot rid us of our own barbarous acts any more than killing a goat can absolve us of our wrongdoings. Projection, like suppression, is just a symptom of denial—an inability to recognize our own flaws.

This is not to say that America is completely devoid of goodness. It is important to remember that the nation has helped the world through times of great crisis, that it is the first responder to natural disasters, and that it consistently ranks as one of the world's most charitable nations. The persona is not a false but rather incomplete part of the personality. Failing to incorporate the shadow results in a state of limbo in which we are constantly running from a monster we can never escape. Exceptionalist justifications for the crimes of Hiroshima, Nagasaki, My Lai, or Abu Ghraib only abet the perpetration of yet more barbarity that must in turn be suppressed or projected to protect our persona. This vicious cycle begets a blind and stubborn society—one that fights to keep Ebola away from its borders but refuses to address the flaws in its own healthcare system, one that rages against the 75 American deaths caused by ISIS in the past 15 years instead of addressing the 300,000 deaths caused by domestic gun violence.

The monster in our dreams, however, does not simply disappear when we stop running. On the contrary, Jung describes *auseinandersetzung*, or the "confrontation" with the shadow, as a painful and disorienting experience. It is a plunge into the darkest parts of our being, a stripping of our persona, and the death of our identity as we know it. In alchemy, this turmoil is known as nigredo, a state of blackness and chaos. In Greek mythology, it is represented by a descent into the underworld. Because of its harrowing nature, Jung advises that *auseinandersetzung* not be undertaken without adequate mental preparation (45).

It is here that the zombies of American mythology can act as maieutic art objects that allow us to indirectly confront our collective shadow. "The first stage of growth is being realistic about who we are, what we are and where we are now," say Billy Childish and Charles Thomson, the founders of the "Remodernist" art movement ("Handy Hints"). Instead of endorsing persona-oriented films like *World War Z* (2013), in which Brad Pitt and a band of White doctors team up to save the world, Childish and Thomson advocate for art that lays bare our flaws and denies the trope of the fundamental hero. *The Walking Dead*, because of the lengthy nature of the television series, provides this degree of vulnerability that is often missing from non-serial narratives. Unlike Gerry in *World War Z*, Rick Grimes is no hero, and throughout the show it becomes clear to both him and the audience that he is no less barbaric than the Governor or the cannibals at Terminus. In Season Five, Rick gives a speech to his dwindling group of survivors in which he tells them that "we are the walking dead" ("Them"). With this quote, the masks that distinguish heroes from villains—fundamental good from fundamental evil—are shattered, and we, much like Rick, become painfully aware that the shadow upon the undead has always been our own.

For most people, it is easier to watch the lovable Gerry save a little Black boy from the clutches of zombies than to have our esteemed image of Rick slip away as he raids a community of innocent people. The jarring images and themes of the show throw us into a state of chaos in which, like the characters, we are constantly forced to ask ourselves: "Who are we?" ("A"). Art thus is the alchemist that melts down our composition, the guide that leads us into the underworld. Though the process is long and grueling, it is only by way of nigredo that ordinary metals can be turned to gold; it is only by dying that the warrior boy can resurrect as a hero; it is only by realizing that we are all infected that we can truly be cured.

WORKS CITED

28 Days Later. Dir. Danny Boyle. Twentieth Century Fox Film Corporation, 2002. DVD.

"A." *The Walking Dead. AMC.* AMC Network Entertainment LLC, Mar. 30. 2014. Television.

Baker, Carolyn. "Trumpenführer: Magnetizing the American Shadow." *CounterPunch.* CounterPunch, 7 Mar. 2016. Web. 9 May 2016.

Childish, Billy, and Charles Thomson. "Handy Hints." *A Stuckist Manifesto.* The Hangman Bureau of Enquiry, 2000. Web. 22 June 2016.

"Ebola Patient Dr. Kent Brantly Walks into Emory Hospital." *NBC News.* NBCNews.com, 2 Aug. 2014. Web. 22 June 2016.

"Glossary." *U.S. Department of State.* U.S. State Department, n.d.
    Web. 9 May 2016.

Invasion of the Body Snatchers. Dir. Don Siegel. Allied Artists
    Pictures, 1956. DVD.

Ivie, Robert L., and Oscar Giner. *Hunt the Devil: A Demonology
    of US War Culture.* Tuscaloosa: U of Alabama P, 2015. Print.

I Walked with a Zombie. Dir. Jacques Tourneur. RKO Radio
    Pictures, 1943. DVD.

Jacobson, Louis. "Is ISIS an 'existential threat' to the United
    States?" *PolitiFact.* PolitiFact, 16 Nov. 2015. Web. 9 May 2016.

Jung, Carl G. *Psychology and Alchemy.* Princeton, NJ: Princeton
    UP, 1968. Print.

Night of the Living Dead. Dir. George A. Romero. Continental
    Distributing, Inc., 1968. DVD.

O'Hehir, Andrew. "Ebola, the 'Heart of Darkness' and the
    Epidemic of Fear." *Salon.* Salon Media Group, 4 Oct. 2014.
    Web. 1 May 2016.

Pangburn, DJ. "'The Walking Dead' Writers Show Just How
    'Terrorist' Boogeymen Are Created." *Death and Taxes.*
    Spinmedia, 4 Dec. 2012. Web. 19 Apr. 2016.

Saito, Natsu Taylor. *Meeting the Enemy: American Exceptionalism
    and International Law.* New York: New York UP, 2010. Print.

Stevens, Anthony. *Jung: A Very Short Introduction.* Oxford:
    Oxford UP, 2001. Print.

"Them." *The Walking Dead. AMC.* AMC Network Entertainment
    LLC, Feb 15. 2015. Television.

Walker, Hunter. "Donald Trump just released an epic statement
    raging against Mexican immigrants and 'disease.'" *Business
    Insider.* Business Insider Inc., 6 Jul. 2015. Web. 29 June 2015.

White Zombie. Dir. Victor H. Halperin. United Artists, 1932.
    DVD.

MERCER STREET

CONTRIBUTORS

Leigh Anderson, '19, a native of Huntington, New York, majors in Journalism and Cinema Studies with a minor in Spanish at the College of Arts and Science. Along with her interest in human rights, law, and public policy, a debate about immigration in one of her Spanish classes sparked her curiosity about the crisis along the U.S.-Mexico border. Enthusiastic about political issues, she prides herself on objectivity and considers multiple perspectives before formulating opinions of her own. She is intrigued by loopholes in our law system that may provide economic protection without staying true to humanitarianism. This curiosity inspired Leigh's *Mercer Street* essay "Latin American Immigration and the Drug Crisis."

Natalie Behrends, '19, is a Washington, D.C. native majoring in History at the College of Arts and Science. She sees expository writing as a way to communicate the joy she gets from studying the world around her. Writing about the fine line between academia and activism in "Outside the Ivory Tower" pushed her to examine the responsibilities that come along with a scholarly life. As an intern at the Smithsonian National Museum of American History, she experienced firsthand how academic interpretation can affect the way that historical narratives stick in public imagination. When not attending NYU or at work in museums, Natalie enjoys traveling and learning as many new languages as possible.

Paula Cantillo, '19, studies Film and Television at the Tisch School of the Arts. Born in Medellín, Colombia, she moved with her family to the United States in 2000, where they settled in the little suburban town of Jonesboro, Georgia. Her diverse cultural background is a major influence on her writing. It allows her to keep an open mind and consider things from different and uncommon perspectives. "The Art of Manipulation" was motivated by a desire to push beyond the superficial arguments about the film *Her* to understand it in a broader, more world-relevant context. Her interest in mythology and the role of television in American culture led her to write "The Shadow of the Undead," finding interest in the "zombie fever" proliferating like wildfire throughout the country. Paula hopes to one day write and produce for television.

Angelica Chong, '19, originally from Singapore, is a Media, Culture, and Communications major at the Steinhardt School of Culture, Education, and Human Development. As someone who has always been interested in historiography, memory, and war, she was excited to write "Hiroshima, Redux." Through her essay, she learnt to enjoy the process of writing inspired by exploration—writing with curiosity instead of certainty. In her free time, Angelica likes to yell about fictional characters, read science fiction and fantasy, and make fun of Nicholas Cage.

Sophia Chou, '19, studies Nursing and hails from Hewlett, New York. An early attachment to science eventually developed into a special interest in health and medicine. After spending time in pharmacies, hospitals, and her high school research lab, she discovered her true passion: nursing. The Spanish film *Mar Adentro* turned her attention to the subjects of euthanasia and medical ethics. Her essay "Politician-Assisted Compromise" stems from this interest. Sophia can often be found with her nose in a book, a pastime that has assisted her in enjoying the countless hours of research put into her essay.

Lisa Dean, '18, is a Flute Performance major in the Steinhardt School of Culture, Education, and Human Development's Music and Performing Arts Professions department. Her essay about remembering trauma and memorializing tragedy, "Scars and Stigmata," was influenced by Marita Sturken's Deans Global Honors Seminar course on cultural memory. Lisa values the relationship between personal experiences and broader historical, social, and otherwise non-academic contexts. She seeks to bring the two together in her writing. Originally from Utah, Lisa chose to attend NYU as a means of escaping the (culturally) barren desert in favor of more hospitable climes.

Hieu Do, '19, from Ho Chi Minh City, Vietnam, is pursuing a dual-degree in Computer Science and Computer Engineering at the Tandon School of Engineering. In addition to his keen interest in STEM, Hieu aspires to strengthen the quality of education in Vietnam. A good education appreciates the achievements of one's ancestors but also acknowledges shortcomings as a key to improvement. History teaching in Vietnam often fails to recognize these shortcomings. Hieu's essay "Teaching History in Vietnam" expresses his concern to the Minister of Education of Vietnam. Hieu was a Davis Scholar at Westminster School in Simsbury, CT, where he was the Co-Editor-in-Chief of *The Westminster News*. He received the Harvard-Radcliffe Book Prize and the Richard K. LeBlond II Honor Award for academic achievement and service.

Xavier Patrick Dzielski, '19, is a Cinema Studies major in the Tisch School of the Arts. Hailing from Buffalo, New York, Xavier comes from a line of proud Irish-Americans. When given the opportunity to explore a film about Irish national identity in Neil Jordan's *The Crying Game*, Xavier was elated. Writing "Layers" allowed him the opportunity to blend his academic interests and cultural lineage into one curiously rewarding project. In addition to his film studies, Xavier is a competitive Irish dancer.

Wenxin (Wendy) Gao, '19, studies Art History in the College of Arts and Science. She was born in Hefei, China, and moved to Singapore as a child. Thanks to encouragement from her teachers, Wenxin grew up writing sci-fi stories and creating her own futuristic worlds. Her essay "The Freedom to Imagine the Past" asserts the right for people of minority experience to tell their stories through fiction, to break free from stereotypes, and to define themselves on their own terms. In her spare time, Wenxin enjoys art, theatre, dance, and sitting by Monet's *Water Lilies* in the MoMA.

Daniel Getzler, '19, is from New York City. Described as the greatest ancient you've never heard of, Xenophon—the focal point of Daniel's Freshman Seminar course—was a prominent Athenian military general, student of Socrates, and political commentator during the early fourth century B.C.E. Daniel's essay discusses the ending to one of Xenophon's most famous texts, *The Cyropaedia,* which tells a largely fictional story about the brilliant leadership of Cyrus and the unparalleled success of the Persian empire. In particular, Daniel's essay, "*Cyropaedia* 8.8: Xenophon's Final Chapter," tries to make sense of Xenophon's motives for ending his laudatory text about Cyrus with the complete collapse of his empire shortly after his death.

Maria Fernanda Gonzalez, '18, is majoring in Media Criticism and Sociology at the College of Arts and Science. She is interested in literature, philosophy, and current events, but is enamored with culture. Living in New York City has opened her mind, and she is especially interested in how discourse shapes the way we understand and produce cultural capital. Originally from Costa Rica, her Latin American background has made her passionate about social justice and environmental issues. She enjoys practicing yoga and watching movies, and writing has been her lifelong passion. Maria Fernanda aspires to be an editor, and believes that consciousness and mindfulness can have a positive and tangible impact on the world.

Jaydn Gosselin, '19, studies Film and Television at the Tisch School of the Arts. In America, he loves the sound of his own voice. Born and raised in Sydney, Australia, he has an accent that lends him the undue admiration of people he meets, even before they get to know him. While learning to craft cinematic art with his own strong voice, he is concerned with finding a way to never drown out the voices of his subjects. With "The Nineteenth Language," Jaydn examines what happens when well-intentioned people with privilege speak for the dispossessed. Jaydn is a terrible singer, an alright writer, and an advocate for knowing when to shut up and listen.

Lauren Hardman, '19, is double-majoring in Drama and Dramatic Writing at Tisch School of the Arts. "O'Say Can You Scan: Surveillance in Art, Public, and Self" was inspired by her own surveillance of "surveillance art" and by her own inner hypochondriac. An aspiring actor and self-described professional people-watcher, she has developed a strong affinity for figuring out why people act the way they do. Through the process of researching and writing her essay, Lauren realized that the greatest potential threat of an all-seeing government isn't limited to the extinction of privacy as we know it, but a possible erosion of the very freedom of thought.

Ashley Hollkamp, '19, originally from Fairfield, California, studies Education, Spanish, and Linguistics at the Steinhardt School of Culture, Education, and Human Development. As someone with strong interests in gender, sexuality, and identity, working with *Boys Don't Cry* in her essay was a natural choice. Grappling with the problem of hate crimes, "Fragile Conceptions: Gender and Masculinity" attempts to shed light on the larger cultural implications of a society that sees difference as a threat. Ashley views writing as a way to educate. She enjoys using it as a tool to further conversations on important social matters (and to eloquently express the strong opinions she's much too shy to tell in real life).

Allison Kiteley, '17, of Annapolis, Maryland, is a sociologist at heart, a Math major in reality. She spends most of her time studying intersectional feminist theory and goofing off on the Internet—usually getting into arguments about the former. Despite being a STEM major, she takes issue with the overemphasis on supposedly objective thought in American culture, in particular as it is used in self-proclaimed 'anti-social-justice' movements that deny alternate perspectives. This commitment inspired "The Internet Shrugged." Allison hopes to continue to write about the internet and its culture because she feels that there is a dearth of scholarship about it.

Nicolas Kugel, '19, is from the San Francisco Bay Area and studies Politics in the College of Arts and Science. His process in writing his essay "A Postcolonial Revision" could be described as a roller coaster of emotion. He initially struggled to piece together different texts and only clearly articulated his arguments after weeks of revision and a few trips to the Writing Center. At no point during the process did he feel confident in the quality of his writing or that he was even following the format of an essay that reckons with its sources. In the end, Nicolas's professor noted that the anxiety of never feeling like his essay was good enough may have made it successful, eventually.

Isabella Loh, '19, originally from Singapore, is a Biochemistry major in the College of Arts and Science. Her essay, "The Blue Death," uses the resources of fiction and was inspired by a real-life account of the 1918 Spanish influenza by Dorothy Deming, a nurse who worked tirelessly to save lives during the height of the outbreak. As a pre-health student with a passion for history, Isabella used historical documents and secondary sources to piece together her representation of one of the deadliest epidemics in history.

Paris Martineau, '19, is double majoring in Comparative Literature (with emphasis on French and the visual arts) and Journalism at the College of Arts and Science. Her hometown of Destin, FL, is frequently referred to as 'lower-Lower Alabama'—a fact she tries hard to forget. As the Deputy Opinion Editor at *Washington Square News*, Paris is proud of the number of belligerent Facebook comments her articles have inspired. She is a CAS Presidential Honors Scholar, and aware of how ridiculous that title sounds. Her essay, "Your Kind-of-Sort-of-Half-Truth is Stranger than Fiction," has given way to a new research paper titled "How to Make It To 46 and Kill Yourself: The Effect of David Foster Wallace's Suicide on His Critical Reception."

Brett Moody, '18, has always been fascinated by the R rating given to explicit films because it implies that stories can change a person's behavior for the worse. After he met Nonny de la Peña, the famed virtual reality journalist, he recognized that stories can utilize empathy to change a person's behavior for the better. For his essay, "School

Shootings in Media: A Pathway to Empathy or a Blueprint for Evil?" he examined how media can evoke empathy and translate it into significant prosocial action so that he could apply these insights to his own work as a Film major. In his spare time, Brett works on service projects, explores nature, plays games, and builds relationships with friends. He lived for several years in Singapore and Houston.

Chelsea Moore, '19, from Berkeley, CA is a Psychology major in the College of Arts and Science. Inspired by her mother, a textile designer and Fashion Institute of Technology graduate, Chelsea took Victoria Olsen's "Rise of the Visual" Freshman Seminar hoping to expand her knowledge of contemporary art and her ability to discuss visual artwork. "White Noise: Overcoming Overstimulation" granted her the opportunity to travel to Beacon, New York, to see the work of Robert Irwin and artwork from many other prominent artists. Contemporary artwork reflects human psychology and Chelsea hopes to continue making connections between artistry and psychology. After graduating, she hopes to return to California to attend culinary school.

Summer Okoye, '19, is a Drama major at the Tisch School of Arts. She calls the peaceful state of Delaware her home. As a first generation American of Nigerian descent who has grown up around multiple cultures, races, and traditions, she is constantly trying to figure out where she fits. However, her most suitable identity is that of an artist. Not only does she love to act, sing, and dance, but she has a passion for writing, poetry, drawing, filmmaking, and all forms of art that allow her to tell stories about the human experience from her own perspective. She has pursued this passion in her essay "The Black Commodity." Though she cannot predict where her creativity, inquisitiveness, and musings will take her, Summer intends for her artistic voice to be heard.

Mae Roney, '19, was born and raised in Manhattan and studies at the Tisch School of the Arts. After studying classical violin, viola, and classical voice for many years, she decided to pursue acting and is now a student at the Stella Adler Studio. The arts have been a vital part of her life, and taking "Writing Art and the World" was a nice marriage of two of her interests: art and writing. With "On Importance: Art as Enlightenment," Mae received encouragement from Professor Jennifer Cayer to use the writings of other established authors to explore the various ways in which art helps people to understand their place in the world.

Sim Yan Ying, '19, is a Theatre major in the Tisch School of the Arts hailing from Singapore. She wrote her essay "Velvet Handcuffs" to understand the relationship between censorship and politics, and a belief in the need for greater freedom of artistic expression in her home country. Being in New York has given fresher eyes and greater objectivity toward the pervasive censorship back home. She aspires to create emotionally truthful and socially relevant works of art that synthesize her experiences across cultures in New York, Singapore, and other parts of the world. Beyond theatre, Yan Ying enjoys dancing, reading, café-hopping, having spontaneous conversations with strangers, and throwing social conventions to the wind.

Nina Svirsky, '19, is a Mathematics major hailing from New York City. She has always been fascinated by feminism, prompting her essay "Solnit's Catch-22: In a Nutshell, Female." One spark for this interest was *Third Wave Magazine*, a small, independent feminist literary magazine that she founded with a few friends in her senior year of high school. She is developing a second major in Gender and Sexuality Studies, in which she hopes to complete a thesis or research project in the coming years. In addition to these academic pursuits, she is an avid modern dancer, taking professional technique class on a daily basis. During the little free time left in the day, Nina attempts to delve into as many varied books as possible.

Minghao Zang, '16, whose hometown is Qingdao, China, is a Business major in the Stern School of Business concentrating in Finance and Accounting. Unlike most Stern students wanting to do investment banking, he is uncertain of what to do in the future. Perhaps he aspires differently. The struggle of being who he wants to be is partially reflected in his essay, "A Struggle of Identity," which is also based on his own personal experience. To Minghao, the essay's goal is not to put readers in any kind of dilemma about who they should be, but rather to encourage them to balance their own fish and bear paw in the way they prefer: to be themselves.

Denise Zhou, '19, grew up in Irvine, California in a messy library, drowning in paperbacks and school-required reading. She now maintains equally messy music and film libraries, bringing artists and genres into organized chaos. Her essay, "Coming of Identities," brings more of her values into the same. Moving to New York tested her sense of identity within the contexts of race and environment. Fortunately, she found solace and perspective in expository writing. She is pursuing a Film and Television major, holding closely to her passion for writing, music, and education. Denise intends to keep an exceptionally messy library for however long she can get away with it.

MERCER STREET

EXPOSITORY WRITING COURSES: FALL 2015

INTERNATIONAL WRITING WORKSHOP I

WRITING THE ESSAY

Writing The Essay: Art in the World

ESSAYS FROM THE FRESHMAN SEMINARS

Expository Writing Courses: Spring 2016

International Writing Workshop II

Progression 1

Writing the Essay

Progression 3

Advanced College Essay: the World Through Art

Progression 5

Advanced College Essay: Education and the Professions

A Spectrum of Essays

MERCER STREET

NOTEWORTHY ESSAYS